THE JOINT

THE JOINT

JAMES BLAKE

PARIS REVIEW EDITIONS

Doubleday & Company, Inc., 1971, Garden City, New York

Selections from THE JOINT originally
appeared in *The Paris Review* and *Esquire*.

DESIGN BY RAYMOND DAVIDSON

Library of Congress Catalog Card Number 68–27110
Copyright © 1970, 1971 by James Blake
All Rights Reserved
Printed in the United States of America

For Nonie

CONTENTS

CONTENTS

THE JOINT

PART I

petit larceny, breaking and entering

Dear Mike:

Thanks for your note and the enclosed dollar. It couldn't have come at a better time, at the end of a long week of diggin' and dyin'.

I'm doing two years altogether here, two six-month sentences on two counts of petit larceny, and a one-year sentence for breaking and entering.

As far as my fall is concerned, the only mistake I made was one of judgment in choosing a partner for my small depredations —we did some boosting together and everything was cool, until he got drunk and was picked up for prowling cars.

Then he was seized with an attack of compulsive garrulity and voluntarily directed them straight to me. I copped out on the larceny charges, figuring to get six months at the most, but they sprang a breaking and entering rap that I knew nothing about. What happened, Don H. got drunk and went on the prowl again, but in the boardinghouse where we were staying. How about that? My presence on the burglarized premises was established, and that was enough to get me a year.

Briefly, my fall partner was a Southerner, with a brother on the force, and I was a Yankee ripe for burning. I got two years, he got six months.

I've been here since last September 20, and it's rugged back-breaking labor on the bull gang. We work out on the road under three shotgun guards. On the occasions when I simply wasn't able to keep up, and tired of trying, I was sent to the Box, a solitary cell, high and narrow ($3 \times 8 \times 8$) with no window or bed and a tin can for sanitation. Five slices of bread a day and all the water you want. At first it just made me mad, but now I'll admit I'm scared of it. As a result I spend most of the time in a haze of anxiety, trying to work hard enough to please the head-guard, Piggy, a fat sadistic Georgia cracker, real high-type southern gent.

All of it has got my nerves to a dangerous point, and I must get away. It's been done by a lot of prisoners, running right out from under the gun. It isn't as hard as it might seem, because one of the guards will grease for twenty-five bucks. Once over the line, only about twenty miles away, there's no serious pursuit, because the County is too broke to finance sending after anyone any distance. So I'm trying to raise the loot and just waiting.

Incoming mail is not opened at all, and it's easy to kite a letter out, as I'm doing with this. We're allowed to receive just about anything except firearms, so if you have a white T-shirt and a pair of old tennis sneakers, I could use them, not only for working in, but they'll be handy when I hang it up. Stamps and envelopes are hard to come by here too, and writing and receiving mail is really the only thing to look forward to.

What I do need though, to help me hold on to my fading wits, is a radio. Being without music is like being deprived of light and air, it is as though all the color and shape and meaning have gone out of my life. Please, Mike, if you can get hold of any kind of beat-up little radio, send it along.

Anything you do, any loot you can send will be repaid—I've got a little over 300 bucks stashed in a safe place nearby, the remains of the proceeds from a gas station we pilfered before we fell. I guess the only reason my voluble chum failed to spill his guts about that was the faint hope that he'll be able to lay hands on it when he gets out, but it's safe enough, the poor child.

Well, that is the whole loused-up deal, and the only good, if it is that, to come out of it is that I now have muscles in my eyebrows and all elsewhere.

And that somewhere along the line in all this tohu-bohu I've come of age. And am I bitter? Bébé!   Yours, B.

P.S. There is another and better way to hang it up, which is to have a car pick me up on the road where the crew is working. I've looked at it from all angles, and it's practically foolproof, since the guards aren't allowed to fire at a moving vehicle. So if you have a taste for a little B-movie action, let me know. Seriously, Mike, I know it's too much to ask but, Jesus, I godda get odda here.

P.P.S. When you get this, please send me a postcard—just checking on the mail connection.

County Jail
MARCH 4, 1951

Dear Mike:

Many thanks for your note and the enclosed buck; I was able to purchase some tobacco to supplement the weekly ration of yak dung they issue here.

For good behavior I get a big four months out of two years, leaving twenty months. As for parole, nobody within memory has ever made it out of here by that route. County needs the free labor, man.

I have carefully considered all the ways of hanging it up, believe me, and the simplest easiest way is to be picked up by a car. The crew is in the same spot every day to fill the water barrels for the road—from there it is simple to follow the truck until it arrives at the work location for the day, and await the proper opportunity.

As I explained, the next easiest way is to grease one of the guards. He's a young guy and under no suspicion of accepting bribes. When all the conditions are right, he'll take twenty-five bucks and give you about ten minutes before sounding an alarm.

Even the hardest way, running right out from under the gun—after you have maneuvered so that you have a good distance between yourself and the guard, and his back is turned —is workable. In the past three months three guys have done it, but even that entails a certain amount of cash for buying clothes in town, and taxi fare into town. (Nobody has ever been turned in by a cab driver.)

Having very little else to think about, I have worked out detailed plans along each of these lines, too involved to be explained here, but I'm sure they would be successful. If not, I would probably get from six months to a year additional, wear the chains for sixty to ninety days, and try again.

You advise checking these plans against reality, which I assume means calculating my chances of success. In an existence of days of heart-tearing labor and nights of dreary bestiality, any chance is worth taking. I'm just trying to get the best odds I can and a little wherewithal will supply that—I don't mean from you, Mike; if you're having it rough, I'm damned sorry to hear it, you were so great to me, and I was pretty much chicken-shit— but I'll get it somehow.

I'm going into a solitary cell at my own request sometime this week, to put an end to that part of my troubles that stems from my fellow inmates and aberrant sex run wild—so I sincerely hope you will find it possible to send a radio. I can't possibly convey how hungry I am for music, how starved for it, and I know it would do so much to fill this horrible gray emptiness, and to relieve this tension, this anxiety—

When I shall have to resort to the ultimate refuge of the inarticulate—it stinks!   Yours, B.

County Jail
MARCH 18, 1951

Dear Mike:

Well, my best-laid plan has gang agley—The Man, in some mysterious way, got information that three of us were planning to run, and I have been transferred to another work crew, and haven't been out from under the gun since I joined it. That does not necessarily mean that all is lost, but it will be some time till I can sniff my way to another crack. I'll keep you informed.

The transfer has one good angle to it, the work is lighter. Now instead of laboring like an ox, I have merely to work like a mule . . .

Certainly I wish there was some way of your getting that stash for me. It's hidden in the room I occupied in a boarding-house, in a place that only the dismantling of the building would reveal, and getting it out will be more or less ticklish if the room is occupied, comparatively simple if it's vacant. I had planned to get next to the colored maid there, who's pretty hip, but not hip enough to be fly, if you know what I mean. If you want to make a stab at it, you can come here first (visiting hours on Sunday 3–5), and I'll tell you exactly where to look.

Merci mille fois for the buck, it's more than ever welcome now that I'm living in solitary—being away from my mentor, the Muskie, and all that sex hassle, has done wonders for my peace of mind and serenity, but it has also put me completely on my own resources. So if you can throw in some stamps when you send that T-shirt, I shall be glad to knock off a filling station in your honor, come The Day.

I hope fervently that you can do something about the radio —Last night I had the Polovtzian Dances from Prince Igor running through my mind, and would have given anything to hear it—before that it was Mary Martin singing "Cockeyed

Optimist"—and it goes on all the time. Please do what you can, and thanks again. I hope you'll decide to make the trip up here.

Yours, B.

County Jail
MARCH 25, 1951

Dear Mike:

Psychologists may be right about the small percentage of junkies that are really hooked, but every case that I have personal knowledge of seems to indicate the opposite. In Lisa's case, the ravages produced by an insufficient supply of the drug were not only mental, but excruciatingly and plainly physical. However, perhaps the book should be recommended to her. I know that she is still hot on the trail of the elusive and ephemeral fix.

From the way things look at present, the heat is really on as far as hanging this up is concerned. Both the guards on the crew are young and discouragingly agile, but I am still seeking the chink of venality in their armor. Patience is indicated, also fortitude.

You do not mention going to the boardinghouse, for which I do not blame you. I can understand your reluctance to become involved in this road-company cops 'n' robbers opus. With the weasel-cunning and hardihood this hassle has given me, I shall yet confound these chinchy rascals, if I can only get a little temporary backing from you.

Thanks for the Yankee dollah, it gets me through the week in pretty good shape. I regret that for the moment I can only reiterate pale gratitude. And many thanks for the package, I shall be looking for it.   Yours, B.

County Jail
APRIL 1, 1951

Dear Mike:

The regimen of unendurable boredom indefinitely prolonged continues in force. If all the digging I have done in the past week could have been devoted to the excavation of a tunnel, I would now be somewhere under Paterson, N.J. The hope of hanging it up is rather dim at present, the new guard follows me about with a truly touching single-minded devotion. I attempt to make a friend of him, but I am singularly inept at that sort of thing, and my overtures sound false and hollow to my own ears. However, I have discovered that he has three kids, one an invalid, and is nearly always in financial straits, which may make him somewhat vulnerable—but I shall have to wait a bit.

My cozy solitary cell was needed for the quarantine of new prisoners, so I am once more back in the dormitory, and plunged even deeper into the joyless overblown sex charade from which I fled—Lord, I will be a demon ascetic when I can extricate myself from this hassle!

All this suffering would undoubtedly be salutary for my Art, if I had an Art, but I am afraid that the tiny pianistic talent I possess is more of a monkey-trick than a Sacred Flame. My problem is how to adapt all this noble suffering to a more sparkling piano rendition of "My Baby's Boobies" or "The You Don't Know the Half of It Dearie Blues." Assuredly too great a heat for such a picayune pie.

I cannot adequately express my disappointment about the radio—I ran across something in Flaubert that seems apropos of all my struggles to say what I mean—"Human speech is the tin kettle on which we beat out tunes for bears to dance, when we would move the moon." Or T. S. Eliot's, "Oh the agonizing struggle with words and meanings!" Mutely yours, B.

County Jail
APRIL 4, 1951

Dear Mike:

There has been a sudden change in the shotgun guards on our crew, and one of the replacements is the young guy who was on the bull gang when I was with it, the venal one who does the little traffic in abetting escapes for a two-bit consideration.

The story is that the guards are going to be switched around every two weeks, apparently to discourage fraternizing with the prisoners. So I have two weeks to hang it up in, the easy way and the best, or else run from under the gun and risk what the boys call a "Rash in the ass," or worse.

I had a chance for a word with him today, and the deal is still hot. Another prisoner, a kid from California, has agreed to run at the same time, but in the opposite direction, to complicate pursuit somewhat . . .

I have a place ready in town where I can hide out and get clothes, and lay low until I can get to that loot I've got stashed. From there I'll go to Rose's in Atlanta, and buy there what I'll need for the trip North.

Can you swing it, Mike? I hate like blazes to impose, more than I could tell, but it will only be a temporary thing, a week at most, and I shall be forever in your debt, even when the gold is repaid. I've got to get out of this blasted deadfall. The way I feel now, I can wallop the world, and I want to get away before jailhouse apathy makes me no goddam good for anything.

Many thanks again for the buck, Mike. And now, sweet Jesus willing, let's see if we can't get me off your back and on my feet again. Je meurs, Armand, je meurs!   Yours, B.

County Jail
APRIL 15, 1951

Dear Mike:

Still watching for my opportunity to take off, waiting until the heat is off a little. This spring weather has set off a rash of plans on all sides to hang it up—two prisoners from the other work gang tried to run, were caught that same night, and are now wearing chains. The sight of those has made me doubly cautious, but the moment will come.

My "protector," Joey D., the Muskie, is greatly exercised at my plans to leave—there was no way of keeping my receipt of the money from him, since we bunk together, and could not be more intimate if we were inside the same skin. He threatens intermittently to take the money away from me, but as yet has done nothing but twist my arms and pummel me some, which I am accustomed to as all a part of the impossible game I have been forced into playing here.

We also have a group of prisoners called "creeps" or "night-crawlers," who prowl the dormitory at night and steal from the other sleeping prisoners. To report these unsavory and totally lost creatures is of course a violation of the rigid convict code, and is called "ratting" or "cheese-eating." Lord, what a beautiful warped bewildered pack of troglodytes. I try to preserve a philosophical attitude towards it all, lest I be provoked into making an incautious move, but the position at times is somewhat untenable.

I hope you will forgive my temerity in asking for the white T-shirt, but it really is a necessary part of the plan, and I have no other way of getting one.

Glad to hear that you were able to ransom your typewriter, and wish I had one too, so I could spare you the eyestrain of deciphering my lurching hand.

P.S. Has that fugitive fall partner of mine shown his face? He hung it up a couple of days ago, you know, and may head for Miami, since his mother lives there. I thought it best to warn you to have no truck with him, he's pure poison.

Yours, B.

County Jail
MAY 2, 1951

Dear Mike:

It's damned annoying and frustrating as hell to write letters and then have them go astray. I presume that's what has happened again, since I haven't had any answer to my last one. I'm quite sure I shall be able to get this one out.

I'm still trying to tell you how grateful I am for your intercession with X. I hope that some day I shall be able in some way to repay that enormous kindness. And I'm still awaiting my opportunity and trying to possess my soul in patience. However, I am still in need of a white T-shirt to wear in place of the prison shirt when I take off. It isn't just an idle whim, but a very necessary part of the operation, and I can't obtain one except by having one sent through the mail.

The loot you sent I have deposited with the house-man of the prison dormitory, a trustworthy elderly prisoner from Miami, who has been a good friend to me. It will be safe with him until I need it. I have convinced Joey (the Muskie) that I have changed my mind about running, so things have quieted down somewhat in that direction. He objected strenuously, and is psycho enough to foul me up in some way, so I had to forestall that.

I'm trying to raise enough dough now to finance my trip North. Not from you, I hasten to say, but from some of my erstwhile friends in Chicago. I shall have to hitchhike most of the way, I suppose, but I should like to get out of the chain-gang territory before I attempt it. I've heard a lot of reports from prisoners telling of the rugged chain-gang sentences they've pulled for hitchhiking and vagrancy, all the way up the coast to D.C., and I don't want to make a Dixie Odd-yssey out of this thing.

And if you can possibly make it on your way North, please stop by for a visit. I shall probably saturate you with salt tears of gratitude, and may not be able to refrain from licking your hand, but I long to see a face from the outside world and to hear an intelligent word.

Let me hear as soon as you get this, so I shall know if the mail gimmick is in working order. It has been in sad disrepair.

Yours, B.

P.S. Please forgive this rather incoherent scrawl. The strain of all this waiting and hoping has me a trifle distrait.

County Jail
MAY 7, 1951

Dear Mike:

The small sadness and resignation in your letter quite touched and distressed me, truly, and for a little I was able to forget my own horrid and disorderly situation in realizing the dis-satisfactions and frustrations of another—Really, my engulfing egocentricity makes me all but blind and deaf at times . . .

It's wonderful of you to visit Lisa; the poor child is desolate —but I am in the hands of these cannibalistic Crackers, my pillow is wet, and the night wind carries my keening . . .

It is Monday night now, and I'm going to try to get this out tomorrow. I shall have to perpetrate some small swindle for an envelope and a stamp, or perhaps bestow my bedraggled favor on some prison-type gent. (Flahrs, kep'n, buy some flahrs from a paw gel? . . .). Yours, B.

County Jail
MAY 13, 1951

Dear Mike:

If you really want to take the trouble of beating the drum and waving the suggestive tambourine in my behalf in Chicago, you could get in touch with J.G., Mercantile Exchange. He is so disenchanted with me that I dunno, but perhaps if you tell him you saw me chained in the stocks in the colored bordello section of Jax, bleeding from the eyes . . .

I shall write Lisa a buck-up note, although it will probably have a strange and hollow sound, issuing as it were de profundis. Something like Jack the Baptist urging Salome to get with it. But give her my love undying when you see her—a babe incomparable and indestructible . . .

You ask who the Muskie is. I thought I made that clear. He is simply the brass-brained, muscle-bound Golden Boy who appointed himself my jailhouse Daddy-o. Between beatings and brainings he implores me not to take off. The situation is untenable, boring to desperation, and dull dull dull . . .

Yours, B.

Addendum, MAY 15, 1951

As you can see from the date, I've held this letter until I could find a way of getting it out. It will be mailed tomorrow night, all being well, and you should receive it Friday.

Received the package from X. containing the shirt and envelopes and the fin—Damn, but it brings me alive again to see a way opening up out of this mess! It may be a few days before I can get a letter out to X., so please assure him that everything reached me all right, and that his kindness shall not be in vain. A bas les Dixiecrats!

Now for the information you requested on the details of my commitment. The judge was substituting for the regular judge, who was ill. I received two six-month sentences on two counts of larceny, and a one-year sentence for breaking and entering. On the advice of court attaches, I plead guilty to all counts. (Though I imagine it will make very little difference now, I was and am entirely innocent of the breaking and entering charge.) My record here, as far as I know, is good, since it has never occurred to me to do anything that would bring down on me the rather dire punishment reserved for re-calcitrants.

As for my involvement with the Muskie here, there was never any question of choice for me. Considerable duress was brought to bear, and I was simply forced to comply wit' his wishes. But though I am helpless physically, I can and do describe some fantastic circle around the beast forensically, and I have him pretty well snowed into believing that I won't leave him.

There is a jailhouse rumor that because of the overcrowded condition of the state pen, they are going to start shipping in some longtermers here. That would mean considerably-tightened restrictions and increased vigilance. It may not be true, but if it is, I shall have to get the hell out before it happens.

Your new pad in Chicago sounds interesting. A good trip, Mike, happy orientation, and please write soon.   Yours, B.

County Jail
MAY 20, 1951

Dear Mr. Algren:

This is to thank you for the T-shirt and envelopes and your contribution towards the success of my small plot. My plans have had still another slight setback because one of the trusties here last night took off for the altogether elsewhere, the joint is jumping, and vigilance is the order.

Your kindness is doubly appreciated in view of the fact that I am a comparative stranger to you. We met once while I was playing piano in the Pink Poodle on State Street in

Chicago. It was in Dugan's Bar, I think, and I made some snide remark about an author collecting color. That was my snide period, a prolonged one. Very oafish I was, but the stupidity of the remark was its own handy obituary.

As an author, it might amuse you, or it might leave you somewhat shaken, to learn the method by which the excellence of a book is judged in the chain gang. The method is simple, brusque, direct—One query only: "Is there any fuckin' in it?" When I think of all the polished painstaking book reviews I've read ("Luminous imagery"—Toronto Star) ("Mordant satire" —Boston Globe) I wonder, is all.

Best wishes for your continued success, and hoping I may be able to thank you personally, once I get through the Union lines.   Yours, B.

                                                      County Jail
                                                      JUNE 21, 1951
Dear Mike:

Well, I tried to hang it up, and with my usual flair, I stepped on my dick. It's a long story, but as long as you and Algren and Jack financed it, I figure you're entitled to know what happened.

I had it all set with the guard. I gave him the loot, twenty-five, and he said he'd give me ten minutes whenever I decided to go.

I didn't get a chance till after lunch—everything fell right and I took off through the swamp, crashing through those goddam palmettos like a water buffalo. All of a sudden I heard a shot, then another. I thought the bastard was crossing me up and I really began to run. Then I heard somebody crashing through the brush behind me, coming fast. I looked around and saw Joey, the Muskie. Jesus, I could have shit, but we kept right on running, and in a way I was glad of the company though I was afraid of getting loused up.

We stopped to listen, and heard somebody coming not too

far back. Joey said we'd have to hole up and wait till dark. We crawled far under a spreading palmetto and lay flat. Joey had a thick length of pine branch and when I asked him what for, he said if the motherin' screw ever caught up to us, he'd wish he hadn't. Oh fine.

We heard the guy coming, crashing through the swamp (we must have left a trail a mile wide). And damned if he didn't stop right where we were hiding, with his back to us—It was the guard I greased. Before I knew anything, Joey jumped out and hit him an awful clout alongside the ear with the club, and he went down like a poleaxed ox.

We ran until we couldn't run any further, finally flopped down in the middle of a prairie of shoulder-high grass, it must have been about a mile square. We decided to wait there for darkness, when we could get to the Seaboard tracks.

Then he started upbraiding me for running, said I was just trying to get away from him, and other denunciations. I pointed out to him that he and his shillelah had put the heat on but good and fucked me up for fair. He hauled off and just about beat my brains out. I'll spare you the rest of that sunbaked nightmare in the afternoon, but if ever I wake up screaming (or laughing wildly) I'll be thinking of that. Erotic dalliance on the veldt, with all those half-witted crackers looking for us and that guard lying back there. The man's insane.

After dark, we made it to the Seaboard tracks. We waited at the top of a long grade, where Joey said all the freights had to slow down to make the hill. It must have been hours we lay in the bushes, but a freight finally came along and we grabbed an empty gravel car and crouched down in the corner out of the wind. That damn thing made about eighty stops, and it was daylight when we jumped off outside Wincross. Another guy dropped off with us, and Joey asked him about getting a train out, and he said there was a freight going to Atlanta that night at nine.

We waited in the woods for the stores to open, and I went into town to buy some clothes. Man, I felt about ten feet high, but I found an Army store and got blue jeans and T-shirts for both of us. (The one I had on was torn and muddy, I was a mess, but the old Jew who ran the joint didn't even look at me. Blessed are the incurious.)

I bought a few groceries and some cheap wine (I needed a drink awful bad). We stayed in the woods all day, and even managed to have a kind of furtive picnic, the wine, of course. And I guess I was light-headed with panic too.

We went into the yards just about dark. There was nobody around but a bo who pointed out the freight for us, and we climbed into a boxcar and lay down flat in the corner. We'd been awake for so damn long and were so exhausted that we both went right to sleep. I was awakened by somebody kicking me, holding a flashlight in my eyes, telling me to get the hell up out of there. Georgia fuzz. They handcuffed us together, and when Joey said "what the hell," one of them said, "You're the half-bad mother-fuckers that killed that guard over in Jetts County." For me, everything stopped—but Joey said we'd just finished working in Ocala and had a job in Atlanta we were going to. The guy said he had us for trespassing anyway, and took us in.

They had us cold, of course. One of the young deputies told me that the guard wasn't dead, but had concussion and shock. That helped some, believe me.

It all moved pretty fast—they took us back to the County jail and we were tried and sentenced in three days—but before we were tried, they took Joey out of the cell one night and brought him back horribly beaten up. Man, it was awful, I cried over it.

Joey absolved me of all blame in the assault on the guard, and got a year in the State Pen. I got six months for running and shackles for my ankles. Being fitted for chains is an experience.

Now I'm back where I started, and Joey's gone. Well, nothing is forever. We shall see.   Ever, B.

County Jail
JULY 15, 1951

Dear Mr. Algren:

Lack of writing material has delayed me from writing sooner
to thank you for your really overwhelming and thoughtful gift
of all those *New Yorker* magazines. They have afforded me
a wonderful escape from the drabness and dreariness of my
present surroundings. The half-zany, half-rueful editorial attitude
of the magazine has always been a tonic to me, and in my
present plight it is more than ever reassuring somehow, to
know that such an attitude exists.

I have made a brief and abortive bid for freedom, which
was considerably complicated by too many people getting into
the act. Everything would have gone according to plan had I
not been suddenly joined by a fellow prisoner who decided,
for reasons too devious to untangle, to go along with me un-
announced. In the ensuing melee, a guard was bashed on the
head with a club and left unconscious, thereby generating a
good deal of heat all around. We were caught in Wincross, Ga.,
on a freight train bound for Atlanta, and returned.

My fellow fugitive absolved me of all blame in the attack
on the guard and was sent to the state pen for a year, while I
was returned here with an additional six months and chains
around my ankles.

I am now being kept in solitary for a period, which is no
great hardship, since I am better able to read without distractions
and am excused from participation in the intramural sex games
of the dormitory.

One thing I miss terribly here is the opportunity to hear
any music, and if anybody up there has an old radio they are
not using, I would be endlessly grateful for it. Since the advent
of the newest American brain-killer, TV, I understand that
everybody goes around in a permanently stunned state of tele-

vision-torpor, and radios are very little used. I know now that
I shall have to build this time, and a little nachtmusik would
add color to an existence that is predominantly gray.

Thank you again for that amazing box of riches.

Sincerely, B.

County Jail
AUGUST 1, 1951

Dear Mr. Algren:

I don't know what to say—I am completely absolutely awe-
struck at your understanding, compassion and generosity.

The radio you sent, and the opportunity to hear some music
again that it affords me, have given color and depth to an
existence that had become a flat and deadly gray.

If that seems lush and fulsome, it is nonetheless true.

My blessing, worn and dubious though it be, goes out to
you, and I hope that when I get out of this I may be able to
show you in some concrete fashion my deep and sincere gratitude.

And so, I must take up once again the burden of faith in
humanity.   Sincerely, B.

County Jail
AUGUST 18, 1951

Dear Mike:

Sorry to hear about your mother's illness and hope that
she will be completely recovered soon. I had been looking
for a letter from the usual spot and was surprised by the St.
Louis postmark. Have you been down this way at all yet?
Over the Labor Day weekend I looked for a visit from you,
in fact I still have striped indentations down my face from
pressing against and peering through the bars for three days,

staring staring staring. On the wet pillow, the damp and shredded handkerchiefs, I draw the curtain . . .

The radio that X. sent has made a world of difference to me here, and has been most helpful in fighting off the engulfing monotony of this existence. I hope I shall have an opportunity to know X. better when I get out of here, and a chance to show how I feel about such wonderful kindness . . .

I think I may get the shackles cut off some time this week. In this matter, I have two powerful partisans in the persons of two nice old ladies who conduct a Bible class every Saturday at the joint. I attended the first class out of a cynical curiosity to see what the enemy was doing, but I was so charmed by their sweetness and earnestness that I became a regular member. Now they are everlastingly at the warden to take my chains off, and it is as good as having the furies on my side. I expect some action soon, since the Baptists pull a pow'ful lot of weight in these hyuh parts. We shall see.   Yours, B.

County Jail
September 23, 1951

Dear Mr. Algren:

. . . The radio continues to be a pleasure and a blessing in the arid monotony of these days. I've become quite a connoisseur in private-eye melodramas, almost to the point where I can tell one from another. Speaking of crime broadcasts, when I was living up in the prison dormitory it was forever fascinating to watch the cons listening to Gang-Busters. Everything was eerily hindside-to, with the prisoners judiciously approving the account of a bank robbery, holdup or some other violence to the statutes, ruefully cursing the triumphant arrival of the law. When it was over they would go to bed pointing out the mistakes of their fellow malefactors and bemoaning their stupidity. It always left me bemused.   Yours, B.

County Jail
OCTOBER 28, 1951

Dear Mike:

. . . A voice has come out of the recent past to present me
with a problem this week. A former prisoner here, with whom
I had some quietly ferocious amorous dealings, has written me
from a Kentucky prison, where he is doing a year, that he
intends to come down here to meet me when I get out. He is
flamboyantly attractive, and the prospect of one last wild ride
on the tiger is tempting to my as yet unweaned mentality.
At the same time I feel that I should bank the fires and settle
down quietly to cope with the menopause.

My status here has become that of a semi-trusty, I still go
out with the work gang, but I am occasionally sent off alone
to do jobs out from under the gun. So I have plenty of
opportunity to take off, but lack the wherewithal. Or perhaps
I have now become like the caged animal who fears to leave
the cage even when the door is opened. But I guess it's just
that I don't feel like doing it the hard way.   Ever, B.

County Jail
NOVEMBER 20, 1951

Dear Nelson:

Thank you very much for the welcome deuce, the stamps
and the postcards. Loot is pretty hard to come by here for
those who don't have visitors, and they resort to a variety of
means to raise it, one of the most popular the lifting of it
from one another . . .

Another institution that has filtered through the bars is the
caste system. ("All animals are equal, but some are more equal
than others.")

At the top are those who are alumni of the state pen. The

other inmates regard these eminences much as a Lawrenceville boy might look at a Princeton man.

The gradations continue all down the line to the "winos," chronic drunkards who are regarded frostily as 30-day interlopers and not true criminals at all. Maybe the winos are disconsolate with nobody to look down upon, or maybe they just settle contented and cozy at the bottom.

I cannot tell—the light is rather dim down there.

The Indoor Ward McAllister, B.

County Jail
DECEMBER 2, 1951

Dear Mike:

. . . Those are rather probing questions you ask about the penal setup down here. Are you thinking of tinkering with the statutes? Here's the story—the County does not have a stockade in town for white prisoners, since the resort owners objected to prisoners, many of them in chains, working exposed to the public, or tourist, view. Such delicacy does not extend to our brown brothers, who do county road work down there. Any white who is sentenced up to a period of one year usually makes the time in the city jug. Over one year, he goes to Raxley. There, if he is under thirty-five and in good physical condition, he is eagerly embraced by the State Road Dept., and sent to one of the many camps throughout the state. Most of these camps are rugged beyond imagining. I know that the state gangs we pass at work on the road have a somber lowering aspect, "dead to rapture and despair," and I always feel a faint chill at the sight of them. When I was held in the Bliss County jail, a Raxley gang was quartered temporarily in an adjacent cell block, and when they came off the road at night, they sounded like nothing so much as wild beasts.

Certainly, from the con's point of view it is better to go out every day and do hard manual labor, even in the broiling sun, than it is to stay cooped up for days on end. Preserves your morale, puts you in top physical condition, and leaves you fit for better and bigger depredations upon release. I know that when I get out I shall be full of such an incandescence and rage to live that I shall probably kick a hole in somebody if I am not able to channel my energies properly.

This prison farm is purely a county affair, for offenders with sentences up to three or four years, and while some of the work we do is as tough as anything they get in the Raxley camps, the hours, food, treatment are immeasurably better. This joint is considered a model county stockade. And now that I have become accustomed to the road work, it is only the grinding monotony of the days that makes it in any way though. And of course, no TV.   Ever, B.

County Jail
DECEMBER 9, 1951

Dear Nelson:

This week I finished a book that Jack O. sent me, Elizabeth Bowen's *Heat of the Day*, and for a couple of days, impressionable ass that I am, I was clipped in my speech and moodily English. That kind of performance needs a discerning audience, though, and if my colleagues noticed it at all, it was to give me a brief, dimly suspicious glance and dismiss the matter, the way a cow does when she looks at you.

—My work out on the road has brought me into contact with quite a number of cows lately, and I've never seen anything to beat the way they can convey quiet contempt. It may be that one brief glance tells them I'm not a bull and therefore beneath notice—Still, you can't tell. A number of the funloving lads on the gang give vivid and explicit accounts of illicit relations with cows, and it may be that the harassed and confused animals have put down the whole human race as warped, or inconstant, or at the very least, impotent . . . I think I shall leave all that to the admirable Kinsey.

Thank you ever so much for the deuce and the stamps and postcards. I was able to get a haircut, buy some tobacco and writing paper, and some food that wasn't drowning in glutinous gravy. Our cook is a con who was a merchant mariner and he seems to believe that if it ain't afloat it ain't digestible. As a result, I am awash most of the time.

I have the published versions of four plays I'd like to send you, if you care to send me about forty cents in stamps, and if you're interested. Not hawking anything, I just would like to reciprocate in any way I can. They are *Rose Tattoo, King and I, Moon Is Blue* and *Gioconda Smile.* If you don't read plays yourself, you might know someone who does.

You ask who is Ward McAllister. That was a feeble and forced little joke at best, and being made to explain it is probably the punishment I deserve. Ward McAllister was a social arbiter of the 90's or thereabouts, who conceived the idea of the elite "400." He waged an apocalyptic battle with Mrs. Stuyvesant Fish or somebody, in an era conceivably less harried than this one. My mind is filled with utterly useless information like that. Yours, B.

County Jail
DECEMBER 20, 1951

Dear Mike:

The silence from the oleander bush is ominous. You salty about somethings Papa, or you in jail? I miss your letters and the *New Yorkers* you have been sending. The magazines are wonderful of course, but most of all I miss your letters.

Haven't heard from Lisa either, and I'm feeling completely abandoned and ill used. "Is it nothing to ye, all ye who pass by?" Verging on tears, B.

County Jail
DECEMBER 23, 1951

Dear Mike:

. . . I had a chance to take off from here a couple of weeks back. Another inmate arranged a pickup and a ride to Georgia, for a consideration, and asked me if I wanted to go along. I wrote to Louie asking him to lend me the loot and got the Old Ignore. Reassuring, somehow, in a world fraught with change, that Louie remains the Eternal Shit-Bird. The guy took off with another con, and they're in Chicago now. Thinking it over though, the risk was perhaps too great, I have less than five months to go, and it would have been just my style to step on my dick again.

To brighten the nights a little, I have started a little bootlegging operation, making "buck" (prison liquor) out of cornbread, cane syrup and water. The result is quite pleasant, tastes something like cider with a mild boot. I plan to let the next run ferment a little longer to increase its potency. The penalty for getting caught at it is ten days in the hole, but my cell, for some reason, is never shaken down, and only one other con knows about the stuff.

The legendary "silence" of prisons ("death to the squealer," and all) does not apply here. The joint is full of cheese-eaters, and The Man usually knows what you're doing before you do. I believe that I and my boy—a strange and somber Irish lad fresh from ten years in stir—are the only two in the whole joint who don't gossip like old women.   Ever, B.

County Jail
DECEMBER 30, 1951

Dear Mike:

I was somewhat rocked to hear that Lisa had shown you the letters I wrote her. Mutual confidences between Lisa and me have always been of the nothing-barred variety, and as I remember I out-diaried Kafka in several of those lurid missives. Shock, perhaps. Certainly, before that savage and doomed affair with Joey, the guy who ran with me, I had never come up against such naked violence (almost indecently apt for what I did encounter) and the fact that it did not unseat my reason convinces me that I am completely imperturbable.

But I know I can never forget the several shattering days of that abortive escape attempt, nor the events that led up to it. Nor Joey. Recently he kited a letter out of Raxley to me—and I am dismayed to realize that the flame burns perversely on between us. Clearly, I am a neurotic glassbrain, mired in "nostalgie de la boue."

In speaking of the letters Lisa so thoughtfully showed you, you make use of the terms "terrific" and "classic." Be it known that I am wary of compliments, particularly from persons whom I suspect of cleverness.

As to why I am more concerned with what goes on outside than with what goes on here, it is because so little of what goes on here interests me. There are a number of drab little intrigues stewing all the time, which I keep clear of as being unprofitable as well as dull.

And always, the running to The Man with tales true and untrue. (I expect my small bootlegging operation to get knocked off any day.) Nothing more clearly illustrates the anomalous character of this place than the fact that such tale-bearing is bewailed but tolerated.

As to the attitude of the authorities toward me and the aberrant sex department, it seems to be a blend of detachment and sophistication which I call sinister. I know they are aware of what cooks (a couple of trusties have told me that the assistant warden refers to me as The Whore.) Maybe they think it's the same thing as keeping a cat around a racing stable.

So I am saddled with a kind of sticky notoriety that I did not seek and do not want.

My present "protector" is a huge bull of a guy from Louisiana with a hair-trigger temper, whom I keep happy by the simple expedient of complying wit' his wishes. He has the cell next to mine in the isolation block, having been put there for beating up on just about everybody in the joint. I feed him flattery that would floor someone more discerning, but on him it just begets a fatuous expression. Demeaning, degrading, de-lovely . . .

On Wednesday and Saturday, Bayou Boy and I are taken out of our cells and up to the main dormitory to use the showers. The guards then go back to their poker game in the office until lights out, when we are returned to our cells.

During the time we are up in the dormitory, we shower first—then Bayou Boy drapes blankets around a tier of bunks in the dimly lighted rear of the dormitory (briskly evicting any occupant of the bunks). This contrivance is called the Wigwam, and . . . well, need I continue?—I don't have to draw a picture.

Thus the extracurricular activities. Is it any wonder that I try to turn my thoughts elsewhere, like a roach trying to climb out of a bottle?

It's no use to piss and moan about it; if I made a Thing of it and let it drag me, I really would flip. I can't do without the shower and I daren't cross Bayou Boy—I've seen others try, and the results were pretty apocalyptic. And I think that in that dim brute-mind there is a notion that his part of *entrepreneur* in the proceedings gives a certain cachet. Oh well.

So I can only sweat it out and remember Whitman's convenient, "It was not I who sinned the sin, the ruthless body dragged me in."

You speak of my "good institutional adjustment." You could call it that, but it's the understatement of the year.   Ever, B.

County Jail
JANUARY 1, 1952

Dear Nelson:

I have been meaning to write earlier to thank you for that astounding box you sent, but the work we have been doing lately has left me so exhausted at the end of the day that I have been asleep when I hit the pad.

We have been widening a right-of-way on one of the county roads, cutting through a solid wall of vegetation. I remember reading once in one of those bleary South Seas novels that Nature in the jungle was almost a malignant force in its ferocious growth. After battling it for a week, being strangled by vines and tripped up by roots, I am ready to believe in the malevolence of Nature.

As to that prodigious box, I have been like a fat lady with a barrel of chocolates or a dog with an array of bones. I have been gorging myself on *New Yorkers,* after dipping into that curious volume "Prison Days and Nights." (That was a rather pixie-ish inclusion. You aren't being flip with me, are you, lad? And wherever did you find it?)

It's absorbing though, and by comparison makes my situation seem like a breeze.

As you have probably read in the papers, the simmering witchesbrew of fear and ignorance (real southern cooking) has boiled over into murder again. The Florida murder of a Negro prisoner by a sheriff's deputy in Tavares and the murder of the Negro leader Moore near Sanford are reprehensible, in local opinion.

For the reason that they bring the unwelcome light of publicity into the dark hinterlands here, dark with the pall of proud and willful ignorance and carefully nurtured prejudice.

With a thick pink smooth Baptist icing.

Incidentally, two Baptist ladies come out every Saturday to hold Bible classes here, Negroes on one side, whites on the other. After the Baptist lady has fervently assured the whites of the heavenly awards awaiting the righteous, she always turns to the Negroes with a kind of hasty "and-of-course-you-too" addendum. In dealing out threats of Hell for the wicked, she gives the colored side the same breezy afterthought treatment.

I always have the curious sensation that she has a comfortable secret knowledge that in Heaven there are toilets and drinking fountains marked "White" and "Colored." In Hell of course, there are no such provisions. Which is what makes it, indubitably, Hell.

Did you know that mothers down here threaten unruly children with "If you don't behave I'll send you to the nigger school?"

So watch it, Junior, or you'll wind up doing Black Algebra.

Yours, B.

County Jail
JANUARY 13, 1952

Dear Nelson:

Of the books you sent, I've enjoyed rereading *Huck Finn* very much and D. H. Lawrence's hotsy-totsy opus *The Lost Girl*, new to me. Some rather shrewd and delightful humor in this Lawrence book, though, something I've encountered in his other things.

One thing I have noticed about Lawrence, though (said the mountain, proudly bringing forth a mouse). I ran across *Lady Chatterley* not long ago and reread it. To my intense disappointment, most of the "hot parts" were deleted, and it was spangled with asterisks—but in both books, it seemed to me that his descriptions of scenes of passion, or bedroom bouts, were almost womanishly fervent. That is, the viewpoint seemed to be female. Curious.

However, maybe it is all "in the eye of the beholder," and instead of being penetrating, I am merely tipping my mitt. The hell with it.

I heard a story the other day that has haunted me since. One of the guys on the crew is a one-armed fellow called "Tub," a cheerful garrulous villain who doesn't do anything but water the men and spin yarns endlessly. He has been in the state pen a couple of times, and on one of his stays there it was his job to drive a mule-drawn wagon that took the colored women prisoners from the prison to the cane fields where they worked. At dinner time, none of the women would eat the beans out of the big pot, as they came from the prison kitchen. Instead each one would carry a tin can, put her beans in that, cover them with cane syrup, and build a separate fire to cook them over—so that there were always twenty-four separate fires going, a woman bending over each one.

Two of the girls on the crew were named Helen and Josie. Josie was a "bull-dagger" or active Lesbian, and Helen was her chosen partner, her "mate." Another girl who was also a bull-dagger had recently joined the crew, and Helen had transferred her affections and her favors to the newcomer.

During the late afternoon fifteen-minute break when the prisoners were allowed to rest and smoke, Josie asked Tub to lend her his knife to trim off the end of some cane she was chewing. And when nobody was looking, she stabbed Helen several times. There was no way to get her back to the prison but the mule wagon, and on that slow rough ride over the rutted roads, the file of colored girls following like a cortege, the beautiful and faithless Helen bled her life out, in the flat and somber back country. A dismal place for a soul to find itself adrift.

I should like to write that story, but I'm afraid even Quiller-Couch couldn't help me.

Once again I must thank you for enclosing the deuce, the envelopes and all those stamps. I long for the day when I can make some practical return, instead of merely emitting clouds of gratitude when squeezed, like one of those plastic deodorant bottles. Yours, B.

County Jail
JANUARY 16, 1952

Dear Mike:

I rather regretted mailing that last letter after I had done so, but you asked for some information as to what went on here, and I thought perhaps some of the racier details of the social whirl were indicated. And that bland mention of my "good institutional adjustment" nettled me somewhat, at a time when I was struggling with an impossible situation.

I was close to despair, really, and determined not to succumb to it. That may explain the lack of restraint that I exhibited.

At any rate, things have taken a considerable turn for the better. In a situation like this, where one's immediate future is so completely in the hands of the authorities, changes can occur with no warning at all, and that is what has happened.

Ever, B.

County Jail
JANUARY 27, 1952

Dear Nelson:

I kited a letter out to you a couple of weeks ago, and not having heard from you, I am wondering if the letter ever got out. That happens frequently around here, convicts being rather tricky and unpredictable creatures. In the letter I sent I mentioned that the power tube of the radio you sent had gone out. I have since given the radio to one of the shotgun guards, who does repair work as a sideline, and in the revered tradition of all radio repair men, he found a number of other things wrong, so that the bill is five dollars, which I must pay before I get the radio back.

Perhaps you are annoyed at my asking you for the loot, for which I couldn't blame you less. But please be assured that I fully intend to repay anything you have sent me. This is not to detract in any way from the warm great-heartedness you have shown towards me and my dingy situation since I have been here; your kindness has been the brightest spot in an otherwise pretty murky existence. But there is after all no reason why you should subsidize me with no thought of any return.

The important thing above all to me is that I may continue to have your regard and good will—they have become rather important to me.

I have about three months and twenty-three days to go—

then I can stop being the eternal suppliant and take a more active part in the scheme of things. The day of liberation still seems remote, but inevitably it must come. It scares me somewhat to contemplate it, but I understand that buck fever is not unusual among convicts approaching release.

I have been given a cellmate, after a long spell of being alone. It has taken a little adjusting, and I miss my precious solitude, but we are getting on fairly well now. He is a massive husky Irishman from South Boston named Tom, has done time in numerous pens, has a bottomless amorality, and is a source of new knowledge, wonder and astonishment to me. Tom has been a jack-roller on Clark Street in Chicago, and tells zestfully of sending untold numbers of "marks" rocketing into oblivion through the use of chloral hydrate. Matter of fact he urgently wants me to send him a supply of the drug from Chicago, for use in recouping his fortunes when he is released. Here, at least to me, is a new twist—chloral hydrate as the be-all and end-all, the "Sesame" to success. I hesitate to abet such a dubious operation, and I am filled anew with wonder at the predatory inclinations of certain of the human species. Yours, B.

County Jail
FEBRUARY 10, 1952

Dear Nelson:

Thank you, father, for the fin and the postcards. Once more there is music in the air in this dullest of all possible jails, and life creeps its petty pace from day to day, but the weight of it somewhat mitigated.

My new cellmate, Tom, continues to be something of a mixed blessing. Before his advent, I had grown to like my solitude, with its opportunity for contemplation and long thoughts, and for reading. Now I find myself a captive audience for the rambling autobiography of a malefactor. I realize now that I have been grievously duped by all the crime movies I have seen, all the books about criminals I have read—I had been led to believe that criminals were tight-lipped, taciturn menacing gents who talked in grudging monosyllables.

Not so. All of them I've run across in here have been as extroverted as puppies, pathetically eager, nay, insistent, to tell *all* about their depredations. I could almost believe that lacking any other listener, they would fasten to the lapels of a policeman and never let go till they had related the gripping story of their misdeeds. Garrulous little buggers . . .   Yours, B.

County Jail
MARCH 16, 1952

Dear Mike:

. . . I am delighted to see Bayou Boy get the parole and wish him a speedy departure. Only then, I guess, can I feel entirely free from his domination. Yesterday, he detained me in the shower room for the old and sickeningly familiar reason, and I was numb with helpless rage for the rest of the day.

I shall be overjoyed when all this sticky nightmare is over. This breed of humans fills me with a vast weariness. I prefer cats, dogs and pianos.   Yours, B.

County Jail
MARCH 23, 1952

Dear Nelson:

Thousand thanks for the fin. My ever-lovin' cellmate and I were really on the rocks. It appears now that I have took him to raise, but the benefit of his protection outweights any financial outlay I have to make. He's rough enough to keep the other characters at bay. His autobiography drones on, and there are times it makes me wish I could vomit at will—it would be a neat succinct way of expressing the desperate ennui that comes over me.

I hope I never come under your sights as did the hapless P.

Bowles. I'd like to read that review, if it's still around. I may
as well admit that my memory of the book is a prurient one—
I remember mainly the goings-on of the heroine and that derned
Ay-rab. But I still think that Bowles is capable of some formidable flights of creative imagination. I assume it is a completely
objective performance. If it is not, he's holding out on his
psychiatrist and the worst is yet to come.

I've completed about half of a story that has been hanging
around in the back of my mind lately. I should like to send it
to you for inspection when it is finished, but I shan't insist.—
Anyway, I have set the thing down in my inimitable lurching
prose, and even if you blast it I shall simply murmur a tranquil
"Philistine!" and remain serene.

They tell a story about Gide and the piano in his studio. He
would sit at it, placing his fingers on the keys, but never play.
Said he was haunted by the fear that somebody would be
listening. It is something like that with me when I try to
write. I conjure up an imaginary reader—his face is unidentifiable,
but I can see the pursed lips, the judicious mien, dawning
slowly into disapproval as he reads. There is a sad wondering
shake of the head. Most unsettling. But I persist.   Yours, B.

County Jail
MARCH 30, 1952

Dear Mike:

I am writing this under something of a handicap, having
sustained a bone-deep cut on the first finger of my right hand
while removing an old rusty pipe from a culvert. However, I
think it will heal all right.

Many thinks for the shipment of magazines.

Fifty days left of this durance vile, and they get longer all
the time. I'm building pretty hard time now, waiting for the
day. At the end of it, I have the problems of getting up north,
but that doesn't dim in any way my eagerness to be out and
away.

Whatever became of your sailor suit? I could make good use of it hitchhiking North. True, I'd probably make a slightly over-seasoned salt, but these are parlous times, and everybody is more or less harried and confused.

County Jail
APRIL 13, 1952

Dear Nelson:

Another great howling box of goodies! Dammit man, you're just too much. I can only say again, sincere thanks.

The salacious pictures on the pocketbooks you sent aroused a clamor in the vitals of the happy mongoloid who is my cellmate, and forthwith he plunged eagerly into them. But he soon emerged bristling with frustration. The literary tone, and you can take it from him, is entirely too high. A student of Spillane and ilk, he seemed to feel that he had been roundly tricked.

The story that I was trying to write remains half finished and I think it will stay that way until after I leave here. I am unable to work with such a distracting presence in the same cell. And there is the lurking suspicion that it doesn't matter a hell of a lot if it's never finished. Even so, I shall persist.

Friday we worked deep in the swamp, repairing a sandy road leading into a fishing camp. We caught a couple of alligator terrapin turtles, an extremely belligerent type with a neck six inches long, which it uses to strike with the lightning swiftness of a snake, and jaws which can snap a finger off. The gang cook enticed its head out by waving a stick before it. When the turtle struck, he gave it repeated vicious blows on the head. There was wrung from the beast a small choked cry of such mortal agony that I shall never forget it. It seemed to come out of centuries of silence. Lord, I was shaken!

I am reading the *Short Novels of Colette*, which I should like to pass on to you, if you want to read them. For one in love, as I believe you to be, they have an added poignancy.

County Jail
APRIL 20, 1952

Dear Nelson:

This will be a tough one to write, so I shall just plunge into it. I am getting out in twenty-nine days, and would like to borrow fifty dollars to get back through the Union lines.

The prospect of having to hitchhike through all those southern counties, all of them eager to recruit penniless wayfarers into their road camps, is about as inviting as a trip across Niagara on a slack wire.

In addition to my fare, I need clothes for the trip. The clothes I had when I came in here have not been improved through laying in a burlap bag in a damp storeroom for twenty months. I was allowed to inspect them yesterday, and they're hopeless. The shoes are cracked and covered with mold, the slacks have been riddled by some kind of varmints.

The official reaction to my outraged amazement was a bland indifference.

I am profoundly ashamed of being such a nuisance, of forever being the droning importunate, but there is nobody else I can ask. The people I'm going to in Wisconsin are far from well off, and will be depending on me to help out when I get there.

I shan't be able to start repaying you for a month or so after I get out. I figure it may take that long to get my fingers back in shape. After that, I can easily get a job in a river town replete with gambling hells and roadhouses.

If you decide to help me (once more!) and send the fifty bucks I need, I shall deposit it in the prison office till I leave. Then I will be able to shed this anxiety and do these last weeks, which get longer as my time gets shorter . . .   Yours, B.

County Jail
APRIL 27, 1952

Dear Mike:

Can't tell you how much your offer of help relieved my mind. I had visions of making every labor gang from here to Cincy, finally trudging along Clark Street in Chicago with a long white beard, looking for the familiar stripteasers, only to find they were all long since married to marks and living in Oak Park.

I had a couple of hectic days as a trusty, when one of the guys in the kitchen was laid up. Because of my short-time, I took his place, and it led to rather an amusing contretemps.

I had previously made friends with one of the colored trusties, guy named Pete M., who used to blow tenor sax in bands around New York and Philly. A delightful guy, pretty hip, and a pleasure to talk with after all the pedestrian conversation I get from the white stiffs around here.

Pete works in the colored kitchen, so we were free between meals to kick around on the extensive grounds of the stockade. He got hold of a little keef, and we managed to fly out on it a couple of times.

Seems we not only breached the color line, but gave it a compound fracture, you might say.

Somebody ratted us off, and I was put back on the work gang. They had Pete on the mat in the office, asking all kinds of probing questions. As he told me later, he gave them the Uncle-Tom-yassuh-boss routine that many intelligent Negroes use in their dealing with crackers, and they were forced to let the matter drop.

They never even came near me. Untouchable, I guess. Anyway it hasn't altered my status, except I get some fishy looks, and I still get out on that golden day, May 20. But I shall tread softly hereafter.   Yours, B.

County Jail
APRIL 27, 1952

Dear Nelson:

"Shall no far April heal my pain, shall no Spring make me whole again?" Twenty-three days to go, and the anticipation of freedom is killing me. When I was a child (shortly after the Crusades), there was always a long endless night that had to be somehow lived through before the coming of dawn on Christmas morning. I am feeling again something of that agony of waiting. On the road every day I work like a demon, tiring myself out so that I shall fall asleep the moment I hit the pad. It is for that moment my traitorous mind lies in wait to run riot . . .

You and Mike are kinder than I can say to make it possible for me to extricate myself from this Dixie debacle. I was in hope that you-all would see fit to lend me enough loot to get the new shoes and slacks I so badly need. There's a guard here, a fine guy, who has agreed to shop in town for what I need if I give him the money. But if it's too much, just skip it, you're doing an awful lot as it is.

Incidentally, I get a big five bucks from the county when I leave here. No peon, I.   Au secours, Jim

———, Wisconsin
JUNE 4, 1952

Dear Mike:

Arrived more dead than alive after one of those cunningly contrived Greyhound safaris—contrived, I suspect, by the railroad interests.

The peace and quiet, the beauty and serenity of my present surroundings may in time enable me to find an answer to the confusion that still besets me. In time, I hope that I may cease to feel like Lazarus adrift.

I practice the piano daily and hope soon to be able to go to Dubuque and find a playing job. It was gratifying to find that not all digital dexterity had vanished.

So all is not lost—soon, in a small corner of the world of music, I shall be playing my small sad keening songs—or my wistfully gay ones, which are even sadder, Mac. It is the moment I lie in wait for, when humans are weakened by night and alcohol, and I can take them back to the treacherous warmth and joy of the past.   Ready or not, Jimie

———, Wisconsin
JUNE, 1952

Dear Nelson:

If you find the timid little manifestations of Nature that surround you now abhorrent, I wonder what would be your reaction to the countryside I find myself in. Great roaring booming hills on all sides, and at night the demented incessant cry of the whippoorwill, or the foxes on the hills, sounding at times like shrill hysterical girls, at other times oddly like asthma victims gasping their last.

In these faintly inimical surroundings, I work at physical labor most of the day—I do not know why exactly, but it seems important to me that I remain physically hard. When I have finished working, I follow the rocky course of a brook to a pool in the woods and there bathe in the paralyzingly cold water.

I practice the piano for a couple of hours every day. All this in an effort to lay the specter I seem to be locked in with— the dogged memory of Joey D., and the year I had with him in the chain gang. With him, for the first time in a disordered jangling dreamlike life, I really came alive.

I want to try to write a comedy about what went on in the chain gang. Enough happened that was ludicrous to make a funny story, and playing it for laughs is really all I think I'm capable of. When I suffer, I sweat.   Yours, B.

P.S. All of which is vaporous nonsense, of course. I have decided to approach the problem of diverting the public with a studious nonchalance. I merely want to make money and leave the travails of Art to the younger and sturdier. I've had it.

——, Wisconsin
JUNE, 1952

Dear Mike:

I shall write this rapidly and mail it as quickly, because I think what I have to say might later seem to me shameful or weak. (Oh, God, I hear you say.)

I am wandering around in these enormous hills up here with a load of guilt or apprehension or whatever it is, meant for a mule. These people are kind and understanding, but there is not a single goddam thing in the world that will help me other than going to work and being in a position to help others, and to repay what I have already taken. I want and need so desperately to break through this wall, and to get back to the land of the living. They are poisonous, vicious, dull, I know, and I want to join them in their nefarious games. Contemplation drives me nuts.

And at the back and bottom of my mind is the realization that I shall come soon to think of the chain gang and the time I spent there as my finest hour. I simply cannot let it happen, I've got to begin quickly to make loud noises to exorcise that demon.

It's too easy to crawl back inside the gates. I want to stay out and do battle—but I need a couple of hammers.

Outside in the night at this moment the whippoorwills, with idiot intensity are singing their urgent questing song. I think I find them soothing because they are more possessed than I.

Jim

PART II

possession of narcotics

DOPE CHARGES
HOLD 'NOVELIST'
FOR TRIAL HERE

January 1, 1954——

James Blake, 35-year-old male nurse, ex-convict and aspiring novelist, is to be tried in Peace Justice Court today on a charge of possessing marijuana.

Detective Denis Quilligan, narcotics squad, said Blake confessed ownership of a small can of the narcotic yesterday.

Blake, born in Edinburgh, Scotland, was jailed New Year's Eve on a tipster's information that he was in possession of the "tea." Quilligan said Blake permitted a search of his dwelling at 3221 6th St. S. and the marijuana was found in a cupboard.

Blake has served an 18-months sentence in Jacksonville, police said, on breaking and entering and larceny charges. He admitted, police said, having been on a one-year probation in Miami in 1949 on a narcotics charge.

Police said Blake has submitted a novel of his experiences on a "Florida road gang" to a well-known publishing house and has received encouragement to revise the work.

Blake told police he had imported the marijuana here

from Chicago when he came to town in October. He
said he had "forgotten all about it" until police found it.

Ex Post Facto

*After the release from the chain gang in 1952, it was my
intention to spend some time preparing to return to night club
work as a pianist. I spent a couple of months in Wisconsin on
a farm owned by a painter friend, living quietly and practicing
piano several hours a day. This period of country living with a
good companion, and the music, did much to ease the anxiety I
felt at entering a strange civilian world, and to give me back
my civilian identity. But when the time came for me to perform
for a night club public again, I found myself unable or unwilling
to face the tensions involved.*

*A friend of mine got me work as an orderly in a mental
sanitarium in a small Wisconsin town. It was a highly reputable
hospital for mental disorders with a remarkable percentage of
recoveries, and I was fortunate to work under an eminent Midwestern psychiatrist. Trained workers were scarce and the work
was demanding, twelve hours a day, but rewarding, and in
working with all manner of mentally ill over a period of two
years, I learned a little more about myself.*

*After two years, however, I began to feel the strain of the job,
along with a recurrence of my old restlessness. It was October,
the Wisconsin trees were flamboyant, but the leaves were falling,
the morning air had an ominous edge, and suddenly I dreaded the
approach of another Wisconsin winter.*

*So I returned to Florida, to work in another mental sanitarium.
The latter turned out to be a very dubious operation run by a
pious Seventh Day Adventist. It was a front for a lucrative
traffic in illegal narcotic sales, where addicts with enough money
could live and be assured of a steady supply of whatever they
were hooked on.*

*These fashionable captives lived in modest pastel villas, dis-
creetly sequestered under palm trees, facing the ocean. Along*

with the gilded ones, however, there were a number of severely insane patients, and my work was chiefly with them.

I found them stashed away in a building behind flowering bougainvillaea. They were in such a heart-stopping state of neglect and filth that I was tempted to turn and walk away, but I couldn't. A few days of hard work with buckets of hot water and soap and Lysol improved their quarters. To clean up the patients, smeared with their own ordure, took persuasion and some persistence. Gaining their trust took even longer, but in time it was accomplished. And after a while a few of them could be taken out singly for walks in the fresh air, along the waterfront.

Not long after I went to work there I discovered the narco hustle in the hospital. The instinct acquired on the chain gang, to run from "heat," told me to get away, but it would have meant abandoning what I had gained with my charges. So I decided to hang in, and be as wary as possible.

The work was so exhausting that I had little personal life at all for a long time. I'd rented a small cottage in a tourist court on the bay, very pleasant, but spent most of my time there sleeping. My one relaxation was marijuana, which I obtained by mail from Chicago. I used it sparingly, smoking a part of a stick every night when I returned from work, and played the phonograph and did some writing. All very quiet and seemingly harmless . . .

However—the head nurse brought her nephew Sam from West Virginia and gave him a job. A sixteen-year-old boy, mentally and physically developed far in advance of his age, and with a sleek poise that was daunting. Almost at once he came on strong to me, soon was paying visits to my small cottage, and we began to pursue a torrid course.

About that time, Danny checked in, an ex-Navy man hooked on morphine. A difficult patient, violently combative, and because nobody else could be bothered, he was given in my care.

It didn't take too long, probably because they gave him the drug, perhaps because I worked hard at bringing him out of it, that he emerged as a different individual—personable, articulate, *literate, and with considerable charm. When he was granted permission to leave the sanitarium grounds for a daily period, he visited me, and to my surprise, brought gifts. In gratitude, he said, for my help. One of the times he came, Sam was with me. This confluence seemed to set off a train of events.*

The state narco agents finally descended on the place, and in the course of the investigation, it was discovered that I was an ex-con. The head nurse had not known this, but made a good deal of it after she found out. I was the heaven-sent, gift-wrapped scapegoat, everybody breathed a sigh of relief, and it all ended in a blaze of mutual good feeling. Excepting for me, Ichabod the pariah.

The fuzz asked permission to search my pad, and I consented, knowing myself innocent of any complicity in the operation. Forgetting all about the pot. My use of it had been so controlled, so nearly therapeutic, that it never occurred to me to hide it.

Anyway, they found it, with many a view halloo, and I was jugged, once again.

County Jail
JANUARY 12, 1954

Dear Mike:

I'm going to kite this out tomorrow morning, so herewith the tale. It all began when Danny was admitted to the Sanitarium as an M addict—an Irish urchin's face (strongly similar to yours), shy, diffident, gentle, though he came in roaring like a lion, due to being strung out, of course. I could see that under the uproar, he was lost and bewildered, and I was touched by it, brought him pajamas and a robe and what reassurance I could.

We became friends and after he was put on the ad-lib list at the San, he visited me often, bringing gifts (cigarette lighter, case, wallet, liquor, etc.). Seemed always to have plenty of loot, from a large Navy pension (three fingers off his right hand at Guadalcanal), the Veterans Administration paying his expenses at the San. He asked me to go to New Orleans with him after January 1, and I agreed, partly to get away from other complications, partly because I felt a genuine affection for him.

He told me of the hunger he'd had all his life for someone, asked me to stay with him and help him beat the morphine, said if he had love and companionship he wouldn't need anything in the narco line.

There was never any sex, he wanted something more than a roll in the hay for one night, he said we had plenty of time the rest of our lives for that. So, warm embraces, chaste yearning, nothing more. Paul et Virginie.

We planned to leave for New Orleans on New Year's Day. Danny went into town the afternoon of New Year's Eve, to make some final arrangements.

New Year's Eve was a happy time for me, one of the best I can remember. I worked at a local night club. I had a piano to play, someone to care for and to take care of, and I got glorious drunk.

New Year's Day two hamheads picked me up, took me in. First question as I got into the prowl car: Are you a pervert, Mr. Blake? No, sezz I, Presbyterian.

At H.Q. they threw the junk charge at me, having searched my room at the San, and I breathed easier, thinking I was clean. They stripped me of my ill-gotten finery, gold watch, ruby ring, lighter, case, gold I.D. bracelet; turned out Danny had been plastering all the jewelers in town with bum checks. They brought him in, someone I hardly knew, a wild-eyed savage hurling accusations of homosexual orgies spiced with all manner of narco. In the face of such a shocking and unexpected onslaught, I was commendably cool, I thought, pointing out that Danny was an undischarged patient from a mental san, incompetent and irresponsible, though it filled me with shame to have to do it.

They wouldn't buy much of it anyway, and took Danny away, still roaring. Formee-dob. What they had done, of course, was withhold the M from him till he was mad with desperation. But why destroy me? Passes understanding.

When they brought him over here from St Pete he was normal again, that is to say M to the earbones, contrite, weeping with remorse over what he had done to me. Said if he was going up, he determined that I should go along with him. Strange kind of affection. So now, even though he has been moved to the hospital lockup, I hear from him daily, and he has been paying for my simple jailhouse needs. I should have stayed on the tiger, rather than seize a wolf by the ears, but how was I to know?

I've about decided to cop out to the charge and take my chances with the judge, citing my good conduct record since my release from Jax and my fidelity to the memory of Flossie Nightingale.

No hope of making it a federal charge, and anyway I figure if I must have another jailhouse experience, it might as well be good and ripe. From what I hear, Raiford jumps—and if it gets too thick I can always try for a road camp and work myself into fighting trim for the time when I come out.

I wrote Dr. Algren about a week ago and as yet no reply. I hope he isn't displeased with me. More than ever I shall need his help. Certainly the book will be finished in a shorter time than it would be if I were out, with all the distractions I manage to find. Now necessity, financial and spiritual, will be the spur. Ever, Jim

County Jail
FEBRUARY 19, 1954

Dear Nelson:

The hurricane has come and gone, leaving me up a different tree than the one I started out in. Shifting the gears, making the adjustment to this most recent blow has been a little more difficult, the creeping years, I wot.

The first sharp reaction was "This means the end of my job with Budweiser." And the realization that the element of choice has been removed from my existence—or if not entirely removed, what remains is a beggar's choice between nothing and less than nothing. Well, one must make do with what is at hand: "If thou must choose between the chances, choose the odd/ read the New Yorker/and trust in God."

Last night the moon was radiant through the bars, and I felt a bottomless sense of loss, knowing that for a long time I would not walk the night and savor it—"I long to walk outdoors in the dark, the day is so shrill and pale."

How long I will be in is moot at the moment. I am told that a narco sentence carries no parole, but that the prisoner is released when considered cured. (Of what?) A minimum term of four months and some days has been mentioned, but this may well be jailhouse wisdom, there's a lot of that around.

There will be a period of waiting after my trial, for commitment papers and the arrival of the Raiford bus, conceivably a wayward vehicle, since it operates on no set schedule, but just as there are convicts to be transported to Moonbeam Academy. And there's a stretch of quarantine at Raiford, two to three weeks, after which I presume I shall be able to get mail. Since mail is permissible only from immediate family, I'll have to acquire some married sisters, and in that way, write to you.

The opus is snailing its way along. Since I sent you the latest pages, I was given at my request a cell by myself in which to work. A type of understanding rarely found in jails, and I've seen a few. I'll keep gnawing at it till I leave, when I'll post it to you.

My condolences on the death of Bubu—cats no doubt die as beautifully self-contained as they live.

One of my neighbors is going out in the morning, so I'll kite this out with him. Ever, Jim

County Jail
FEBRUARY 20, 1954

[Postcard]

Dear Nelson:

I had a preliminary legal skirmish today, but I dunno who
won yet—My head has been shaved and my pants leg slit up
the side. What do you suppose is up? I have devised a defense
measure for if I go to the Academy—I shall carry the MS everywhere I go, and read it to anyone who offers to chat. As
the word gets around, it will be as if I carried a ticking bomb.
Ever, Jim

County Jail
FEBRUARY 24, 1954

[Postcard]

Dear Nelson:

I landed a three-year contract with the Commonwealth today.
Could have been worse. Now if only Doubleday was as free
with *their* contracts. Well, if they boot you off one level,
onliest thing to do is look for kicks on the *new* one. Just
waiting around for the bus now, probably ten days or so.

County Jail
FEBRUARY 27, 1954

Dear Nelson:

The last bus for the Academy ran the 22, so the next one
will be mine. Usually ten days or so apart.

I'm rather surprised and gratified that anything emerged from
that gelatinous prose I inflicted upon you. The period of

transition from jailbird to accredited convict has an air of impermanence about it, waiting for the other shoe to fall. Once the matriculation at the School for Scoundrels is accomplished, and I am installed once again at the bottom of the ladder, safe from attack from beneath, things should level off and move either forward or sidewise.

Some of the questions you asked I answered in a previous letter, but I'll run it again if you want.

The length of time to be shook on a sentence like mine is indeterminate, from all I can learn, that is, I can be released when pronounced cured of my addiction.

And what a glorious golden day that will be! To be free of the nagging craving for the weed with roots in Hell! When I think of the good jobs I've lost through being a slave to the weed—assistant manager at the Walgreen's, ladies' foundation buyer at I. Klein, (though there was a lot of tension there)—the prosperous balloon-rental agency (till it went up in the air), the glacier warning service in Miami— Gone, all gone, in the smoke of the hell-spawned weed.

The offer of a radio is more wonderful than I can say—it may be that the labored quality of the stuff I've been putting down lately is due in part to the lack of music—it is an integral part of me. Fortunately, radios are permitted at Raiford, and I'm told there's a band there, and it may be I can charm some body into letting me play. My need for music is basic, without it I am a lamentable lopsided figure.

You can best be the judge of the proper time to tell the agent and publishers that the Black Maria came for the White Hope. I should think they'd be pleased, a captive author (or embryo thereof) free from all distractions and blandishments.

The quarantine period is fairly rugged, they say, but conditions improve after assignment of a permanent job and I've heard that a couple of cats I knew in the chain gang are up there, so I'll know somebody, at least.

As long as there are people around with motivations, inhibitions, reactions, to observe and speculate on and marvel at, things will never be entirely dull. And since I am bound for a repository for persons with motives most devious, inhibitions most fragile, and ganglia similar to those of a frog, I daresay I shall find something to occupy me.   ever, Jim

Ex Post Facto

The Florida State Pen at Raiford is some fifty miles south-west of Jacksonville, in the desolate melancholy piney-woods country of inland Florida. The prison sits in the approximate center of a huge plantation of hundreds of acres, and has the appearance of a 1900 New England mill or shoe factory unaccountably set down in a subtropic setting and painted a glaring white. The prison has no high outer walls, but it has instead a series of three wire fences, fifteen and eighteen feet high, spaced six feet apart, the center one electrified.

In the county jail at Clearwater, the prisoners who had been in Raiford before had taken a grisly enjoyment in painting the horrors of the penitentiary, and so I approached it with dread. But my first reaction was one of disappointment. From jailhouse movies, I had expected a place bristling with tier on tier of bars, and clanging with electric bells. Instead, each cell was set apart from the next by concrete walls, and only the doors and outer windows were barred. Three floors of cells, called "ranges." The ground floor was made up of large cells, holding from twelve to twenty men apiece. There were stationary bunks around the walls, three high, comfortable enough bedding, and the sheets were clean. (Two sheets!) Though the prison itself was like an old shoe in its comfortable run-down condition, and rather sloppy, the convicts all appeared very clean: there was a laundry (worked by Negro prisoners) and clothing change three times a week.

We were taken off the prison bus (a converted panel truck) and led down a long dark hallway (an overhead sign said, NO LOUD NOISES AT ANY TIME). A more or less constant din banged and echoed off the walls. We were to spend two weeks in "New-Cock Court," the quarantine section of the prison, where newly arrived prisoners are kept while they're *mugged and printed, examined for scars and tattoos, tested for unspeakable diseases and suspect attitudes—and endlessly interviewed on their careers in crime.*

In a bare room we were told to strip; our civilian clothing and belongings, with the exception of cash and toilet articles and shoes, were taken from us. Then we were issued baggy gray coveralls (which I was to wear for a week without change). The coveralls and our underwear were our only clothing. These coveralls had a wide white stripe down the legs, and marked us as new-cocks.

We met Mr. Mac, the official in charge of ID—fingerprints and mug shots. He gave us a brisk talk, giving us to understand that we were less than dogs and weasels and were now going to pay the price of crime. Each neophyte was questioned as to how much money he had brought in. I'd been forewarned that all over ten bucks was confiscated, apparently never to be seen again, and had only the ten permitted.

After fingerprinting and photographing, we returned to sitting on long benches against the wall in the corridor. During this time I noticed that Mr. Mac had several convict assistants, who walked about with a great deal of freedom and assurance, dressed in spotless white trousers with a blue stripe and smart shirts, apparently from civilian life. One in particular I recall, the runner, or errand boy, of the ID office, a strikingly good looking young man who took a sort of interest in me and asked me about myself. He seemed obviously to have a homosexual understanding with the older con in charge of taking ID pictures, and that part of the photo lab which was their private area was tastefully furnished and held an easel with an unfinished painting on it.

I remember wistfully watching these glamorous creatures, the convict trusties, like an urchin looking at movie stars, so low did I feel on the totem pole, envying their apparent ease and freedom of movement in surroundings that were to me inimical and inhibiting. I wondered if, in the three years ahead of me, I would ever attain such dizzy heights.

The next ten days were spent attired in coveralls, in an

open quadrangle in the cell blocks, a dusty littered area where we had to sit on the ground while awaiting the next stage in our indoctrination process.

There were interviews of all kinds, some conducted by so-called "free-men," civilian employees of the prison; sometimes I was questioned by white-trousered convicts, who I learned were trusties, prisoners of privileged status who had been in the joint for years.

It was in these encounters that the relationship between interrogator and subject was most confusing, ambiguous. Their attitude switched from avid personal curiosity to official indifference and back. It was a breed I had never seen, their personalities seemed curiously muted, veiled, and I felt more intimidated by them than by the officials.

Whenever we were convoyed from one place to another in the prison for a new kind of examination, and passed through the prison population, there were wolf whistles, bawdy remarks, stares that were frankly sexual, measuring, calculating, speculating. A time of almost intolerable pressure for me, but my state of shock shielded me and I went through it all in blessed numbness.

At night, my assigned living quarters were in a large cell on the ground floor with seventeen other prisoners. Bunks were bolted to the floor, three high. The top one, considered least desirable, was for me the best, the furthest away from the whirling bedlam of the cell which began when we were locked in at night and continued until the bell rang for Lights Out. There were the usual extrovert bullies and loudmouths in the cell, and I kept to myself as much as possible, reading whatever material I could pick up. After Lights Out one night, one of the younger, weaker occupants of the cell was gang-raped by a number of the others, and sounds accompanying this noble group therapy were something to saw the nerves in half. The boy was removed to the hospital in the morning, his anus torn and bleeding, but nothing more was said about it. And I took bleak counsel with myself.

My cell was near the end of a long narrow corridor, and to reach it I passed Cell G-5, a notorious den I'd heard of in the county jail. Here the overt homosexuals lived in perfumed, screaming lurid celebrity, wearing earrings, their faces garishly painted. A line hung across the cell was draped mysteriously with feminine undergarments. I marveled at the official attitude, which seemed to be one of contemptuous tolerance.

The strange did manage to roam at certain times, I later learned, and were able to rendezvous with the jailhouse lovers, who provided them with cigarettes, makeup and the things that make a girl's life easier. They were known as pussyboys, galboys, fuckboys, and all had taken girls' names like Betty, Fifi, Dotty, etc., and were universally referred to as "she" and "her."

One of them, called Fraulein, vaguely Teutonic, affected some sort of mongrel accent, which seemed to enhance her allure among the "tush hogs." Fraulein was standing in the prison yard one day drinking a Coke, surrounded by swains. One of them whispered something in her ear, and Fraulein, who made a mad pretense of chastity, took umbrage, and hurled the drink in his face. Dripping, spluttering, he blurted, "If you wasn't a broad I'd stomp yuh!"

The Queen of the Rock, a really beautiful faggot, was Bobby —a feral, venal, coldly poised and enameled creature who filled me with awe. It was said she extracted staggering prices from her lovers for her favors.

One Saturday afternoon, Bobby and her current lover were discovered flagrante in an upstairs two-man cell, and taken to the Rock Lieutenant, known to cons as Uncle Ben. An old weary, bored, sardonic Cracker, his legendary profanity was said to scorch the eyebrows and sear the brain. He could have sent the guilty pair to the Flat-Top, the sinister building where the rebellious were methodically starved. Instead, he procured a chain six feet long and fastened one end around Bobby's ankle, the other around the ankle of her lover. Saying: "You so goddam fond uh one anothah, ah'm gonna give you a chance to get fondah." For two weeks they went around the joint chained together. Their arrival in Mess Hall was always eagerly awaited. Bobby would come in the door, the chain looped around her wrist, the crestfallen lover following like a sullen bear. Then she would drop the chain with a loud clank on the concrete floor and sweep regally down the aisle to the steam tables. No time, nowhere in the world before or since have I seen poise to match.

Small wonder that whenever in the course of official interviews I encountered the question "Are you a homosexual?" I calmly and casually answered no. There were couples living in prison wedlock all over the Rock, just less flamboyantly. The officials and everybody else knew the score—they had a sample bag of deviates as Horrible Examples for visiting brass or visiting busy-bodies. Among the officials, as among the convicts, the code of conduct seemed to be "Don't get in my face with it." Anybody who was caught was punished not for sex deviation, but for stupidity, for violation of the code.

It was in the future for me, all this jailhouse knowledge, being able to negotiate the treacherous currents of a penitentiary, and particularly this oddest of prisons. Sitting in the dust of New-Cock Court in a state of suspended animation, I knew little and felt less. About the sixth day of my incarceration, however, things took a sudden turn. Late one afternoon, I was suddenly braced by a burly red-faced civilian ("free-man"), chomping a cigar stub.

"You Blake?" I looked up, nodding. "Yes, sir."

"I'm Carl Hatch, I run the band. You're a piano player. You read notes?" Getting to my feet, I nodded. "Come with me."

It was close to dinner time. Carl Hatch took me into the mess hall, past convicts lining up for chow, up to the balcony bandstand overlooking the huge noisy hall. The band was assembled, twelve of them, preparing to play the nightly program of dinner music.

Hatch hustled me to the piano, through a barrage of curious and measuring stares. He sat me down and said, "Let's hear you bang out something."

At my right hand, a thin emaciated convict in horn-rims, holding an alto saxophone, turned and said, "Willie B.'s my *name, I'm supposed to be the leader of this outfit. Just play what's set up there."*

He beat off the tempo and we began. Stricken with stage fright, I was relieved to find they were using simple stock arrangements. At the end of the set, the alto man turned and said, "We'll jam a few. How about a blues in C?" Just a combo of five men played. They were all pretty good, and when it came to my solo choruses, I could tell they were listening hard. On my third chorus or so, I became aware of the drummer, behind me on my left, playing a strong driving beat, getting under me and lifting me up, exhilarating.

When we finished I turned timidly, furtively, to get a look at him, and met a pair of cold amused demonic green eyes. His skin burned brown and stretched taut over the angular bones of a face almost skull-thin, surmounted by an aggressive widow's peak and thick sun bleached yellow hair. He wore a T-shirt and his abnormally long sinewy arms were almost completely covered with tattoos.

In a peremptory, threatening tone he said, "Sometimes we play 'Laura.' You know 'Laura?' "

I nodded dumbly. The alto man turned to say wearily, "Don't fuck up another piano man for me, J.P."

Jerry Parker. His vibrations made the air crackle around me, and even with my back to him as I played, I could feel his intensity. When the band finished playing and descended to the mess hall to eat, he took unmistakable charge of me, while Willie the leader scowled. There were a lot of questions, the most pointed of which I evaded.

Next day he came into New-Cock Court, in defiance of the rules, and said, "Let's walk and rap." So we walked the dusty oval, talking. He handed me a book. "See what you think of this." It was a copy of The Prophet *by Kahlil Gibran. I scanned some pages and handed it back to him. "This is rubbish." He pinned me for a moment with the green eyes, then threw back his head in wild barking laughter. "Yeah! Yeah! Yeah!" he shouted at the sky. And again that blazing survey. But he refused to explain.*

The last step in the matriculation routine was what the new-cocks called Graduation Day, when we went before the Classification Board to be told what our job assignments were to be. An important decision—it made the difference between pulling easy time or hard time. Not unimportant was the fact that it was also the day on which we shed our dirty smelly coveralls for clean prison uniforms, and were no longer marked as new-cocks.

The convict clerk called my name and I went into the big room where officials and department heads sat around a long table. I took the victim's chair at one end of the table as I was told. The chairman perused the folder before him (my rap sheet, the record of my stay in prison) and the men at the table in turn inspected me. After an agony of silence, the man said, "Blake, I think we'll put you in the band. Have you any questions?" "No, sir," I stammered, "Thank you, sir."

In the hall Willie the bandleader was waiting with J.P. They took me to the clothing room, where I was issued three changes of prison uniform. The white trouseres and white shirts of a band member and a trusty. I had begun my penitentiary career as a wheel.

NOTE:
Inmates of Raiford State Prison were permitted to correspond with members of their immediate family only. Thus it was necessary to invent married sisters with the surnames of the friends I wished to write to: Amanda (Mrs. Nelson Algren), Lorraine (Mrs. Mike Moran). "Gertrude" is Gertrude Abercrombie, a Chicago painter. Though the original letters were addressed to "sisters," the subsequent letters herein have been addressed to the actual recipients, for the sake of clarity.—Blake

Blake ♯52603, G-9
Box 221
Raiford, Florida
MARCH 13, 1954

Dear Nelson:

Two weeks of silence and grinding suspense, waiting to hear the publisher's reaction. The long silence is ominous. I can't imagine what made me so confident that a contract would be forthcoming—perhaps because by free-world standards it seemed such a picayune sum to ask for, though it would be adequate income for a convict, and the difference between shaking easy time and difficult.

Now the erratic pendulum of my mood has swung to profound hopelessness and stuck there. I've been fooling with a short story but have been handicapped by a lack of paper. (There's plenty in that box of clothing I packed for Raiford, but I haven't received it yet.) Any further work on the book will have to wait on the publisher's decision on the pages they have—if it is adverse, I expect it will take an effort to continue. One gets the weird futile feeling of having a waltz with oneself. Though as you know your encouragement has been the chief reason for my having any faith in myself at all.

I've discussed "Golden Arm" with several junkies here. They, not I, brought it up as an excellent example of a hip treatise. I didn't claim friendship with the author, not wishing to be thought a bumptious name-dropper, but I experienced a sharp glow of vicarious pride and pleasure.   Later, Jim

(James Blake ♯52603)

Raiford, Florida
MARCH 17, 1954

Dear Nelson:

Well, I've been at the Academy for about a week now, and very few of the lurid tales I've been told about it seem to be true. Not exactly the Rooney-Plasma, but it's not gloomy either.

The first day we went into chow hall, I was astonished when a band burst into dance music, live music, baby doll, not a jook. The orchestra plays at dinner every day, giving it a festive air and for me sometimes a vagrant touch of sadness. There is a trombone man in the band that is the living end, great big round bawling mournful tones, really heart-clutching at times. Yesterday I was called out, asked about my piano experience and played a set with the orchestra. I was pretty rusty, and I thought I was fairly inept, being about four years out of practice, but the boys in the band seemed, I would say, satisfied, and I may get the job. Nothing at all definite but I have hopes.

As for the mss pages I sent you from Clearwater jail, I knew they were rather lifeless and flat—I think perhaps being boxed in for so long a time caused my mind to go dead. My mental attitude seems to me a trifle livelier now that I'm getting out every day and seeing something more than a jail cell day in and out. I shall not have an opportunity to resume work on the book for perhaps another ten days, when I shall be out of "New-Cock Court" the quarantine section, so to speak, of the Rock. So I hope that what I've done so far will satisfy the publishers enough to write a contract for that big fifteen a week. And mighty big it looks to me in here, with my simple tastes.

Life has indeed been reduced to its simplest terms, a state of affairs not completely unpleasant. So many of the trimmings that go with life outside have often been merely confusing to me. The food here is simple but entirely adequate, as are the pleasures. Sunday night we had a movie, "Titanic," which was perhaps a shade *too* simple, but that would be Hollywood's doing. The orchestra played some fine jump music as overture and postlude, and there was a feeling of gala in the evening.

Feel good, have lost the jailhouse pallor and creeping apathy of Clearwater, and hope to resume work on the book shortly, along with the orchestra work, if I get the job.

I could use some stamped envelopes and paper like this, if such is to be had. Please observe the rules governing correspondence.

ever, Jim

Raiford, Florida
MARCH 21, 1954

Dear Nelson:

. . . There are a number of Jax (chain gang) alumni here, some who appear in the book—seeing them gave me a start, like suddenly materializing ghosts. Having them about to observe will perhaps add a certain depth to the characterizations, though my furtive scrutiny may make them uneasy.

There is evidence of a certain amount of literary ferment here, the bi-monthly magazine Raiford Record prints short stories, one of which I thought very fine, the rest at least creditable. I feel I shall be able to produce some writing here, once I get into less crowded quarters . . .   ever, Jim

Raiford, Florida
MARCH 31, 1954

Dear Nelson:

. . . I've been assigned to the band and orchestra. In the band, which plays every day at noon in the visiting park, I play the bass drum. An inimical intimidating instrument which, nothing loath, I belabor with vigor and verve, rending the air with such stately pandemonium all earth and sky are shook with the wonder of it. Sometimes it's even on the beat.

Then in the mess hall at night the orchestra plays for the dinner trade, and I play piano, a somewhat friendlier instrument. Last Sunday was my first night of playing with the outfit at the movies in the auditorium. I had a fine case of flop-sweat, which is excusable, the guy who played this spot before me was held over for three years. Some booking . . .   Later, Jim

Raiford, Florida
APRIL 15, 1954

Dear Gertrude:

No doubt you've heard by now how I stepped on it, I imagine Nelson or Mike has told you. I gave your name as one of those I'd like to correspond with, sister mine, so I hope you'll write now and then, when you're not painting. Or running that free pad for wandering minstrels.

My job assignment here is playing piano in the band, how about that? Pretty good outfit, several of the members were professional on the outside. All we have to do is play (and practice every day). We play dinner music in the mess hall every night and on weekends blow at the ball games. Nobody digs that, but it goes with the gig. That's the military band, something else. I play bass drum, you believe it? This swingin' group plays marches every day at noon in the visitors' park. Sunday night we play before and after the movie, and that's the big performance, we point all week for it.

After all, we have a captive audience of around 1500 for that, and they're pretty demanding. J.P. the drummer is easily the star, the leader lets him showboat at least once every movie night, and the convicts raise the roof, it's a fan club.

He's a big blond cat from Coral Gables, junkie, and he's been trying to make me play with more drive. The leader's an old-timey legit musician and he keeps us pretty much confined to stock arrangements. He says more guys get to play that way, and he's right.

So J.P. and I go up on the bandstand in the mess hall a couple of hours before we're due to play for dinner, and we jam, just the two of us. Most of the time he makes me play over my head, the way he backs me up on drums. Maybe by the time I get out I'll be a jazz musician—you always claim I'm not.

J.P. has been a help in other ways, too. Somebody to talk to, he's intuitive and perceptive, and we walk around the ball field for hours and rap about everything. Laughs too, which God knows I can use. The cat's a wild man and an outrageous ham.

We live with the band in a dormitory arrangement, a big room on a Trusty Range. The rooms on the floor remain open, only the floor is locked off at night, so there's considerable freedom of movement, the range is longer than a city block.

J.P. says we should get a two-man cell together in another part of the Rock, where we could have a radio and phonograph and be able to hear some music. I'm inclined to agree—after being with the band members all day, it would be a good idea to get away from them at night. But two-man cells are hard to get, the joint is crowded. And the band leader doesn't think so much of the idea, he says he doesn't want any "clicks" in the band. What's a click?

So that's what's happening in de jailhouse. What's happening out there in the cold cruel world? You painting much? Who's playing around Chicago? I hope you'll write, little sister. This isn't all that much of a ball, there are some very bad stretches, and I need to hear something from Out There.   Love, Jim

Raiford, Florida
MAY 2, 1954

Dear Nelson:

These past weeks have been a time of groping my way through the dense complexity of this strange and new society. Impressions, sensations, hustlers, coming at me from all sides.

Mostly it involves people (something like 3000 convicts here)—trying to figure which ones would be good to know, which ones costly, which downright dangerous. Willie the bandleader, an old career con, has been advising me from time to time. He's like an elder statesman in the community—which reminds me of a small town, except the population is markedly bizarre. One sees the same people all the time, and there's a lot of gossiping.

I've been lucky enough to find a friend and companion; the drummer in the band, he's called J.P. A brilliant musician, an intelligent articulate individual. He has a wry, sardonic outlook, on the surface he's a bitter clown, but under that there's a raging romantic, which shows in his playing, and in other ways.

I was living in the big dormitory-type room on a Trusty Range where all the band members are quartered. In the evening there was a lot of noise and horsing around, and it was hard to get any reading or writing done. So when J.P. suggested we move out and get a two-man cell (called "locking"), I agreed. Willie opposed it, but J.P. defied him. (What's the use of being a star, he says to me, if you can't be arrogant?)

The small cell is a lot better. J.P. got a phonograph and records, and a radio (a rich indulgent grandmother in Coral Gables), so there's music, we have privacy, time to rap endlessly, and I'm doing a lot of reading.

We're still in the band, of course, and that occupies most of the day. In some ways it's like a college fraternity. Or like a family, with Willie as the father figure. Or maybe he's more like a Proctor in prep school. Unlike the other squads, the band has no custodial officer assigned to it, no guard. We're on our own, and Willie says the only way to keep it like that is for him to keep everybody in line. He regards J.P. sourly as a problem child.

The Band Hall is a long shed made of corrugated sheet iron, one big rehearsal room and some smaller rooms. We check out of the Rock at Squad Call (8 A.M.) with the other work details, and walk a couple of blocks (inside the fences, of course) to the Band Hall.

There we're allowed time to make coffee on the hotplate, or for those with money, to order breakfast from the Canteen. (Every squad has a Runner, in the band a trombonist, who runs all the errands for the group—to prevent unauthorized wandering.) Then an hour of individual practice, and that is formidable cacophony, after which band practice. We play marches, sometimes attempt concert pieces. Me on the bass drum. I'll never learn to read drum music. Mostly I try to fake it, till Willie catches me.

Then we goof till it's time to go to the Visitors' Park and play our noonday serenade to the convicts, filing into the Rock for lunch. The gulf between our brisk optimistic music and the indolent shuffling of the cons can, in my opinion, never be bridged.

We play in the center of the park, which has low pavilions with tables and benches like a picnic area. The bandstand is an exact likeness of those one sees in the square of small southern towns. Gingerbread and all.

After lunch, orchestra practice, and then the members are free to pursue their hobbies. Several of them have impressive vegetable gardens behind the Band Hall, along the high fences. A trumpet player builds steamboat models, which he sells; a saxophone man paints, which he tries to sell; others make leather wallets and purses for sale. A trombonist is digging a swimming pool, under the watchful bemused eyes of the tower guards, who wait for it to turn into a tunnel.

It's a wildly mixed bag of personalities—professional musicians in for narco or bum checks, and high school band musicians, in for auto theft, etc.—and clashes are inevitable. (The tuba man was unhappy when they filled the bell of his horn with water.) But comparative order is maintained under the jaundiced eyes of Willie, arctic in their terminal disillusion behind thick lenses.

The important thing is, it's a group, more or less cohesive, with a common identity. In terms of convict values, a prestige group, and as such a shelter of sorts from the sinister wind that often blows through the joint. Also, becoming J.P.'s cellmate seems to have been a political move that I made all unaware. It's amazing, and acutely disconcerting, the cordiality I get from the hardnoses because of the association with J.P. Slowly, I learn.

I seem to be back in show biz, but I had to do it the hard way.   alors, Jim

Raiford, Florida
MAY 10, 1954

Dear Nelson:

Baby, such gloom! I feel worse about having disappointed you than anything else. As for Doubleday's rejection, I feel a number of things, all confused. (Shall we examine how I feel?)

Well, as far as the answer from Doubleday goes, makes me feel like a man who has resigned himself to hanging, has ascended to the scaffold, only to be stabbed by the hangman.

Or like one at the guillotine who kneels and offers his head, and receives an electrifying boot in the rear.

I don't understand why you counsel not going on with the book for a period. I feel that I'm being patted into bed and offered cambric tea, calf's-foot jelly and eel broth. Lemme up, I'm better nigh ever was! Really, though, could I have particulars on the debacle?

Waiting all that time to get the thing done hardly appeals to me under present conditions— need bread, baby. My thought was to bull ahead with it and try to realize what loot if any could be had. There was a time I thought I had an amorphous idealistic thing to say on the subject, but it seems to have disappeared under a bed somewhere. It may turn up.

Do you advise finishing the book as soon as possible, then, with that viewpoint? If nothing else, I'll have had the practice.

The "long summer" sounds idyllic. My heart is on the Calumet, my heart is not here.   ever, Jim

Raiford, Florida
JUNE 15, 1954

Dear Gertrude:

Down here on the plantation, I'm becoming the well-rounded musician. For one thing, I have to practice every day, and for another, I have to read music. Not to speak of the bass drum.

The drummer in the band, who is also my cell partner now, had been forcing me to play more aggressively, more percussively if you will. And since my inclination has been to play lyrically, I occasionally offer some opposition. In my own covert way, of course, my obstinacy can be devious and take many forms, as you know. I can see that sometimes I hang him up.

It's not all one-way. He's a complex cat, J.P. I hope you can meet and hear him some day. I've never seen such a split between the public and private person. Around the joint he's the flamboyant celebrity—brash, headlong, the performing clown. He has a group of satellites around him, a coterie I guess it is, who applaud him indiscriminately, urging him to even wilder excess. They apparently miss the savagery, mockery, desperation in his comedy. Maybe they don't, maybe that is what nourishes them. Maybe the dismal truth is that he throws a lot of bread around and they have expectations.

Their attitude towards me is interesting—deference, disdain, doubt. A certain resentment, too; they seem to have a possessive attitude towards J.P. I don't know how to come on to them at all, so I take refuge in vagueness. The thing that actively bugs me is that our cell is always in turmoil, stooges drifting in and out. It isn't until night and they're all locked up that there's any quiet.

Then J.P. becomes his other self. Quiet, thoughtful, at times morose and withdrawn. When I feel that I can do it safely, I try to probe his need for all those ciphers, all the exhausting tohu-bohu, but I meet a wall, he won't talk about it. It's got nothing to do with us, he says.

I had the intention to pull this time as quietly and anonymously as possible. Between thought and act falls the shadow. It's a long shadow, little sister.

I'm learning to play the organ. Willie the bandleader is Chapel organist and choir director. Now he wants me to play the organ while he directs. So he gives me a couple of hours off every day to go to the Chapel and practice. It's a nice Hammond, and I'm learning, mostly it's a matter of operating the pedals, and in time I should be an organist.

I speculate about Willie. He's a wise old crocodile, hip in the ways of the joint. He has cautioned me obliquely a few times about my present course. Now he gives me the opportunity to be alone for a few hours every day, with a challenge. It's peaceful and soothing in the empty church, just me and the organ, and I come away from these sessions calmed, refreshed, recharged.

If only I were not so insanely curious. I can feel the wind rising, I know there's too much sail on—but I'll probably ride it out, to see what happens.

Remember when I was playing at the Croydon Hotel in Chicago, how those Mafia types used to intimidate me? I was in Mother's arms and didn't know it. Write me, baby, and if you can send some bread, beautiful. Education is expensive.

love, Jim

Ex Post Facto

After I was assigned to the band, Willie the bandleader arranged for me to move from the new-cock cell to a large dormitory room on the third floor of the prison, where the band members lived. This range was a trusty area called 3-T; the rooms were never locked and it was possible to circulate over an area longer than a city block.

J.P. was living in the band room, and on the first night he initiated me into the practice of staying up all night and eating "cotton." This was a roll of absorbent material inside a nasal inhalator, which was impregnated either with amphetamine or

*desoxin, which induced a kind of tense euphoria, mental alert-
ness and wakefulness.*

*We swallowed chunks of this substance, chased it with hot
coffee, and sometimes stayed awake for two or three nights in
succession.*

*The bandleader was opposed to my association with J.P. J.P.
dismissed it: "Where's he going to find another piano man like
you, or a drummer like me, in a joint full of morons?"*

*So I became the tail to J.P.'s kite. We stayed up at night,
sitting in dark corners of the range, endlessly talking. Discovering one another, and the growing magnetic attraction between
us.*

*One night about a week after I moved to 3-T, J.P. led me
down the long darkened hallway to a vacant room with four
empty beds. The convicts who lived there worked at night in
the steam plant. We turned on and, in local idiom, "made the
scene." It was a hot night, and when we left towards morning,
the bed was drenched in sweat. The convict who had permitted
J.P. the use of the pad complained loudly, bitterly and openly,
and it was public knowledge that J.P. and I had become lovers.*

*I had to contend with the reproachful attitude of the band-
leader and the coolness of the other musicians. And with the
ominous sudden familiarity of J.P.'s hardnose friends, one of
whom startled me by referring to me as "J.P.'s old lady."*

*Bewildered, I told J.P. about it. He was amused. "That's how
it goes. Either you're my old lady or you're a whore. If you're
a whore, they'll grind you up. As soon as I can buy a two-man
cell, we'll move out of here and lock together."*

*Thus began a turbulent four months, an intensity engulfing
and exhausting. We had companionship, love, laughter—excitement and fulfillment in music. But there were many abrasive
moments and quarrels. J.P. was dedicated to staying constantly
stoned on whatever stimulant was available, and insisted that I
join him in his obsessive pursuit. It took all our money, and
incessant scheming and hustling to get more. If I suggested
cautiously that we moderate our erratic way of living, he turned
sullen and abusive. By the time he was released from the joint*

in September, we had become deeply involved, and his leaving shattered me.

Willie had watched the evolution of the stormy affair with weary distaste, and now he helped me pick up the pieces. He pointed out the tactical error I had made as a newcomer to the joint. In that tight closed society, I had drawn attention, I had "put heat" on myself by becoming the intimate of a notorious and rebellious figure. With the officials I had marked myself suspect, with the convicts I had marked myself available.

He explained that the more useful I was to the officials, the more tolerance I could draw upon. So, in a maneuver to improve my image, possibly because he wanted me around as band pianist, and because he was tired and in poor health, he turned over the job of Chapel organist to me.

That helped to cool me with the officials. To protect myself on the other flank, I induced a burly weight lifter from New Jersey to move into the cell as replacement for J.P. Eddie was a simple cheerful giant, easily dominated. I was learning to be a prison politician.

Raiford, Florida
FEBRUARY 7, 1955

Dear Gertrude:

Such a lovely meaty witty pithy provocative and satisfying letter. And it seems always to arrive when I am in the soupiest of dull gray moods. Chief contributing factor: Our jazz combo has been limping along for want of a proficient percussionist—the boy we have is a nice guy, but has the approach to jazz of a non-union hod carrier. The beat is everywhere but in the slot. And to make it more excruciating, J.P., our former drummer, has returned to the joint with a fresh bit, after only four months or so on the street, and we've been unable to get him back in the band. The thought that help is so near and yet so far keeps me agonized.

A glee club has been formed here (by me), members of the

combined black and white choirs and we are busily preparing
our first program. Chaplain sponsors, and he's letting us ring
in some popular stuff. I've arranged some five-part harmony
on "Dream" (a tune chosen for the safe innocuity of its lyrics—
the fact that there are two sexes is one we must apparently
circumvent, and love lyrics might be inflammatory). We're using
a tenor sax and guitar behind the vocal, and it shapes up pretty
well.

Of course, we have what is probably the world's toughest
audience. Their basic and abiding resentment at incarceration
takes odd forms, such as seemingly senseless booing at random.
Such a reaction at first startled and outraged me, but "com-
prendre tout, c'est pardonner tout," and now I feel only a mild
annoyance.

How I wish I could have heard Frank lecture at that sociology
scene. The naivete of some theorists is as bad as the calloused
cynicism of some veterans in penology. Although my observation of the run of convicts here indicates that it would take
a superhuman to strike a balance between too much sympathy
and too little. Whether the same is true of other joints I cannot
say, being a comparative novice at this game, but the population
in here is by and large a jackal pack, to whom goodness is
weakness. For instance, most of the hacks here are pretty decent
—but to the cons (not all, of course) that decency is a chink
in the armor, and they mark it as such. What is the ultimate
solution for such malevolent misfits? Is there one?

Our black brothers' combo was lacking a pianist for rehearsal
recently, and I filled in. It was an opportunity for me to get
closer to people I've looked at from afar with a gnawing
curiosity. An illuminating and frustrating experience, which
showed me with brutal clarity that the bop medium apparently
will ever remain for me a foreign language. I can understand it,
but I can't speak it. The same seems to apply to communication
with my brothers. I doubt if there is a Berlitz remedy for this.
Maddening.

My literary efforts remain stalemated. I've been tinkering in
my bad moments with a tasteless jape which deals with a home-

sick pederast from Piccadilly, whose favorite tune is London Derriere. Alas for an idle mind.

I don't know if I've mentioned my new cellmate (whose typewriter this is), young Jewish lad from New York, in for 15. A CAN charge, Crime Against Nature (which ignores the infinite variety of Nature). A bright spirit, intelligent, and at long last someone who shares my mordant view of my compeers of the compound. He's an erstwhile member of the Eastern tootoo set, a friend of ——, the playwright. The conversation at times attains a brittleness that is formidobb— what Taloo said to Ezio that made him belt her with the kippered herring, what gives with Tennessee and the reclaimed Arab camel-boy— at times it reminds of two Schrafft's-type harpies awash in Alexanders, in full cry, and the prim prison air is rent with demoniac eldritch cackles.

Complications loom, however. J.P. is back (and when I saw him in the prison yard, I understood how heart attacks can occur) and he's confident of moving back into the cell. The awful clutch was there, but I had a wrenching time, both during and after, and I'm somehow reluctant to live in an eggbeater again. I've made a lot of points with Willie the bandleader, and I could spend them all in one false move.

Fondest, warmest, Jim

Raiford, Florida
FEBRUARY 28, 1955

Dear Gertrude:

For the wonderful package, warmest thanks, mes petits, I was like a child with one of those Christmas stockings of red netting, pulling out one bright and shining and astonishing thing after another. The clock was a special delight, I'd been going through the days always with the harassing feeling it was later than it was (philosophers tell us it *is*), and the ticking box has restored a small corner of peace to my mind—no mean thing, as matters stand. . . . You say, "I wonder what is really happening to you in that southern retreat"—a remarkably perceptive shaft, to be sure, though I didn't know that my graveyard whistling was so apparent. What is happening here quite probably might happen to me elsewhere—though there I would be free to flee from it if I chose. In fine, I'm in a perpetually simmering stew, the ingredients of which are the same as kept le tres cher Andre Gide in such a swivet all his life. (Though I do not presume to indentify myself with him.)

The cause and object of all this fever I've mentioned to you before. I realize I've put myself in emotional pawn to the point of bankruptcy, and I struggle constantly to regain my old self-sufficiency. A shattering experience, but instructive, in that I have discovered new heights and depths, new facets to the constant puzzle of human relationships—an exploration highly recommended by the poets. When it has ended, as these things must always end, in a frail diminuendo of frustration, I may be wiser. Or I may simply be wearier. At present I am a drunken balloonist in a high wind. And it has driven me to work, since in my worst moments of blind longing and black hopelessness, work is the only thing that restores my identity to me. If I burden you with this, it is only that in telling it I am able to exorcise some of the malevolent magic.

In a lighter key— I may have mentioned to you our new trumpet man, a shy romantic little cat from Pittsburgh, blows a lot like Chet Baker and writes tender wistful little tunes, the music to which is mostly good, lyrics mostly bad. I'm going to try to help in that department, bringing to bear my long years of distinguished failure as a songwriter. But we play together tunes like I Fall In Love Too Easily and Time After Time, and are always discovering new ones we love in common. All is not black. First bell has just sounded, so for now, good-night, bless you.   Jim

Raiford, Florida
MARCH 3, 1955

Dear Mike:

The silence from that direction is worrisome, I hope you haven't been kicked by one of those Hialeah horses. Or contracted the fatal magnetism for policemen which is my special affliction. May I be reassured?

I've been industrious recently, having finished a short story and nearly completed another. Tomorrow I must take the finished one around to the front office to have it approved for mailing to the agent. I anticipate no difficulty, it's innocuous escape stuff, and the only grounds for objection I can think of would be literary.

Called "A Burglar Is Only A Man," it is an exceedingly simple thing, suitable for an exceedingly simple magazine, of which there is no dearth, so I have hopes. It's an O. Henry-gimmick type story, however, rather unfashionable since the New Yorker created a vogue for the short story that trails off into a low moan. Mine may perhaps be too brisk for the fashion.

There's another apprentice author here, Tom Rolfe, whose acquaintance I've scrounged—intense introspective sort of cat, a little on the solemn side, as most of the prison quasi-intellectuals seem to be, for some reason. Everybody wants to instruct somebody. About his writing, he's stern and dedicated, approaches it with the lugubrious and methodical manner of a man building his own mausoleum.

He intends to prepare himself for the craft (he's in for 15 and there's no pressing need for haste) by writing for pulps. Somebody has assured him this is the approved Murcan way for all authors to begin.

It well may be. I know I've missed a boat somewhere. The other day he told me, in a manner that brooked no contradiction,

that Frank Yerby was a genius, a concept so novel that I am at
a loss to know where to begin to grapple with it. But he's
stimulating company and takes my mind away for a time from
my fustian Proustian ruminations about my unfortunate pre-
dilections and what at all is to become of me.

With your consent I'm giving your address to a student who's
graduating shortly. Not only because he'll be bearing tidings,
but because I think you'll find him vastly intriguing. He's evil
from the toes up, but it's a kind of light-hearted wickedness
you don't see around much any more. Belongs to the spike
society, shoots angles all his waking hours, dreams them the
remainder, and speaks a patois all his own. I think you'll be
diverted. I needn't tell you to be wary as well as beguiled.

The time approaches for your northward migration along with
the wild goose, and I hope you will give a thought to falling
by here for a visit. If so, write for a pass good on weekdays,
I don't have to tell you how much I yearn.

No further word from Doctor Algren, intrepidly gold-seeking
in California. I expect he's much involved with all the Hollywood
starlets, harlots and varlets.   alors, Jim

                                        Raiford, Florida
                                        MARCH 27, 1955

Dear Gertrude:

I am so proud of Frank I could bust—speaking before that
group of penological types, I mean. Aside from the aplomb,
the poise it must take to do something like that, I feel an
almost personal glow of pride in the way he is spreading the
gospel of tolerance and understanding. There's a tremendous
gratification in knowing there is somebody who is taking the
time and effort to tell the people on the outside how things
really are. Especially in the field of penology, where so much
gaffle-baffle obtains. And there is also a vicarious satisfaction in
contemplating such an orderly life as this, of pleasurable pursuits
balanced by service.

A life of service seemed indicated for me the last time I finished the cooling period that society had prescribed for my overheated spirit. Accordingly, I sought and found a certain salvation through working among the mentally ill. The brutal and gratuitous invasion of my privacy by the forces of right and might, however, shattered the glowing image I had of myself as a combination of F. Nightingale and A. Schweitzer, and proved fatal to my tenuous hold on the do-gooder principle. Henceforth I shall be found closer to the side of the imps than that of the angels. (Remaining a disenchanted observer of both.) Tired of chirping with the bluebirds, I am going back to hanging upside down with my friends the bats. The perspective from that angle seems the most comfortable and suitable for me, and it may well be the truest.

You may say that such an attitude springs from bitterness. And, baby doll, you would be positively poetically right. This pilgrim may not be the smartest around, but he is going to be the wariest.

Your farewell to the late Charlie Parker was a warm and gratifying thing, intensely moving and tender; the tears came as I read it. A great artistic soul has gone, whose equal we may never know again. And though I hate to inject commercialism into a subject on which you have so personal a feeling, I'd like to suggest that you expand that so touching eulogy into a full-length article. Somebody is going to do it, and better it should be someone as close to the subject as yourself.

J.P. has always been an adorer of The Bird and he was enormously impressed by your tribute, so much so he insisted I make a copy of it for him—he said he wanted to read it every morning for a while. Things like that, so typical of this erratic quicksilver spirit, compensate me for having traded my peace of mind for turbulence.

We're having a difficult time, J.P. and I. It was sheer misfortune that Bob, the kid from New York, moved into the cell almost simultaneously with J.P.'s return. I'm hung up in a grinding dilemma: I'd like J.P. as a cellmate again, but I hesitate to go through all the hassle we had before. The tentative, clandestine meetings we have are harrowing and totally unsatisfactory, and J.P. keeps pressing me to move Bob out of the cell. And then I got Willie the bandleader narrowly scoping me to see if I'm going to jump off the end of the dock again. All of it keeps my wig in turmoil.

The manuscript is proceeding slowly, and I'm now in the final third of it. It is the most crucial part, the part which must offset the preceding flabbiness, and I suffer constantly from stage fright. Let me hear soon, small one. J.P. and I again thank you for the definitive word on Bird.   Goodnight,—Jim

Raiford, Florida
APRIL 18, 1955

Dear Mike:

I would have thought my pleading wails for a visit would melt a heart of stone. I guess you haven't got a heart of stone.

To give you a piquant glimpse of what you missed—I am now the glockenspiel soloist in the faintly military-type aggregation that plays every noontime in the visitors' park here. Had you been a visitor you would have heard me wail on this iron contrivance.

Some time back, the bandleader suggested that I play in the military band in addition to my duties in the jazz outfit. He tried me on bass drum, but my cringing psyche was simply incompatible with this forthright instrument. Despite this disaster, he kept after me, and I had to tell him (sadly) that I didn't play any instrument they had on hand, but that I was hell on the glockenspiel.

Never trifle with a literal mind. They bought me a glockenspiel.

One ages quickly enough without such complications. The other day I made the appalling discovery that the hair on my chest is turning gray. Doubly intolerable since the hair on my head remains a flamboyant shade of indecisive orange. The latest, and most painful, in a long line of gratuitous insults from Fate.

Aside from this ambush, life flows more or less smoothly and monotonously behind the fence. I have found my apparent niche in this tight little society as a sort of graduate student on campus soberly immersed in community activities—music, the organ job at the chapel, the literary magazine. On the lighter side I enjoy watching the sleeveless intrigues that abound in the local pachuco set, an expanding population of PR's and Cubans. A mildly racy group, they seem to be the hippest citizens around, though sometimes rather determinedly so. J.P. the yellow-haired drummer has returned with another bit—a creature of flame and quicksilver, volatile and personable, with an intuitive beat as much a part of him as his bones. Because of his wayward behavior, he has not been permitted to rejoin the band, an excruciating frustration for both of us. The best we can do is to have two-man jam sessions, in the face of official disapproval from the bandleader. Thus flops the mop.

Another valued friend is the aspiring novelist from South Carolina, Tom Rolfe. He's writing a novel of violence with his fists, feet and teeth. He's a former pro boxer, and once had a fight in Mississippi where he kicked his opponent in the scrotum when he couldn't conquer him with his fists, then wept tears of frustration. I consider this arresting. His book, incidentally, seems to me to have authority, and the kind of drive that made him boot the boy in the, ah, scrotum.
And so it rocks. Please write:

> Sticks and stones may break the bones,
> Hurled with angry art—
> Words can sting like anything.
> Silence breaks the heart.

ever, Jim

Raiford, Florida
JUNE 18, 1955

Dear Gertrude:

Such a pleasant coincidence. This Saturday afternoon I've locked in, in preference to attending the Negro ball game.

(Though these contests are hard to beat for opera bouffe.) All week I've been sternly throttling hope, against disappointment, when the mailman appears. But with your letter, which has only just arrived, the sun has come out and there is birdsong. Good thing, too, the letter I was about to write would have been a weeper, one of those hangdog numbers—you know, not angry, just hurt.

Happy stuff first. The black population of the Rock is preparing a variety show for July 4th in the joint's auditorium, and I'm the only ofay asked to participate. Not to lose sight of the fact they have no suitable black piano man, I still think it's a gas. They do a number to "Taboo," in which a black con from the boxing team dances, that is a marvel of muscular grace and invention, a revelation in fluid physical expression.

Also several blackouts (surely they should be called white-outs?). These have a thigh-slapping, chortling quality of humor, the essence of which I can only just glimpse, but they bring the house down at rehearsal. I try to empathize, but I fall short, baffled.

I have the use of a radio for a while (a friend of mine has been withdrawn from the population into never-never land) and I've been able to catch some sounds. The station at the nearby University of Florida plays some good things, and I was delighted to hear Lena Horne's new record on Love Me Or Leave Me, with that tight pure bass fiddle obbligato behind Lena's vocal, which she phrases as if she were blowing a tenor chorus. All silky and foxy. The flip side is Porter's I Love To Love, with a very fly lyric.

Speaking of Cole Porter's lyrics reminds me of those deathless lines in the tune I Am In Love (in that portentous beguine tempo he favored): What is this sudden jolt?/ I'm like a frightened colt/ Hit by a thunderbolt./ To which a pianist friend of mine used to add, "Pass the Old Overholt."

Listening in on the musical world outside, I am not reassured, rather I'm dismayed at the signs that popular music is still sliding backwards downhill. I have a personal interest in this alarming trend, since I've decided to go back to playing the piano when I get out next year. All the playing I do in here, piano and organ, has put a sharp edge on my technique.

I'm still embroiled with the glockenspiel, which I blow in the Raiford Sedentary Marching Band. This outfit plays at the Sunday afternoon and Thursday night ball games. The nights are the worst, particularly at certain phases of the moon—the glockenspiel takes on a malign identity of its own, and some horrid sounds ensue. I have enough trouble controlling it in the daylight. This iron contrivance and I are not compatible. Perhaps I should go back to the bass drum. We had our differences, but life was more gemutlich.

I'm trying to finish the opus by August. Nelson has offered to take it to New York with him for hawking, if it proves acceptable. All I yearn to do now is to write Finis to it—my opinion of it fluctuates, but I'd say it's mostly pessimistic.

Incidentally, the good gray Doctor A. is in process of finishing a work called (tentatively) "The Legless Rider of Iberville Street," apparently set in New Orleans. I think the title is masterly—arresting, evocative, with a magical suggestion of curtain-going-up. Le Maitre is one of the few contemporaries who is not afraid of poetry in his prose, one of the few who can handle it, salting it as he does with an oblique and rueful wit. I hope you are over your pique with him.

I've been lonely and desolate this week, at a loss. J.P. went to the Flat-Top (bread and water) for drinking, for an indeterminate period. However, the new Security Officer we have here is laudably humane in meting out sentences of this kind, and I look for J.P. to be out possibly a week hence. By which time the records may have arrived, exactly the thing to restore the roses to his cheeks. But this infraction of the rules has made us lose ground in the campaign to get him back in the band. Lord knows we need him, the percussionists grow steadily less ept. I've grown weary of futile protest and have adopted an attitude of que-voulez-vous. So now we play boneless borscht with a buried beat.

The reclamation and exploration of this impassioned percussionist, poet and painter continues to be an obsession with me. This dervish presents so many disturbing facets, I am reminded of the fable of the prince who, in order to learn some magic truth he sought, had to seize an enchanted swan by the neck and hold it fast until it told. The swan changes into a hissing snake, a screaming eagle, a crying child, all manner of evasions. The prince, we are told, prevails.

By the way, what is this peripatetic compulsion that has seized everybody? Frank in New England, Mike in Delaware, Algren hopping from Hollywood to Gary to Montana to New York. And me bound and gagged in Dixie, I could spit.

This has been a rather forlorn number, after all. The week has been lonely and interminable, with the golden one in limbo. Next time will be better, I'll bring my banjo.　　　　　love, Jim

Raiford, Florida
JUNE 26, 1955

Dear Gertrude:

The records haven't arrived yet, but your description of them has me thirsting. Rough about the Sinatra records—you are one of the few who seems to share my enthusiasm for the Gaunt One. If he never did anything else, his intuitive understanding of the lyrics of Larry Hart, the turbulent one, would endear him to me. Aside from Lee Wiley, who approaches it from a different slant, nobody comes close to Mr. S. in projecting the wry mixture of sneers and tears that is Larry Hart.

How'd I get way out here? Maybe the picture we had here recently, "Young At Heart," where Sinatra played a night club pianist as it should be and ain't (the piano music at times got a little creamy, portentous crashing tenths in the left hand that sounded depressingly like Libbie with the Let-Down Hair, but one does not carp). The striking thing about his portrayal of an embittered shut-out was the way it caught and held many of society's wards in this particular joint—sharp identification with the film character, savage howls of masochistic pleasure as he spoke of the world and its hatred and mistreatment. ("It's the story of my life!")

The black variety show is coming on like Buster's gang. A professional director for the operation has appeared out of the population, a gent with years of experience in the Silas Green shows. Add to the already heady mixture this brash approach from the carny lots, and I think we got a hit. A pity we can't tour with it, but the management here seems to think that absenteeism among the actors would be rife.

Among the dancing numbers and comedy bits, there are quite a few vocalists, and all of them seem to imitate Billy Eckstine. If anyone can flatten a tune under a load of "style," it's an Eckstine imitator. Maybe I should be glad they've stopped imitating that emasculated tenor in the Inkspots. Lately I notice the effect of Sammy Davis, Jr., who saves his too belting delivery by a sly oblique junkie-type humor. In any case, it's good to see the descendants of the kidnapped learning their way in the neon jungle. They fascinate me, and sometimes I get the impression it's a mutual feeling.

J.P. got out of the Flat-Top after a week, and he dug your letter with me. A letter from you is always an event here behind the fences, and we always feel further rewarded when there is news of who's blowing what and where and how. He was struck, as I was, by the ebullience and joie de vivre that came through so strongly. He looked sidelong at me (with those arctic green eyes that seem to have needlepoints in the center) and grinned ruefully: "The bastards. They're having a ball." But said it fondly, and I felt the same; fondly envious.

At present we have to live with the constant frustration of not being able to share the joy of playing music together—for me not only joy, but instruction. In the rare two-man sessions we're able to have, piano and drums, I always have to overcome a vast diffidence. J.P. has such a sure, comfortable, intuitive command of jazz, I always feel like a floundering novice, though he is always kind toward my efforts, unobtrusively suggesting to me, with deft examples, how a jazz piano should be played from the standpoint of rhythmic patterns.

In these sessions, I have sometimes turned while playing to encounter his eyebrows raised in silent surmise. Disturbing, but challenging. "Surp," he calls romantic music, meaning syrup; to move him it must have the bracing tinge of acid. I keep trying to undermine this resistance of his to tenderness in music, this percussionist's distrust of emotion, through assiduous repetition of tunes like The Boy Next Door, Here's That Rainy Day, others like that.

All your letters bring with them a breath of outside air, and I sniff it eagerly—for no matter how busy I keep myself with musical duties and pleasures, or how hung up I get swimming and splashing in these swirling tides of human relationships, I'm unable to shake the dogged feeling that none of it is real. It is a frantic guignol, there is an aspect of bustle about it, a superficial air of movement, of activity, of life, in this turbulent teapot of cross-purposes and dubious motivations.

But life inside has an oddly static quality, a sort of suspended animation—existence seems like a boat anchored in a river, poised on the surface while the stream of time flows around and beneath it. Perhaps because all the activity transpires before scenery that never changes. It is like an interminable play with only one set.

That's enough Tinker Toy philosophy.   Later, Jim

Raiford, Florida
JULY 4, 1955

Dear Gertrude:

Impossible to convey how gassed we are over those records. The two of us, J.P. and me, have had more kicks, digging the sounds in quiet sessions, than we've had for too long. It's really too bad that J.P. could not have known Bird personally—the deep affinity he has for Bird's music is something that lights him up from inside.

Bud Powell is fantastic, as always, though hearing him usually fills me with a faint despair, knowing I can never attain that commanding slashing brilliance.

The Sarah record of If You Could See Me Now has a special association for us. Hearing it together afforded one of those magic moments that are all too rare between humans. . . .

Later, Jim

Raiford, Florida
JULY 11, 1955

Dear Gertrude:

. . . July 4th was a holiday here, a high fete day with watermelon for all, and a day-long program of events (potato races and like that). The band has to start the day by assembling around the flagpole on the recreation field, where we played patriotic airs while the flag was raised. There was considerable mutinous muttering in the ranks, and Willie the leader had to use the lash. The few cons who were out that early stared briefly at us, then lowered their eyes and hastily moved away, as if they had surprised us in group onanism.

Was it Caesar who said, "Give them bread and circuses, and they won't look for cake?" The spade show in the morning was moved out of doors, which diffused it somewhat, some of the impact was lost, but a certain loose al fresco charm was added. A ball.

The day's windup was a double-header baseball game which seemed interminable. I have been promoted to Assistant Band Director—the duties of the post are vague and the encomiums even sketchier. However, I made my debut as an outdoor conductor during the second ball game (to the sound of blood-lusting cries from the sport-loving cannibals in the stands). I learned what a transparent hustle conducting is, nothing to it but waving a stick in time with the band, and stopping when they stop. Probably the most outstanding thing about it is the insane sense of power it gives to know that one can make all hell break loose simply by giving a downbeat. Standing in front of the Raiford Sedentary Marching Band, armed only with a baton (it's the same as a lion-tamer's whip), I evoked such demoniacal sounds I felt like master of revels on Walpurgisnacht.

About the records again—J.P. is so familiar with most of Bird's choruses that he can sing along with them, improvising strange and wonderful combinations of words. He has a sense of imagery that is a constant source of shock and amazement to me. A timid swimmer am I, to be so far out in unknown waters, but I mean to explore this holiday from native Scottish caution if it ends me.   Sois tranquille, let me hear, Jim

Raiford, Florida
JULY 26, 1955

Dear Nelson:

This will be brief, not because I have little to say to you—the medium of censored communication is not the most satisfactory, as you have undoubtedly gathered from the hollow jocularity of my other letters. It is difficult to be innocuous and informative at the same time.

I had hoped to be able to send you the completed manuscript of *Chain Dance* by now, but it isn't ready. Part of it was written during a period of stress and upon rereading seemed even to my indulgent eye not worth keeping, so I'm back at 235 pages. I've applied myself to it, at times with a dogged tenacity necessary to offset the jailhouse apathy that creeps over me too often. In fact, I fear that my very persistence has resulted in passages of trudging exposition. The editing will be a job I'm reluctant to burden you with, since you'll be busy with the stage treatment of "Man With The Golden Arm." I'm overjoyed about that—and when is the book about New Orleans due to appear?

This bit has been a numbing experience. It's true I've learned a good deal about the species and its antics, but I'm weary of thinking about hopelessness and degradation—perhaps later when I'm away from it, I can get a fresh slant. Being up to my eyes in it doesn't give a very clear perspective. The only good thing that has come out of it so far is the warm comfort of J.P.'s friendship. That is a thing that will endure, for even should the actuality come to an end, the memory will be a good one.

This is a lugubrious one, I know, but I lack even the spirit to apologize for it. This fog will abate, it must, but tonight I am foundered.   ever, Jim

                                              Raiford, Florida
                                              AUGUST 8, 1955

Dear Gertrude:

The ambivalence in my wig has been terrific these recent days. I've wanted to write numerous times, and at the same time I've been in the grip of a fog that drifts from nowhere and envelops me in a helpless state of apathy and Weltschmerz. So I've hesitated to burden you with sad songs. Nothing definitely wrong, just a creeping malaise.

I've been keeping busy writing arrangements for the small cocktail combo—I guess that's what it's called, though it's a vapid enough appellation in the free world, certainly a wild misnomer in this austere society, where all the attractive appurtenances of vice are only wistful memories. Anyway, it's one of those tenor-band setups, a fairly foolproof instrumentation that Willie the leader and I evolved. Two altos, tenor, trumpet, guitar, drums, piano.

No bass fiddle, the faculty member in charge of refusals told us if we wanted a bass we should use the tuba player we got—I'd like to see Gerry Mulligan toy with that for a while.

We get a somewhat professional sound from the combination. Doesn't swing, for lack of a competent drummer, among other missing components. Willie and I are the only ones left in the outfit with any professional background. The others are high school musicians unaccountably gone astray. They read the stuff with fair accuracy, but no fire, their interpretation has all the verve of a seal blowing My Country 'Tis Of Thee.

My writing efforts have been spasmodic, chiefly I think because my personal life has been at such an emotional boil as to make any literary contrivances seem pale by contrast. I'm still hacking away, but way behind schedule. Nelson offered to take the manuscript to New York with him this month, but I haven't heard from him, and I'm rather ashamed about not meeting the deadline I agreed upon. I can't blame the weather for my lassitude—I've become accustomed to southern summers, where the air is like the inside of a sponge and tropic rains fall vehemently from the skies daily.

Not having J.P. in the band with me is a consistent and cumulative drag for both of us, more so for him, a guy who lives to blow as he does. He's on an outside work squad, not at all physically demanding—they go outside the fences every day to do light farm work—but it's mentally numbing. As a result he is often in a difficult and morose frame of mind, and it takes some ingenuity to lift him out of it. Though I must say that most of the time his own blithe spirit is what saves him from despondency.

Not for a minute do I see myself as the calm omniscient healer—so much of the time I am the moody one. In the time we have together in the morning, between breakfast and the whistle that orders us to work, we find a quiet spot in the baseball grandstand and resume the fascinating process of discovering one another—thoughts, ideas, attitudes, likes, dislikes. It is a voyage of exploration in strange country, with new enchantments beyond every horizon. And if sometimes our eyes meet in grave surmise at how far we have come, there is no dismay, nor thought of turning back.

It has been a time of grinding frustration for both of us, not being able to play music together, and not being able to be together; but in a day or so, we'll be cellmates again. After long and sticky and demeaning negotiations with my present cell partner, I've finally persuaded him to move. The relationship has been for some time an abrasive one, his big-city ways had become too way-out for my peasant simplicity. His purple reputation was beginning to rub off on me, and I've worked too hard on a good record to carry heat for somebody else, especially when there's nothing in it for me.

To be candid, I'm not without trepidation over resuming with J.P. Apparently I never can learn that life extracts payment for whatever it bestows—for the jewel I have found, I've had to surrender the contemplative attitude of bystander, and I find that it has inhibited my writing efforts to a degree. It seems difficult to convincingly stoke a literary conflagration when my own wig is in flames. I'm hoping that the hiatus is temporary, that time and custom will dim the aching bewildering wonder of it into something calmer. I miss the impassive Blake.

Flammably, Jim

Raiford, Florida
OCTOBER 3, 1955

Dear Gertrude:

The news that Frank has pushed another book to completion leaves me stunned. And corroded with envy. I'd ask how he does it, but I know I'd get some disgusting answer like "hard work."

I've been rather hung up over an ending to my opus, also. But about four o'clock in the morning a few nights ago, as I lay wide-eyed and sleepless, thinking long miserable thoughts about the nature of love, a poem of Emily Dickinson's popped into my head: "Much madness is divinest sense/ To a discerning eye/ Much sense the starkest madness/"—Turning the words over in my mind, I was struck by a revelation, and I knew what I'd been casting about for. I couldn't leap up and shriek Eureka, ebullience is frowned upon in these prim purlieus at any time, but I made some notes as soon as it got light, and felt pretty good about the whole thing. All I got to do now is beat my brains out getting it down.

Another hangup that paralyzes me in my writing attempts is the daunting realization of my flimsy background and meager education, an awareness brought home to me all too sharply all too often. If I could hole up somewhere for a couple of years and read all the things I can't lay hands on here—Camus, Sartre, Colette, Faulkner, Welty, everybody, the list is endless—I might emerge with a sounder grasp, a sharper blade. So inadequate I feel to express what I so bustingly want to say.

As for applying myself more diligently to writing, that problem has been suddenly and disastrously solved for me. In the fabric of my existence, a gaping hole has been torn. J.P. was sent without warning to a camp of the State Road Department, and I am benumbed. It comes to me with the stark surprise of a knife thrust that the old poetic cliche "aching void" actually describes something. In the fury of work I hope to find some sort of balm until this catastrophe can be assimilated. The yawning gulf that opens before me frightens me as nothing before in my experience.

I gave him your address, so you should be hearing from him before long. In that manner we hope to keep in touch— you can relay what he says, though not the actual letter—and drawings may be forwarded. He sometimes communicates, enigmatically, in that fashion. By writing to him, you will enable me to continue the project that is so preciously important to me—the reclaiming of a shining talent from an abyss of doubt and insecurity. If you could know (as you shall in time) the valiant spirit and high courage that is his, when it is not obscured by the fog of uncertainty that a wavering sense of identity brings from time to time. He is a creature of quicksilver and flame, but he has many black moments and dark misgivings, and needs reassurance desperately and often. Until the time when he's out of prison and blowing with a band—then his talent will assert itself and he will be on solid ground, headed in the right direction.

He read your last letter, the day before he was shipped out, and glowed. So more of the same is certainly indicated. Where he is, he will be out of touch with music, so I presume to ask you to send him Downbeat, and to keep him informed of what's shaking musically in Chicago. His sole interested relative is a grandmother with a lot of bread but no real understanding of her turbulent grandson.

And if you will pass this word to him when you write: "Nothing will be right until I see you again, but I'm taking refuge in hard work on the book, working toward the realization of the plans we made and the vision we share. ("He who a dream has possessed can know no more of doubting.") That is the talisman I keep in my mind and heart. I continue to play the piano as if you were listening to me—in that way, I hope in time to play as you would have me play. Be cool, come back soon, I'll be around—Uncle Wig"

So, dear one, will you assist me in The Cause?

En avant, Jim

Raiford, Florida
OCTOBER 10, 1955

Dear Mike:

Received the M.O. for the bread. Couldn't have been more opportune, the clamor at my heels was growing daily more shrill. I can stop panting and start breathing. Many thanx.

Nine months to go on this interminable bit—the nineteen I've already shook stretch out behind me into the mists of antiquity. It is frighteningly difficult for me to picture with any clarity the world outside the tall triple fences that bound this microcosm. I look forward to experiencing the beautiful claustrophobia of elevators and air-sickness on escalators. Panic in the subway rush hour. Ah, the urban delights.

The days slip by placidly enough, but they lack the contrast of dark and light to give depth to their passing. Being constrained always to live in the shallow insipid light of day has been a loss deeply felt. I miss the benevolent darkness.

My Day begins at six AM, when the convict turnkey comes down the long range of two-man cells, dragging a stick across the bars like a kid passing a picket fence. A half hour to dress, and the long drawbar is pulled back. Our range is among the

last to be opened, so there's always a long line in front of the
Mess Hall. (Locally called the Pandemonium Room for the
clattering of metal trays, the roar of conversation, and the steady
grinding of thousands of molars in hundreds of jaws, relentlessly masticating.) And I've always had an inversion to eating
with even two or three people.

Mornings are trying anywhere. Here, with the cons milling
about in clots and groups, talking the same perfunctory tripe,
it's gruesome, so I make my way through the low underpass
that leads on to the spacious grassy field that fronts the Rock.
If I have bread, I stop at the Canteen and queue up for coffee
to take with me. If I don't have bread, I may look around for
a likely prospect (locally, "mullet") to buy it for me. However,
this entails the real danger that the mullet will want to come
along with me, thus beginning the day with a spate of paralyzing
conversation.

So I usually make it solo and give myself a short period of
communion with the sunrise. This is not too bad a time of day.
As on the street, it is the hour of hiatus; the bipeds are just
beginning to emerge in pursuit of their devout absurdities. Until
recently, it was the daily custom to meet J.P., my drummer
friend, on the deserted field in the morning. But a week ago,
he was shipped to SRD. Losing the joy of his companionship
has been a bitter loss; I've been floundering ever since. A rebel
with a discerning eye and an acid wit. I live in hope that he may
return soon, he made this joint bearable for me.

To continue with My Day: Breakfast is a fairly indifferent
though sufficient meal, after which there is a period of waiting
around on the big field till the whistle blows to go to work.
During this period also, conversation in the milling groups of
malefactors burgeons and billows, inanity hangs in the air as
thick as cheese. Drab liars telling dreary lies, soi-disant experts in
every imaginable aspect of mediocrity, all in full cry. To avoid
these asphyxiating colloquies, I find a quiet corner in the baseball
bleachers and barricade myself behind a book.

When the whistle blows, the squads line up in twos, and march
out the gate at the end of the quadrangle, to disperse to various

buildings on the prison grounds. The band has its own small
building, an unprepossessing structure of corrugated sheet iron,
but it has a wide lawn behind it for sprawling and sunbathing,
plenty of room for the restless to pace, and a small pool
built by the musicians. The pool is a blessing in the smothering
heat of an inland Florida summer.

There's also space for gardening—this year I did well with
tomatoes, lettuce and melons, despite the dreamy assistance of a
tall blond daffodil from Alabama, in for being caught flagrante
delicto on a beach with an inflamed soda jerk or bicycle mechanic or that ilk. The daffodil threw seeds around like nuptial
rice and smiled charmingly the while. Oddly, everything came
up, tomatoes on top of watermelons and lettuce all over everything. My gentle assistant made tossed salads deftly, with an
ominous ease, and for a while the living was high. Unfortunately
he got out via the bug route and is now cooling it in a plush
sanitarium while they pump him full of hormones and the urge
to mate properly.

The band is the softest touch in the Rock, which may explain
why we've attracted so many no-talent clowns; the jazz outfit
has gone to hell for lack of replacements. It fell apart when
my boy J.P. went out on expiration of his first bit. He came
back after only four months on the street. (Funny, we talked
about every conceivable subject, but it seemed that neither of us
ever wanted to inquire too closely into the reasons behind
his quick return. There was some hostility towards me when
he first came back.) I was able to overcome it, but now that
he's away from me on SRD, and probably making hard time,
I'm horribly afraid there'll be another boomerang of resentment.
I hope I'm wrong, I don't want to lose what it took so long to
find.

Anyway, he was unable to get back in the band, the official
in charge taking a sudden antipathy for him and his affinity for
the spike. It was a deep loss; personal and artistic; I learned
more about playing progressive piano while working with J.P.
than I'm ever likely to again. And I was beginning to perfect a
taut astringent style that was new for me. I think I'm going to

have to go back to the music racket when I get out, for bread. In my spare moments I've been writing some original stuff along the Matt Dennis line, not as polished maybe, but similar. I think my appearance is better, the glow imparted by Florida sun and months of nauseous clean living. I've run out of space.

So later, Jim

Raiford, Florida
OCTOBER 18, 1955

Dear Nelson:

Here is a part of what I have been able to do on the magazine article "The Bughousers." I'm sending it to find out if you think I'm on the right track before I go any further with it.

The past three weeks have been desolate. My friend and cellmate has been sent to an SRD camp, and I'm bereft. Idle to wonder if I made a mistake in bisecting myself, only to have the other half take off. It was something that seemed as inevitable as sundown, and "glad" or "sorry" hardly enters into it. I'll be seeing him again somewhere, it's that kind of friendship, a thing I've looked for all my life. But right now it's rough, I feel crippled.

. . . Also enclosed, a poem. (I have been driven to poetry.) See what you think and say what you think.   subdued, Jim

Raiford, Florida
OCTOBER 26, 1955

Dear Gertrude:

October days down here are poignant—Summer fades almost imperceptibly, there is not the flamboyant awesome color riot that marks the dying season up North. Rather it is a wistful slipping away, day by day, pastel and Camille-ish. Mornings the sun shines pale through a delicate haze. By afternoon the mist has burned away and the sky is a blazing blue bowl. The beauty of the long drowsing days only deepens my loneliness. I wander hungry-hearted, haunted by a question without an answer.

Willie the bandleader has made me his assistant, and also Band Runner (courier, errand boy). The job gives me a Trusty Card, so I can leave the compound of the Rock proper, and move about the extensive prison grounds. But wandering with a phantom beside me can be a sad business—I am the prisoner of my obsession. Still, I have moments—in the afternoons, the radiant October light makes everything luminescent, the sky is electric translucent blue. With that vast music all around, there are indeed moments.

Even in mourning, the necessity to operate remains. Being vulnerable, I've had to look around for an immediate replacement for J.P. as cell partner. I found an almost completely physical type, suitably innocuous and tractable, one who can be easily moved, should J.P. return. He's Jack Fleming, a cat from New Jersey, has the reputation of being an expert hotel jewel thief. He's relaxed, amiable, with a special quality about him I can only call quaint. At present he's engaged in a mad surge of picture hanging and general homemaking activities. The bracing acid effect of my mordant temperament has not yet begun to bleach his boyish effervescence. These things take time, I'm sure all will be well. And anyway, I'm merely awaiting the return of the sojourner. So much is in abeyance.

besotted, Jim

Raiford, Florida
SUNDAY, 1 A.M., OCTOBER 30, '55

[Not Mailed]

Absent One:

The first white worms of doubt have begun their blind, silent gnawing at the hope and faith I have lived by since you

went away. (Though even now I write this and tell myself that
I will show it to you when you return, as you said you would.)

The doubt was there almost from the beginning, I guess. It
sprang from the rueful acknowledgment I had to make to myself
that it was folly ever to expect you to return my love in kind—
foolish to hope you could ever feel such intensity and abandon.
I told myself it was unfair to expect it. I reminded myself that
I had told you more than once that I would make do with
whatever you cared to give me. I meant it, I still do—but it's
hard to make do on nothing at all. More than a month now,
and there has been no word, though I furnished you with a
way to write to someone who was in sympathy with us, who
would quickly pass on any message. So if I'm falling prey to
doubts, it is because you have been so ominously silent.

It's frightening to face the fact that I may have read too much
into what passed between us. Perhaps I can be pardoned such
presumption—you see, I looked for someone like you all my life.
I'd given up searching, banked the fires, and settled back resigned to the knowledge that such things were to be found only
in the minds of poets and in the lyrics of love songs.

Then one day, at possibly the lowest point of my existence,
I was auditioning with a mediocre band in a wildly implausible
setting—the noisy mess hall of a down-at-heels southern penitentiary. And I heard behind me the unmistakable and sure
artistry of a musician, clear and sublime through the surrounding
musical muck.

It was as if a hand reached out and claimed me. —"Do you
know 'Laura'?" Even in my fright and confusion I was touched
by the abrupt gruffness in your voice, which I recognized as a
cloak for shyness and a fear of being rebuffed. Your eyes, when
I turned to look at you, matched the tone of your voice; frosty-
green, arrestingly oblique eyes, almost hostile. But as I heard
in your voice the undertone, so I saw in your eyes a question
that had no connection with the one you spoke aloud. That was
the beginning.

Today being Sunday, I know that there is no chance of your

arrival, so I shall have peace, a peace that is like dying a little. But on Monday I shall once more resume hoping.   Goodnight—

                                        Raiford, Florida
                                    DECEMBER 20, 1955

Dear Nelson:

Not hearing from you is disconcerting. I don't know whether you're busy, salty, or maybe just weary. I heard from Moran (off-and-running Moran, that is) shortly after his arrival on the Hialeah scene. Nothing since, I hope Mike hasn't fallen under a horse or been apprehended putting amphetamine in the oats.

Principal reason for this letter, besides wanting to know what's shaking, is to send you a Xmas parcel permit, in the hope you'll send some reading material. Seasonal concession from the P.O. They also allow any jars of instant coffee you may have laying around. Coffee, with my present nocturnal writing struggles, is of the essence. I do slightly better if I'm awake, I find. If it's possible without hassle for you. If not, not.

The yuletide seizure is upon us here, and I've been occupied with rehearsals for the Xmas play. I accompany the choirs and supply heartrending organ music behind the narrator's spiel.

This year's vehicle, as before, is a morality play, with the moral and the plot alternately elbowing one another aside. This adds movement, but only sidewise.

Doesn't really matter, it's sure to be a smash, because the female convicts from the Women's Building are in it. The ravenous cons won't even know what's it about, or care. However, it deals with a modern family (I presume, the young folks in it are pretty flip about religion). There's a grandmother who crouches behind her knitting basket, making what looks like a thuggee cord, and balefully quotes Scripture (nothing later than Elijah and Isaiah and the doomsday boys).

Grandma terrorizes the whole crew, egged on by two little granddaughters. (Played by two female inmates whose aspect is nostalgically reminiscent of some of the narrower streets in

Port Said.) These debauched moppets ply the crone with provocative questions, obviously trying to nudge her into a voodoo
fit.

The inmate who's directing, an unfrocked Arthur Murray instructor, has astutely heightened this miasmic atmosphere. Under
his guidance, there is a telling nervous flux in the action, suggesting incipient mass hysteria. The players congeal from time
to time into sudden frightened huddles, goggling in frozen dismay across a yawning stage at Granny, while she sprays them
with apostolic spleen. After each tirade, they flutter and skitter
aimlessly about the stage, only to regroup in the same despairing
cluster, like sparrows with a snake in the nest. The obvious moral,
so starkly drawn, is that there is no safety in numbers or in anything else.

I haven't seen the last two acts, having discovered that the
music rack on the Hammond will also accommodate magazines.

Season's greetings, Jim

Raiford, Florida
DECEMBER 28, 1955

Dear J.P.:

I met Leo Z., a cat from your camp, he was back here to have
some dental work done. He says he's due to return to the camp
in a day or so, and I'm kiting this note out with him.

Glad to hear you're keeping in touch with Gertrude and
Frank. Not only are they hip talented people, they have all kinds
of connections in the music business which will be helpful to
you later, when all this nonsense of building time is a dim
memory.

I know how adaptable you are, but I can't believe there's
enough intellectual stimulation in that CCC-type joint to keep
you happy. So a connection with the world of music and allied
arts is a good thing to have.

I've been working hard on the book, it will be ready to send
out some time in January. It's like having an only daughter leave
home to enter the South American whore traffic.

Other occupations— I got a piano pupil now. Remember Sandy, the sullen kid who played cornet in the band? Wanted to be a hard-nose badass type, and Willie decided he was going to reform him or kill him. Very good, but he turns the kid over to me and says, you do it. He gave me the job of Band Runner, with a Trusty Card, so I can't beef, it lets me swing a whole lot wider. So I take the kid down to the band hall on the afternoons the band isn't there, and teach piano. From the looks of things neither he nor I is going to live long enough. He tries, but, man, what a struggle.

Sammy is a steady companion (the kid from Pasadena?) and Tom Rolfe, the bellicose bard from Carolina. Good talk from both of them. And the new cellmate, Jack Fleming, is fantastically generous, which enables both of us to stay well insulated against the pain and strain.

So from the pieces that were strewn around, I've managed to construct a life of sorts again. It's quieter, it lacks the color and depth (and hysteria, I miss the all-night safaris, but it's tough all over, I hear). I had a long spell of blackass, but it's lighter now, I can cut it. And unlike you, I don't demand happy stuff all the time—you gotta have valleys to have mountains, right?

But I still scope every bus that rolls into the joint, and there's not a day I don't say to myself, "Maybe today." Be happy, hang loose, keep the faith.

                                        Raiford, Florida
                                        JANUARY 2, 1956

Dear Gertrude:

Thanks ever so for the books, a beautiful present, I was really hung for something to read. I've been curious about Mezzrow's *REALLY THE BLUES* for some time, but I'm sorry to say I bogged down somewhere around the 82nd chorus of "Muskrat Ramble." It's probably a faithful picture of a period and a certain type of musician. But I'm afraid if I'd been around at the time, even if I had two raccoon coats, a monogrammed hip flask and a closetful of Charleston trophies, I'd still have fled Mezz like the pox.

I kept wondering, why am I finding this cat so distasteful? He seemed innocuous enough, if a bore. It wasn't until I got to the part about Bix, and what a shame it was that he was led astray from the righteous music by furriners like Stravinsky, Debussy, etc., that the veiled resentment at the artistic growth of another musician suddenly put it into focus. Ol' Mezz was relentlessly dogmatically ignorant. He'd learned to play the one-string banjo and didn't want anybody else playing the harp.

His cloying indiscriminate embrace of the black race must have been a trial to intelligent spades—forever carryin' them back to Ol' Virginny and the rotten plantation they were trying to shuck.

Mezz had good fortune in Paris, though. Unerringly he found a soulmate, the humorless, ponderous, one-track pedestrian Panassie, a man devoted to fitting boots onto butterflies. Oh well, I make too much of it, it's a pathetic tale stiffly told. I'd much prefer to read Dave Tough writing about the scene. The musicians might emerge as something more than hapless cretins barely able to dress themselves.

Willie the bandleader has dropped another job on me, a combination of psychotherapy and baby-sitting. We got a new man assigned to the band recently, a kid about nineteen, who escaped from the state joint for adolescents, Appalachee. He and two other kids stole a car and wrecked it in their bust-out attempt. So they brought them here.

When Sandy came down to the band hall, he glowered, sulked, scowled, wouldn't practice his horn. (Plays trumpet and cornet.) We tried talking to him, tried to put him at his ease, but he was rigid, scornful, contemptuous. He didn't want to play in the band, he wanted the 8-Spot, the shovel squad where all the badasses go.

Willie finally blew it. He told the kid he would either practice and play in the band or he'd go to the Flat-Top on bread and water. And Willie can come on like a scorpion with his tail up. He told me afterwards that he was convinced Sandy's attitude was only front. We're going to turn that little bastard around, he says. Laudable, I say, praiseworthy.

I'll turn him over to you, my leader tells me. He says he wants to learn piano. Maybe you can reach him that way.

I had the same feeling Willie did. Sandy didn't seem like the malign mindless punks who float around the joint, radiating malice, oozing ugliness. He was tall, gangling, awkward, a hang-dog posture denoting inner anxiety, huge brown eyes lighted by intelligence, thick emphatic eyebrows, a rare fleeting lopsided smile.

My diffidence and deference bugged him for a short spell, till he decided I must be harmless. (I was supposed to be a wheel, but I didn't come on like one, so I must be stupid.)

That helped to lower his guard some, and when I could I cautiously probed. He was an orphan living with relatives in a trailer park in one of those strangled dusty towns where the center of wickedness, corruption and hope of degradation is located in the all-night diner.

I think he's coming along. Not on piano, unfortunately, but I've seen a few spontaneous bursts of animation, and he plays his cornet in the band with an encouragingly matter-of-fact attitude.

It's a project to take my mind off my maudlin preoccupation. And I find that I feel definitely involved, to my surprise.

Later, Jim

Raiford, Florida
JANUARY 22, 1956

Dear Gertrude:

How nice to get three letters in one. They made a charming little Christmas chronicle, a picture of simple, vanished joys. I had a twinge of nostalgia, but it didn't last, folkways are beyond recall for this pilgrim, and I consider them well lost.

Xmas has been for a long time a tribal fete I successfully

ignored. On the street, I'd hole up in a hotel room with books and stay in bed. Or find a funky bar somewhere. This year I got dry-gulched. My cellmate, the international jewel thief, told me considerably in advance that he wanted to decorate the cell for Yuletide and did I mind. I said no, he has a way of presenting bizarre proposals in such a bland, tentative salt-free manner that they seem remote and unreal, and I usually concur with only half my mind. He outlined his plans for this festive adornment in detail, but I thought I was listening to a wistful nostalgic fantasy.

But when a huge box arrived from his mother containing Xmas tree lights and ornaments, I began to feel that I hadn't dreamed it. Preposterous, I told myself, but simultaneously I was thinking, this cat makes up his mind and then he makes it happen. It's not the first time I've had to take a narrower look at him. On our nocturnal safaris I've encountered the same eerie, diffident, dogged tenacity. But dissembled, it's a new kind of flimflam. He makes Sisyphus look flighty.

How the hell he did it, I don't even want to know. But there it was, a small spruce on a triangular shelf in the corner of the cell, so lavishly hung with ornaments, tinsel, lights, etc., it looked like a female impersonator en grande tenue. Even a wreath on the barred door. Even those ghastly letters on a string spelling out Merry X and Happy New Year. It all seemed nearly worth it when a guard stopped outside the door and looked in and said, in genuine awe, "She looks purty in theah."

The therapy regimen with the young cornet player Sandy continues. Early on it was apparent to me that he had no affinity for the piano. To keep him interested in the sessions, I suggested coaching him in how to be a pop singer, and that seemed to grab him. So I've taught him some tunes, showed him how to phrase and project, and we've been working on that.

Sometimes I get scared. It's a little frightening to see a young spirit grow, unfold, reach out. I try, very tentatively, to shape his taste in music and reading, terrified of having too heavy a touch, such delicacy is required. Often I've had to examine my motives, question my actions, ponder the direction of this thing.

Then I remember the pure unequivocal dependency and trust I've seen, and all the rest is confetti. Such response to a little attention and affection—do I have a right to withhold it? I can see the Pygmalion syndrome waiting for me, if it hasn't already got me. But J.C. said: "Don't put your hand on the plow if you're only going to take it off again." It was good enough for J.C. and it's good enough for me.   alors, Jim

Raiford, Florida
FEBRUARY 7, 1956

Dear Gertrude:

. . . Had some cheering news the other day, a letter from the agent to say that The Paris Review had decided to publish a short story of mine, *Day Of The Alligator*, and also the letters that appeared in *Les Temps Modernes*. This time in English. I feel rather bucked by it, I've been enormously impressed by the quality of the issues of The Paris Review I've seen. Nelson says that appearing in it will add prestige—I'm hoping it will facilitate the sale of the book *Chain Dance*.

Not that I've heard from Algren, I think he is salted with me because I fell down on the magazine article "The Bughousers." It's a task that has left me frustrated, but I'm still trying to whip it, because the bread is so good. And so veree veree necessaire. My entry into the big world is only four and a half months off and I'll need some cushioning against the blessings of free enterprise. No flop-sweat yet at my impending entrance on the civilian stage, but from experience I know it will come. . . .
For now, Jim

Raiford, Florida
FEBRUARY 8, 1956

Dear Nelson:

Your idea of trying The Paris Review with the letters was an astute one. They've agreed to publish them, along with the story *Day Of The Alligator*. I'm ecstatic, and all of it I owe to you, *très cher maître*.

I feel a goodish amount of constraint in writing to you, since you scorned my letter of December 20, and as yet I've heard nothing from the one I wrote around January 31, enclosing a couple of manuscripts and a photograph of the Raiford Christmas Pageant. I get about as much reply as Emily D. with her Letter To the World.

I've just sent off a biography of your correspondent to The Paris Review. Leaving out the part about how I was kidnapped at the age of sixteen, while on holiday from Harrow, and sold to a raffish Riff in a Marrakech bazaar. You know how people misconstrue.

The agent thinks I'll realize between a hundred and two hundred. Since I'm a rising threat on the literary horizon, I thought perhaps you might care to advance a loan on the great expectations. Bitter truth is that I devote so much time to scuffling pennies in order to get by, writing hillbilly music for rich hillbillies (among other dismal expedients) that I have nothing like the time I need to finish the book. It's maddening, when I so badly need the money I might realize from the book as armor for my entrance into the free-enterprise arena, which is four and a half months away. ever, Jim

Raiford, Florida
MARCH 5, 1956

Dear Gertrude:

Something less than four months to shake off this bit, and my thoughts are increasingly concerned with the world Out There and my Adjustment to it. I remember all too clearly the stage fright that afflicted me at the approach of expiration day in my previous incarceration. And I was much less cloistered during that period of penal servitude. This stretch has been like a sojourn on the moon, so remote has the world beyond the fences become. Once again I have to negotiate the perilous passage between imprisonment and freedom, that suspended moment when the animal leaves the safety of his cage for the narrower freedom beyond.

And having for the second time paid a debt to society, I am wondering whether I'm ahead or behind in this ludicrous game, and just what sort of fink accountant is keeping tab. Lovely to be a paid-up member of society. My private opinion is that it's a rather broken-down outfit, but it seems to be the only one. ("There's a hell of a good universe next door.")

I haven't yet decided what I'm going to do, but I've been practicing the piano daily, and will continue, in the event I decide to play professionally again. I feel a certain hesitancy, chiefly because of the close entanglement with the Public. An active detestation of The Herd and the disparity of our tastes in music were the factors that brought me to a blind alley once before. The rub of the frustration took me narrowly close to flipping completely. Before I risk my sanity a second time I want to think it over carefully.

My position in this tight frenetic society is now, I think I can safely say, assured. I've progressed from lousy lowly piano player to church organist, glockenspieler, bass drum thumper, and Runner. (A runner is a sort of glorified errand boy and sheepdog. It is my duty to convoy the band squad from the Rock to the band hall and back, and to run any necessary errands within the prison enclosure.)

However, I realized suddenly that I had not really arrived until this past week, when the official in charge of the band informed me he had received a number of anonymous letters about me, none of them fan letters. Nothing particularly alarming about this development, it is more or less routine in jail. The wonder is that I have so long been able to keep myself inconspicuous enough to escape the attention of the abandoned souls who deal in this type of correspondence.

It bothered me, though. And when I ran into the assistant Warden who circulates all the time within the prison I asked him about it. He was amused. Said not to worry, they simply file the letters with your rap sheet and wait until they catch you doing what the letters say you are doing.

Naturally, I was outraged when the Boss told me about it, as indignant as only a criminal can be when accused of the wrong crime. It's like having a snake slide across your face when you're sleeping.

I think I know where the letters came from, and I think I know what to do about it.

I hope you've heard from J.P. by now. As far as sending any word, I feel I've said all there is to say.

Nelson's remarks about Frank's book were startling. But not inexcusable or inexplicable. Integrity has nothing to do with tact. I received a postcard from him—says he is plagued by the nightingale, beset by the loon—but it hasn't slowed the creative fury. Later, Jim

MARCH 21, 1956
Raiford, Florida

Dear Gertrude:

. . . Now that I am a Trusty I have to eat in the Trusty Dining Room, outside the compound of the Rock proper. It is a mixed blessing. The food's better, but when I ate in the big mess hall it was forever absorbing to look at the faces—the smoldering vitality of the brute beings, the weaselish alertness of the sharpies, whose eyes are like peepholes for the avid watching animal within—the blanched listless vacuity of those for whom prison is a kindness.

I miss all this in dining with the seraphs, who are office, hospital and chapel workers—ribbon clerks they seem, prim and pallid, one sees such smug docile faces in the subway rush hour. Seeing them here I marvel at what unimaginable upheaval, what dull desperation could sting them into transgression. Their life-long conditioning appears to be intact, the regard for appearances and the proprieties remains, and the bedraggled banner of caste still waves.

By comparison, the wrong-headed brawling savages at the bottom of this microcosm are infinitely admirable. The savages in their head-down, bull-like assaults on the social order, the sharpies with their oblique flank attack, their childlike belief in a society of marks inexhaustibly gullible—these hapless warriors will go down, while the Rotarians in their pious mediocrity survive. The defeated ones will have fought a good fight, with brawn and brain, and by their own lights will have kept faith with themselves. And by their protest, however ill conceived and abortive, will perhaps have contributed more to the race than the cravenly repentant ones.

Marx said that criminals have a function in society, to provide employment for policemen. Does it follow that criminals who cravenly reform at the first sign of misfortune are shirking their job?   zut alors, Jim

                                                    Raiford, Florida
                                                    MARCH 26, 1956

Dear Gertrude:

Your letter as always a tonic, your comment on my approaching debut most heartening. My feelings are more than simply the numbness of stage fright. There's a steady and joyful surge of anticipation when I think about the Outside. I think of the freedom to walk in the night under the stars in the blessed dark, after these endless months of living my life in the shrillness of daylight—savoring again the poignancy of twilight. When I think of how shining new the simplest things will seem to me, I am filled with excitement.

You mention the gratification that working with your hands gives you, a pleasure that was astonishingly revealed to me during my stay on the chain gang. Amazing what peace and serenity it came to give me, in time; how clear my mind was, what long thoughts I had while my hands and muscles worked with a shovel, an axe or a sickle. For me, the discovery of my physical self in the Florida swamps was an important one.

You may remember Sandy, the young cornet player whom Willie and I were trying to prevent being just one more snotty punk. He has become the vocalist with the combo that plays at the movies in the auditorium. The howl of admiration and approval that comes from the cons when he sings is something to hear. (There may be another ingredient in that howl of adulation, but what the hell.) The great thing is that Sandy glows, he sparkles, and the assurance and poise he has gained is enough to make one believe in fables. I think perhaps I have expended more of myself than is wise— I think maybe the physician has contracted a fatal malady. Nothing is for nothing.

I've encountered a certain amount of flak and static from Sandy's cell partner, a converted Jew who poses as some kind of an evangelist on the campus— I think of Savonarola, I think of Rasputin—and while I have never been a man of violence, I have always been a man of ingenuity and cunning. We shall see.

I'm sharing a cell with Tom Rolfe now. The South Carolina cat who writes. He has a southern accent that renders him unintelligible to me, but I have a hunch he's bright, he has a novel finished, ready to send off. In the terse Cain tradition. It's the first time I ever met a novelist who, when stymied, picks up his typewriter and hurls it against the wall. I'm not sure this is in the best literary tradition. Would Faith Baldwin do that, I ask him, would Pearl Buck? Some day I'm going to get killed.

I was thunderstruck by the re-entry on the scene of J.P. The joy was a little dimmed by your news that he has a federal sentence to serve. I try not to be cynical, but I wonder if you would have heard from him if he had not been thus grounded. Whatever the circumstances, I was still glad to hear and even if the overture may be a shade calculated, it doesn't diminish his need for understanding nor detract from his talent.

Pauvre petit. I guess I scared him. It beats me why I always expect to be held over in these engagements, when I so unfailingly overblow the gig.

Soon I shall be in need of some articles of clothing to make my exit from these hallowed halls. Like a sport shirt (M), an odd jacket (38) and 9½ shoes. They give the graduates a couple pair of pretty good slacks, but I'm afraid the rest is please-don't-rain.

Soon, little one, soon! Borned again!   scared, Jim

Ex Post Facto

The affair with young Sandy was something I didn't seek, couldn't foresee, and never regretted. As Willie the bandleader diagnosed it, Sandy needed only a little attention to bring him out of his alienated state. After I began taking him down to the band hall with me in the afternoons and had an opportunity to talk to him alone, it seemed to me that he also needed love. That it was homosexual love was, in my opinion, of no importance. It was the only variety available and the need was crucial.

So we became lovers. Our being alone in the band hall so much brought a lot of comment from the other musicians, and from other convicts. Willie asked me about it, and I told him the truth. His answer was merely that I should be careful to protect myself and Sandy.

Sandy's cell partner was a glib, sinister con artist, a Jew who had become a converted Baptist and posed as a Bible-toting evangelist. A type convicts called "Bible-Back."

Sandy told me that this charlatan terrorized him with threats of perdition, quoted Scripture at him, and at night in the cell sodomized him.

If I was performing fellatio, it was because Sandy wanted it, enjoyed it—there was never any question of duress. In time Sandy became the dominant one in our relationship. It was of little importance to me, and I felt that it gave him confidence. In the matter of music, I remained his teacher and required him to learn.

When the band supervisor told me that he was getting anonymous letters about Sandy and me (and because he liked me and I was useful to him, his attitude was one of amused tolerance), I knew they were coming from Sandy's cell partner.

*The population of the prison was huge (3,000); the bureau-
cratic confusion was formidable. Under cover of this confusion,
it was possible for alert convicts to operate to a remarkable
degree. So I went to a friend of mine who worked as a secretary in the custodial office and made a deal with him. On the
street he had been a church organist and had ambitions to
succeed me in my job as chapel organist.*

*In return for letting him use the chapel organ and recom-
mending him to the chaplain as my successor, he agreed to
extract the folder ("rap sheet") of Sandy's cell partner from
the master file and place it in the road-transfer file. This was
the list of inmates marked for transfer from the main prison
to one of the state road camps.*

*Accordingly, one morning at daybreak, Sandy's cellmate was
called out and placed on a bus for transportation to a road camp.*

*It was tough for me to leave Sandy when the time came
for my discharge, but I was proud of the change in him, and
Willie promised me that he would look after him.*

*Much later, I heard that Sandy had done what I had always
told him he would do—returned to the small town he came from,
married, and started a family. Happy, or reasonably happy, ending.*

*Sandy's former cell partner is now in a state hospital for the
insane in a southern state.*

PART III

the happy islanders

Charleston, South Carolina
JUNE 30, 1956

Dear Nelson:

Well, I left the Academy after a simple but moving graduation ceremony, with a big sawbuck courtesy the State of Florida, and literally hit the road. Impossible to describe the mixed emotions I had walking away from the penitentiary. For a considerable stretch, I could still see the Rock, where I had spent two and a half years. Could still see the big recreation field and the path around the edge of it where I had walked so many miles in confusion and anxiety. I could even recognize some of the convicts on the field. And I did not, for a fact, know whether I had been cast out of Heaven or Hell. I had left behind the young Sandy, in a grinding scene of farewell that left a knot in my gut.

But when I crossed the bridge over the river and the road took a sharp turn, I was in the world I had not been able to see from behind the fences. I took a deep breath and said to myself, ready or not, motherfuckers, here I come, and felt exhilaration on top of the apprehension.

The nearest town to the prison, Starke, is about five miles, and I guess I walked about half of it. Just dawdling along, looking at the fields, looking at the cows (feeling myself watched as I passed the few houses along the road). A pickup truck came along and gave me a lift into Starke. One of the guards at the prison, a decent sort, but there was some grisly conversation that gave me the feeling of being half In, half Out. From Starke, a bus to Jacksonville. I didn't pause there, it's a miserable town at best and on Sunday it's chilling, and I wanted to get on with it, so I took a city bus to the northern city limits.

I planned to go to Atlanta, and I expected to wait a long time for a ride, Sunday being a bad day. To my surprise, I waited only a little while at the side of the highway, when a bigass Chrysler stopped. I ran towards it and discovered, with a shaft of dismay, that the driver was a spade, very black and very rough looking. Not for nothing all that training in the Rock. I jumped in, with a "Thanks a lot, man."

I told him I was going to Atlanta, he said he was bound for Charleston, but would give me a lift as far as he could. It took me a couple of minutes to surmise this cat was getting blocked. When he told me to open the glove compartment and there was a big jug of Canadian Club, and beer in a cooler on the floor in back, I knew he was getting blocked in a very methodical fashion.

I had a couple of drinks and a beer, and started to get carefree, I hadn't had any real juice in over two years—man, I was *clean*. By the time we got to the turnoff for Atlanta, I had decided to go to Charleston with my buddy. What the hell, I had never *seen* Charleston.

After a bit, though, the paranoid caution I'd acquired in the Rock began to take over, and I started to worry about his driving, which was becoming fairly free-form. A pusher friend of mine in the joint had given me some bennies as a bon voyage gift (talk about pagan decency) and I started to ply him with an antidote to all that juice. It seemed only to intensify his anarchical mood.

He was called Stony, he told me, he had been to Jacksonville trying to get his wife to come back to him. He ran a shrimp boat out of Mount Pleasant, across the harbor from Charleston, and was on his way to acquiring another boat. Devoting himself to rising above his station had cost him his wife, and he was a bitter somber black man.

By this time, we were well into Georgia, and started hitting all the small Deep-South towns; somnolent at their brightest, on Sunday they were graveyards with traffic lights. We stopped in one for gas, Darien, I think it was, at a combination gas station and general store. The usual loafers and stooges were hanging around. Stony's manner as he ordered gas was peremptory (the air of a "smart nigger") and the air was full of knives.

We got away from that, though expecting them to call ahead and have the state troopers on our ass. It was odd, too, how the vibrations between Stony and me changed for quite a while after we pulled away from that pool of ugliness.

Somewhere along the road in the afternoon, we saw a truck, decorated with bunting, parked on the shoulder of the road. Stony slowed down, saw it was some kind of black picnic (it was a church outing) and he stopped. Instantly all kinds of black gals, high on beer, were sticking their heads in the window. ("Lookit that beautiful breed. Come outa there, boy!") I found myself surrounded by shrieking satirical black women, found myself dancing with one on a stretch of concrete from some abandoned building, while a radio brayed rhythm-and-blues.

When we finally got away from that, after an eternity of strain and embarrassment for me, Stony said drily, "You don't dig broads, do you?"

"I don't mind broads. I just don't like loud broads."

"Uh huh."

When we got to Charleston it was night, and raining like hell. Stony knew that I was just out of the joint, had no bread, and no place to go. Without a word he drove through Charleston onto the long high humpbacked bridge that crosses the Cooper and Ashley rivers to Mount Pleasant. It was pitch dark, and I could smell the fish and salt smell of the ocean. I followed him out on to a wharf, and we were on board his boat. I spent the night there with him. By the light of the oil lamp in that small fishy cabin, I felt a tenuous security—and a strong sense of brotherly love such as I had not known before.

In the morning we faced the facts—it was impossible for me to stay there. He drove me back to Charleston, and I spent the day missing the strength of Stony, and casing the town. There was no doubt in my mind I had to move fast and I looked for a joint to break into.

That night, prowling, I was picked up on suspicion (I didn't know that Charleston had two fuzz for every citizen) and taken to the station. They shook me down and found my discharge from the Florida joint. The sergeant was indignant.

"Just got out and trying to get back in, huh? Well, you ain't gonna do it, not here." He calls up a mission on Skid Row and tells somebody I'm coming over. They even gave me a ride.

And that's where I am now. An Irishman, the Reverend Ryan runs it, and he seems, I would say, intrigued by my case. Besides, I worked like a dog cleaning up the dormitory they got here, and I play piano for the phony services he holds every night for the winos and drifters. (It's a highly polished grand piano, in good shape, and when all the saints are away, I get to play it.)

I have moments of speculation, about my friends. Permitting me to be run though the grinder, once again. (Out of curiosity, to see what I'd look like, reconstituted?) I think you could say I'm a little different.

That bridge, incidentally, between confinement and freedom —it's a suspension bridge, and it hangs by a thread. Very difficult from the one that leads the other way. That is a triumph of engineering, solid as a rock. I seem to be on the other side of the bridge now, but I'll be goddammed if I know where I am.

Charleston, South Carolina
JULY 26, 1956

Dear Nelson:

Remember the song that "nothin' could be finah than to be in Carolinah"? Lies, all lies, the guy that wrote it lived in Far

Rockaway. In fleeing from the Reverend Ryan and his counter-
feit Christians, I've become entangled in a new set of Carolina
complications. I got so depressed and fed up with the Rev and
his Holy Bobble that I swung with the collection one night (a
cool 83¢) and went out looking for trouble.

I figured I'd given the Rev more than 83¢ worth of happiness.
Twofold happiness, in fact. When he first saw me, he thought
he'd found the 13th Disciple. Later, when the true nature of the
beast became apparent, he was able to say he had personally
encountered the Anti-Christ. So it was kicks coming and going.

Anyway, I went looking for mischief, and found Dan Cooper.
He owns a night club called the Magnolia Room, which is the
haunt of the racier element in Charleston aristocracy. And when
it comes to genealogy-conscious stuffed owls, Charleston can
show the Beacon Hill interlopers a thing or two; everybody I
meet descends from a Huguenot.

Dan is one of the Charleston pioneers; the Coopers were on
hand to greet the Huguenots and sell them the acres of malarial
marshland they settled on. Only Dan is a renegade; instead of
living in genteel decline, and hocking the family ormolu, he gets
rich running a saloon.

He's a combination of Old South punctilio and dockhand aggressiveness. Thirty-eight years old, stocky, muscled, rugged-
ugly, with an unsettling charm that comes from a poetic, perverse, avidly curious mind. Disturbing because while his talk
is compelling, fantastic, hypnotic, I can never be sure how
much of it is mendacious and satirical.

Last night he transfixed me with a tale of shooting a kangaroo
in Australia. He shot him (he said, with passionate sincerity)
against his finer instincts. Which also forbid him to shoot deer
and elephants. "You couldn't make me shoot an elephant," he
declared, and eyed me accusingly as if I had tried. "An elephant
is a gentle tender animal."

The kangaroo, shot squarely between the eyes, gave a prodigious leap of more than thirty feet, and died.

"Imagine, a death leap," he said. "But you couldn't make me
shoot *another* kangaroo, not for a million dollars!" And he

surveyed me challengingly, as if I had the money ready in my pocket.

What bothered me was that I knew he actually had spent considerable time in Australia, and that he was a crack marksman. He practices often on a pistol range he has out here. But I speculated that this yarn was simply a savagely contemptuous way of proving to himself that I was a gullible fool, or too cowardly to say I thought he was a liar. He and I have had this particular passage before, with variations. Then too, it's a peculiarly southern thing, they have perfected the fine art of lying with flair.

Anyway, when I drifted into the joint (with the price of one beer in my pocket) and auditioned, he hired me to play the piano. For the first week, during intermissions, I sat and drank with him, while he questioned me about myself. Did it so deftly, deviously, sympathetically, that I gave him more of the truth than I otherwise might have.

His drinking is a methodical, curiously joyless affair, leading to moods that veer from lyrical to sardonic to ugly. The next day, with the same cold precision and concentration, he lifts weights, rides a horse, shoots a pistol, swims, and shows no trace of the night's dissipation. I drink only moderately now, and I don't join him in getting bagged. In a way I'm afraid to.

I had only worked a few nights at the club when Dan informed me that he didn't want me living at the Reverend Ryan's. Actually I'd been prowling a little on my own, and wanted to move into the Dock Street Theatre building (Charleston's bohemia; I met a couple interesting types there). But he moved me out on the island with him.

It's about twenty miles out of Charleston, in the Sound, the open ocean nearby. These are the haunted brooding Carolina lowlands, the tidewater country where the stalwart pioneers displayed false shore lights in order to wreck and plunder ships. Our Murcan heritage. Dan pointed out another island, low on the horizon, which still has Civil War fortifications. The South will rise again.

I'd say this island is only some twenty-five acres, if that.

Dan owns the whole tiny continent, the fief of his ancestors. There's a big house where Dan stays, beautiful, ghostly, decadent (sinking into the sand), and I live in an old slave hut "fixed up." There are never any callers, not so far, and we are the sole inhabitants, outside of the "Nigras." All day the stillness is massive, pervasive, dense, except for the pistol shots when he practices, and these trifling noises seem to drown immediately. The atmosphere seems to be waiting, waiting.

From my windows I can see for unbroken miles— miles of water and sky and lonely marshland. Nothing moves but the fishing birds, wheeling languidly in the air, and the palmettos, fanning themselves in the heat. Waiting, waiting.

I try to tell myself *toujours l'audace*, but I don't like at all what I feel. You should have sent me the bread, and by now I'd be safe with some Rush Street Mafia hoodlum in Chicago. I don't know about these southern aristocrats. There's an old Arabian proverb I just made up: "Lie down with the adder, get up sadder."   alors, Jim

Charleston, South Carolina
AUGUST 3, 1956

Dear Gertrude:

Because I'm thinking of you and wishing I could be with you in Chicago this morning, I'm making do with this. If it gets rather magenta, forgive, this exile is a much-tried pilgrim.

It is five a.m., the birds are stirring in the palms outside and from the windows I can see the first smoke-gray light of day, turning to silver the dark quiet waters of the sound.

The grizzly who owns this island departed about an hour ago, pleased with himself and his world, and I'm left vibrating and wishing myself far from him and this hostile geechee country.

His name is Dan, one of the Huguenots of Charleston, thirtyish, muscled, an arresting ugliness, befurred like the bear. Nor was it the physical charms that put me where I am. Rather it was the cunning, intelligence, deviousness and imagination of the scoundrel that arrested me. That and the need for bread to maneuver on this burning deck.

He owns the Magnolia, the joint where I play. It's a reproduction of a Carolina-style patio, common brick and wrought iron, deep leather booths, murky darkness, and I furnish the unobtrusive piano music. Aside from a discreet sign outside, there's no indication at all of a night club. Underplayed all the way, which results in SRO all the time, and the host's consistently inimical attitude towards customers merely charms them the more.

Wouldn't you think, from all this, as many gutters as I've been in, that I would gather there was a mind at work? Not that there was a hell of a lot of choice at first, I fell into the joint one night, a month or so out of jail, broke and on my ass, played the piano, was hired. Beautiful piano, sharp club, cordial reception from the aristocrats assembled. Terms were attractive, and I felt I'd finally landed, escaping disaster and the looming threat of return to jail. Somewhere over the rainbow bluebirds fly.

I wish now I'd never left the Rock in Florida, but this maniac didn't come on like a maniac at first.

I should have suspected something from the attitude of the rich rebels that haunt the joint, touched with awe, pathetically glad when he warms to cordiality and offers them a drink. Methodically, he plies everyone around him, occupying his booth like a throne at a levee, the wit and charm flows freely, and there is laughing it up while he sparkles.

Not till he drove me home the first night, sober in an instant, did I discover the wiliness, the savagery of his method. In their innocent faith and drunkenness his companions were but specimens for observation. With cold satisfaction he estimated in what way this or that friend was vulnerable and dispensable, how far from ruin and collapse. This engaging misanthrope was compiling for them a dossier of doom.

I was intrigued by such bland villainy, but chilled, and decided to keep as much distance as was compatible with keeping the job.

It took some skating. Being lonely and strange, I looked about

for something interesting in a southern gent. They all seemed to
adore my playing and were eager to be friends. I settled on a
couple of actors from the Dock Street Theatre. The older one,
improbably called Julian Ravenal, had a face ancient with weary
satiety; his beautiful young companion a face of placid dreaming
wickedness. There was not a doubt in my mind that we three
could wind up in some piquant erotic arrangement, the winter
seemed made, so hungry was I for just such raffish companions
after a long starvation.

The three of us seated at the bar, Dan passed by, swept us
casually with a glance, stopped, said to Julian, "I want to see
you." Julian murmured, "I know what the son of a bitch will
say." I never discovered what that was, but that night after
work, Dan said, "If you're really in earnest about wanting to
write, Charleston's not the place for you. I want you to see
where I live."

He brought me out to the island that morning. It was still
dark, the stars were on top of us, the Atlantic breeze murmured
in the palms, the waters of the sound whispered liquidly.
Naturally, I was enchanted.

He brought out the liquor and stayed to talk (in the small
house he said I should "try"). Talked amiably, winningly,
mostly of the arts, and without halting the flow of urbanity,
complained of the heat and stripped to his shorts. (It may have
been the record, "Alborado del Gracioso.") He kept the talk
spinning, but the bronzed hairy maleness of him was making
the air crackle around me, as difficult to inhale as noodle soup.
And while the bastard was gauging his effect, my treacherous
face was selling me out. Even while I reached frantically for a
coherent reply to some damnable observation he'd made on
Christopher Fry, I could read a small tinge of pity in the green
eyes as they weighed the imminence of my collapse.

Oh well. I encountered some variations he must have picked
up from a Bedouin camel-skinner in one of the murkier streets
of Tangier. Even in the holocaust, it crossed my mind that he
could not bear to be bested in anything and was satisfying himself that in this, too, I was a mere dabbler. It was an excursion

into eroticism along roads I never saw on any map. The calm steady dispassionate degradation and debasement, sure, strong, relentless. When it was done—this silent, contemptuous and curiously onanistic performance—the first daylight was rising over the water. I had been coolly employed, crumpled and discarded like a Kleenex.

Sated, sure of one more egg in the basket, he paced the floor, outlining a program of reclamation and renovation. Regarding me with mixed distaste and pity, "Your hair is too long, too —musicianish." Twined spatulate fingers in it, nearly lifting my scalp. "Uglier than I am," he mused. "You're a find, a positive find." Then, "Cut your hair. At the Magnolia, you won't look hired. You should look like a performing amateur, like a guest sitting down to amuse your friends. Then your professional sound will come as an irritating surprise to your listeners."

He looked at me with distress. "And your clothes . . . well, tomorrow we'll cut your hair and get you some sunburn." On, and on.

He paused, only then aware of my anger and embarrassment, and measured it. I had a strength he knew nothing about: I was wishing I was back in jail. Sensing the hidden reserve, he retreated. "It's only sensible, Mr. Blake—" He brayed the long A as Charlestonians do, and drew a smile from me. "I won't have those moribund bastards sniping at you while you're working for me. I intend to see you succeed in the job, and while I'm behind you they won't dare anything but like you. And nobody but me understands what you're doing."

A formal bow. "I'll be over in the afternoon, if it won't disturb you at your writing. If you need anything, press the button, and one of the Nigras will come."

The Nigras. . . . Thus I was appropriated, another weapon in his war with Charleston. When I awoke, it was to gunfire. He was killing the phantom enemy on the pistol range.

Numb with shock, catatonic with dread, I ventured timidly into the kitchen to make myself some coffee. There was brandy left in the bottle, I had a couple of Dexies, and I gulped it all against the fearful appearance.

When he showed it was in riding habit, looking as wide and high as Cyclops. He coolly recorded the degree of my confusion, but his manner was bantering, lightly paternal, there was no sign of the previous night's fever. "Jupiter and I had a good ride, I feel great." He looked closer at me. "Maybe you should eat something. I thought we'd go into town later."

Benevolent commands. The grand seigneur and the poverty-struck transient he has just remembered sheltering in the storm. A nuisance, but noblesse oblige.

Rattled, distrait, I scrambled to escape. "No need to hurry, I brought some trunks, thought we might swim a little first. It's good for a hangover."

So we swam and lay in the sun while he talked quietly, putting the unaccountable waif at ease. Showed me the big house. "My brother left some clothes here. He's about like you. Try them on, those trousers of yours sag in the ass. Is that what they gave you when you left the pen? A shame."

I stand for inspection. He appears to have forgotten me. "Oh yea, much better. By the way. Did you register as an ex-convict when you came into Charleston? State law, six months and a fine. I can probably arrange something. The cops in this town are venal as hell. I wouldn't worry about it."

I look at him. The velvet threat.

So here I am—trapped, beset, lonely, bored, frightened and confused. I don't know anybody except momentarily. We live alone on the island with only the jigs, all starry-eyed for Mistah Dan. "Pappy wuhk for Mistah Dan's daddy. He a caution, Mistah Dan, yuk, yuk, yuk."

But you know something? When I play piano, he listens. And he understands. *Que voulez-vous?*   Later, Jim

Charleston, South Carolina
AUGUST 22, 1956

Dear Gertrude:

. . . The natives of this geechee territory eat rice three times a day, and all the time in between, and they talk about a certain kind of black that is a "good southern nigra, always uses 'Mister.'" Ugh. The fools. I do not think they have taken a good look at blacks as persons for some time, these ingrown insular aristocrats of Charleston. I look closely at the spades as I walk the streets—they are really so much better looking than whites, black is a more suitable color for skin, and in the great majority of them, I sense a secret merriment, an amused contempt. Charleston blacks, many of them, ride around in gigantic new automobiles. I daresay this is because the economy is rather frantic down here, and credit is easier. For everybody but musicians.

I think perhaps the spades are better off here, the weather is kinder, and certainly there is something softer about the Catfish Row type of thing as contrasted with the grim phalanxes of tenements one sees in Chicago. At least there is room for small kitchen gardens, and there is not the grinding pressure of urban existence. Then, too, the blacks have taken refuge in the masquerade of "good nigras" and if there is anything satirical in calling everybody Mister the benighted whites are not hip to it.

I've met several students at the State College for blacks at Orangeburg, rather straight-up types, in a way, from the ones I knew in Florida, but of course that's understandable; the spades I knew in the Rock were felons. These are waiters at the Magnolia, and they seem to be on the track of onward and upward and easy does it. From them there is little talk of revolt and equal rights, they allow the Carolinians their heavy paternalistic role as protectors of "good nigras" from the NAACP. It's possible they don't relate to me because they know my relation with Dan. But one of them who hangs a little looser told me that Dan pays their tuition at college. According to this cat, Dan told them, "If you're going to hang around here, you're not going to remain niggers all your lives." It's a clue, but what do it mean?

I've been dabbling around with writing a few little things, but my obsession with Dan hangs over me and keeps me off balance, and I'll probably never do anything until I'm away from him.

To please him (or rather because I daren't displease him), I have become the complete piano player of the Magnolia Room, clipped, sunburned, my summer suit as rumpled as any on the Battery. He is pleased at his handiwork, sardonically amused when the frosty Charlestonians inspect the Outlander who has come so mysteriously to resemble a native, an object of speculation instead of "Dan's itinerant."

Maybe if we were not so much together . . . I go into town with him in time for work, come back in the morning with him. We turn the phonograph on, leaving the music to wail as accompaniment for anarchy in the dark. He uses the sexual pull he knows he has for me like Pentothal, on the theory that what I evade in the light I will confess in the dark. It would be idle to disabuse him of this notion, in view of the fact that I'm so bloody hooked.

And yet when we lie quiet and the shaggy heat of him is beside me, I feel a precarious love and desire for this tormentor, and I could cry at the wrongness of the reasons we are together. Once I pressed my lips into the tangled hair of his wrist, a silent plea for him to be different. It made his furious, his scorn was horrible, it withered me, and petrified me lest he send me away.

Thus the happy life of the carefree childlike islanders. How many times I have wished myself back in the joint, the perfect peace I had and did not value. The time to read and write, and goof in the sun, to play the piano indifferently or ferociously as I chose. There are nights at the Magnolia when I'm hacked, or simply inert, and can't play, and he stops at the piano and says, what's wrong with you? And there are other nights, when I have really been wailing. The joint closes, he locks the doors, and I play for him. His taste is impeccable, it is a joy. And I think, this motherfucker is attuned to me, but for what, *à quoi bon?* For the sardonic, hateful regard we have for one another?

Sometimes I think all this tohu-bohu is superficial, meaningless, that I am pointed inexorably toward Florida and fated to return there.   Je meurs, Jim

Charleston, South Carolina
AUGUST 24, 1956

[To Tom Rolfe, Raiford State Prison]

Dear Tombeau:

You're a horrible person to get letters from. Sample: "You told me plenty in your last letter—more than you know." What kind of a crack is that? I went around all day mumbling, What I Say, What I Say?

All that blackbird-croaking about my not writing. I'll get to it; right now I'm making a living playing piano, and some other things. Meanwhile I learn, absorb, suffer, exult. Much to explore in your native state, ponder, inhale, examine.

It is 7 a.m., The Boss has just left, we've been listening to classical records and talking about the club and the demented, depraved and just plain dull people that infest the joint. Relations with my boss have improved; it's perhaps only a temporary truce, but nice; I should like to live without the small abrasions that we gratuitously inflict and are inflicted with. But I feel a necessity to do battle occasionally—in the past, as you know, I have mislaid my identity by subordinating my own interests to those of another, and I'm determined that, if possible, never again. . . .

The Paris Review has come up with the bread at long last (and how desperately I needed it in June, it could have changed the course of history), the stuff will appear in the upcoming issue. I've waited so long, hoped so much, all I feel now is depleted.

I can't get a straight opinion on the mss for *Chain Dance*, everyone shuffles his feet and looks away like, you'd think I was inquiring about a bed-wetting aunt. Having taken a hard look at it, my own feeling is I should start all over with it, pitch it higher, higher—the goddam thing trudges, when it isn't yawing.

I will tap a can of beer and go for a swim, and perhaps together they will rout the sleeplessness that has been dogging me and making me tight and irritable. I can't afford it. Friday night is heavy at the Magnolia, the debutantes and blades of Charleston will be thick in my hair. I wish I didn't find it so damnably hard to be affable, but honestly I look at people and all I see are jaws, wagging wagging. How I envy your peace and quiet. How does one go about applying for entrance?   Your buddy, Jim

Charleston, South Carolina
AUGUST 28, 1956

Dear Gertrude:

The dismaying rush of partisan feeling I had when I read your description of Dan ("pistol-popping sadist") told me all I needed to know about where I stand. I feel trapped—all right—I'm struggling. But if I disparaged him it was in a puerile attempt to find strength in a petty resentment, the witless malediction of a scolding crow.

I know this about myself from past involvements, from boats I have missed, challenges I have ignored—that when strong demands are made upon me, demands that disconcert and frighten me, I find a way to evade. And having found it, I find a way to explain my cowardice.

It was a selfishly motivated, incomplete and inaccurate picture of Dan. Behind all his behavior, I think, is the fact that pretense enrages him blindly, and he wants to shake me out of what he considers my dream of existence. After one of those soul-scouring encounters, I will admit that I feel some of the mistiness of my mind has been seared away. What I feel is beyond shame or guilt, or even embarrassment: I know that his homosexuality is like my own, in that it is a matter of attraction between two masculine minds, and not a tinsel thing in which one of them must pretend to be a woman.

Cruel or not is irrelevant, there is a vast uneasiness and torment in the man, a bottled loneliness. Of course I know that the desperation implicit in this kind of alliance will strangle it as a matter of course, and that will be the end of it. Meanwhile, there are the times when we talk and know mutual understanding. For me, slippery and rackety as I am, it has been a revelation to find someone so obsessed with honesty. I don't mean the B. Franklin thing reputed to be the "best policy," but scorching scalding merciless truth. He fights the world for it.

If he is determined to find out what makes me what I am, there are two ends to that telescope. This is a highly charged articulate man who has not yet brought himself to utter the secret of his disenchantment.   love, Jim

Charleston, South Carolina
AUGUST 26, 1956

Dear Nelson:

I was just barely within reach of sleep this morning about daylight when there came a diffident but insistent tapping on the door of my small house.

I had whipped myself up to fiddle-string tautness the night before, playing in the Magnolia Room of Dan's Indoor Gutter —through the judicious use of chemicals of one kind and another—and had exhausted myself, physically and otherwise, performing for my public.

Really it is ridiculous how these provincial bog-trotters have me confused with Liberace or somebody—everybody pays such *livid* attention. I'd prefer to play as the mood moved me, carefully or haphazardly, with passion or indifference, depending on how I was feeling, but my god how these bankrupt individuals *listen*. It makes the air ache.

Indecent, and quite wrong. In all my previous experience, the pub-crawlers and barflies have always been too preoccupied with greasy little private intrigues to pay much attention to the piano player. Which is as it should be. This popeyed, pathetic inhaling the music is something new to me.

It's a burden, I have to be "on" too much of the time otherwise, things being as they are. This fierce hungry interest from

an audience is disconcerting. I find myself constantly overblow-
ing the gig.

All of which is merely to say I was very tired when the
tapping came at my door. When it increased in volume to a
peremptory pounding, I really grew apprehensive, it had the
sinister sound of fuzz. But the rising daylight gave me courage,
and I went to the door.

It was Ralph and Rosalie. Looking for a handout, displaying
the bland cockeyed optimism they always assume on these occasions.

Ralph is a big white gander and Rosalie is sort of a buff-
colored goose with the massive complacency that suffuses a
female who is confident she's a good lay. They are the leaders
of a flock of geese Dan keeps on the island. For kicks, purely,
and they are all of that. A more militantly opinionated reaction-
ary mob you never saw. But volatile. They can go from swag-
gering waddling assurance to gibbering panic in a single blazing
instant for no discernible reason.

And they have embarked on a calculated campaign to undermine me. I can't pass them, as they patrol the island on their
restless aimless excursions, without they try to make something
of it. They suffer me to pass with only a vague bridling and
ruffling of feathers, and a certain sotto voce muttering—and
then there arises a chorus of anathema and alarm like a hundred
spinsters discovering burglars under a hundred beds, like all the
Sabines hollering rape.

Ralph and Rosalie, being more diplomatic and devious, ab-
stain from this maneuver of terror and intimidation. Being
practical fowl, they do not indulge themselves in open enmity
when, with a superficial show of affability, they can get cheese-
crackers, sausages and pretzels.

So we have established a wary detente, we three. Ralph
drops by at odd times, elaborately casual, accompanied by his
paramour, informs me by clearing his throat that he's out there,
and lets the unvoiced threat hang in the air. And I sustain the
charade, greet him with forced joviality and pay enough tribute
to placate him.

But his calling at the ungodly hour of daybreak was really overplaying his hand, and while I evinced no surprise at the hour, I think we both knew he had weakened his position. He took the pretzels I gave him with a certain shamefaced air.

The fall of a prince, even a despot, is saddening, and the bleak loneliness of the hour made it even more poignant. Sic semper tyrannis.   Later, Jim

Charleston, South Carolina
SEPTEMBER 23, 1956

Dear Gertrude:

I've just returned from seeing Great Man off at the airport; he's invading Miami for a couple of days. I shall be alone here for a while, well not alone exactly, the nigras are about. It's profoundly sad, how they are, the crushing paternalism of the Caro-leenians has emasculated them. Dan doesn't share the attitude, I don't know how many times I've seen him in a bursting rage at them, hollering, "God damn you, are you going to stay a nigger all your life?"

I got a glimpse of the old-school outlook on the race thing the day I met Dan's mother, very grande-dame vague sort, with the kind of measured politeness that seems like a studied insult. She lives in one of the monstrous architectural atrocities that overlook the Charleston harbor.

She had quite a bit to say concerning the loving care Carolinians have always given their black charges. Added, with exquisite courtesy, and deadly grace, that of course I was a Yankee and that my outlook was perhaps "different." Meaning wrong. As she spoke of the halcyon days of her girlhood on the plantation, I seemed to be looking down an endless and hellish-dark tunnel of years to the leisurely sunlit scene her words evoked. Banjos strummin', darkies a-hummin', EEEEE. I felt chilled.

Since she pressed me for my views, I tried as calmly as possible to present the musician's attitude, that if a man can't blow his axe it don't matter what shade he is, and if he can, let him be striped. That handsome old beast nodded with every evidence of warm agreement. And later told Dan not to bring any more nigger-lovers home with him. Naturally, I knew before I went into it that the whole meeting was an arrangement to give him his kicks. That's my main man.

Anyway, I intend to fly a little while I'm on my own, though I know the darkies will be a-hummin' to Dan when he gets back. I've met three Navy musicians, and I invited them out to the island today. All fine musicians and wonderfully disparate types. They're stationed here with the Navy band. The bass man is from Tallahassee, built like a fullback, but he is swingin' murder on the bass. He brings his axe into the club often (Dan hates him) and we gas one another. Though I take issue with him from time to time on the current vogue for bass men to play a line which has only a distant connection with the harmonic structure of the tunes. I don't mean to beef, but whatever happened to the tonic and dominant?

The other two sailors are trombone men from New York, and do pretty well at the Kai-J.J. kind of thing. One's a tough, muscled, belligerent Polack, the other—who really delights me— is an incredibly gentle and earnest boy with enormous wondering brown eyes and a lock of hair that falls over his forehead.

Name of Lou. He has a hi-fi outfit that is his pride, which he keeps in an apartment in town which he and the bass man share. I wanted to give them a record, and cast about for something that would be really provocative and also show them what a cultured sonbitch I really am. I settled for an album of The Firebird and Pictures At An Exhibition. Lou put it on the machine and I settled back to bask in the touching wonder and gratitude of these lovable peasants. My effect was marred by the fact that the Polack could sing Pictures note for note, and they were all far more familiar with Firebird than I have ever been. Sometimes I stupefy myself.

No hurricane yet, though I keep hoping, and so does Dan. It may be that he has gone to Miami to see what's holding it up; he takes a firm line in these things.

Ralph and Rosalie, the demented panhandling geese, have permanently adopted me; they live outside my door and wait for the happenings. If I ignore them too long, Ralph bangs on the door with his nose. Also a mouse has moved in with me, called Motherfucker. He picks the moment when my hangovers are crucial and I am in my bare feet to scuttle across the floor on some cataleptic excursion. My heart will stop one of these times, never to go again. And when I'm trying to sleep he's busy in the kitchen, moving furniture, slamming doors, dismantling the stove. How such a tiny critter can sound like six burglars beats me.   zut alors, Jim

Charleston, South Carolina
SEPTEMBER 25, 1956

Dear Mike:

There you are, Horseman. About time. Stay your steed. Nelson told me you been horsing around (sue me) from coast to coast. I missed you. Lots of happenings, chiefly grim.

Remember that hurricane in Miami? It's 3 a.m. here and my small island home is being clobbered by a storm from Hurricane Flossie. Outside, there is a cosmic uproar—rain lashing, surf crashing, palms thrashing—and over all the howling of the wind.

Inside, all is snug. I've put The Buried Cathedral on the phonograph and its serenity nicely complements the roaring without. All I need is a taste of grass, alas.

This island idyll may soon cease, however. Weather bureau says that high tide will be higher by ten feet. The crest is due in about five hours. I don't know the elevation of the island, but since my little hut sits perilous close to the water, I may end up in a palmetto.

Dan, my boss, my heartsease, my cross, is away in Miami for a few days, and I'm sole inhabitant, except for a gaggle of nigras, all Toms. Dan says he emancipated them long ago but they're hanging around waiting for the word to murder us in bed.

It appears that turbulence is still the pattern for me. However, against the upheavals I've been trying to gather a getaway fund, for when it gets over my eyebrows. The stash grows slowly, but it grows. As soon as I've got it to the point where I can feel reasonably secure, I'll do something about returning some of the bread you sent me. But I hope I never again have to run as fast as I did when I got out of the joint. Bit snug in the crotch, that was.

If I can ride this riff through the winter (and it's iffy) I'll stay here. If not, probably I'll make the Miami scene. Don't dig that Yankee weather any more. My playing is stronger and more assured, I think, than it has ever been. (You called it "peo-zallid," remember?) Which is ironic, aside from listening to others blow, I have little interest in jazz any more.

A number of people up there I would like to see again— there's a lot of loneliness in this exile bit. But if I'm ever to stand alone and get something done, I have to learn to find strength in solitude. The sad wild beauty of this place is a help— I feel a need to measure up. Like to hear from you again, dear Michaelo. You coming South this year?   later, Jim

                                    Charleston, South Carolina
                                    OCTOBER 17, 1956

Dear Gertrude:

Mahler ♯ 1 is on the radio from D.C., that all-night program of cultured stuff sponsored by an airline. I find the program plays in most large cities within range of my radio. And it makes me wonder, knowing that business types like airline wheels are notoriously astute. What I want to know is, whom, please, are they aiming at? Well, dig. They're looking for a customer who is presumably up and about at the dubious hour of 4 a.m. And one who likes to hear classical music at that ungodly time. It seems to me that anybody with these qualifications is up to no damn good at all, and certainly he'd be a poor risk for any decent airline. Lot of money going down the drain there.

Another storm has been announcing itself. The wind rising all day yesterday, whipping rods of rain before it. Till now it's howling and singing in the palmettos outside. This is not the grimy sly wind that whines around the buildings of the city. This is the wind where it gets a chance to wail. Roaring in off the water, miles of open marsh to run in, it hits the trees with a strong wild song, it pulls me inside out to stand in it and listen to it.

I ran into a horrible bird the other day. Here in this country the sky is never empty of a hawk or a vulture, always delicately gliding, always watching. Since there's a number of giddy fowl on this island, the hawks make it a point to keep an eye on it.

I was walking down the road to the mailbox, hoping for opium in the mail. Walking along, I met the geese, strangely silent for once, and running for their lives. If you've never seen anything with webbed feet getting out from under, they travel, it's a kind of rubbery haste, but they make it. —I had a terrible hangover, the air seemed to be made of spun brass— and the sight of the terror-struck geese didn't help at all.

Up in the air, hanging directly over me, was a monster of a hawk, a peregrine. Remember Wescott's "Pilgrim Hawk," I thought of it as I looked up at this hovering giant. He didn't seem at all pleased to see me. And followed overhead as I walked. He'd rise and soar for a few minutes, then come whistling down out of the sky, and brake, as if he'd changed his mind. Then continued hanging over me, and by this time I'm stumbling in the sand, keeping an eagle eye on this hawk. The second run he made, I knew this bastard had me in mind, and I looked frantically for something solid to whack him with when he came down.

And oh my god my head was splitting and I thought what a raunchy way to go. Finally I spotted a stout stick, and standing in the middle of the road I brandished it like Prometheus inviting the lightning. This cat really had me scared shitless, I had visions of my eyes pecked out by this flying serpent. And above all was the picture of myself fighting this preposterous bird, the utter appalling humiliation of it. I mean, so *feathered*.

I fought the sky that day. later, Jim

Charleston, South Carolina
OCTOBER 26, 1956

Dear Nelson:

I just dug The Paris Review, and want to thank you for all you did. The way it's edited, it makes me look like Jean Harlow. And placed next to Genet. Not only a damaging comparison, it's like being buried next to the Pope.

It may be damaging, I dunno. Reading him, I was struck by how perilous it is to be a poet.

I'm still trying to make it here and resisting the awful temptation to go back to the peace and quiet of the Rock. The Owner is, for him, more or less patient and sympathetic, but I've met a couple Navy musicians who complicate things some.

The bass man is a great hostile neanderthal, plays his ass off on bass, and thinks I stink. And there's a large brown-eyed trombone player, who thinks I don't. I don't think he does either.

At the Magnolia, I'm supposed to play chic chandelier music, I think it's called inconspicuous, unobtrusive, something like that, and when the bassist and trombonist come in, things take a turn jazzwise, and the Owner prowls unhappily.

You got any idea where I can book a trio, bass trombone piano? hung, Jim

Charleston, South Carolina
OCTOBER 28, 1956

Dear ———:

I'm several kinds of jerk for not writing sooner to thank
you for the heaven-sent god's medicine. Things just move too
fast lately. I'm trying to keep the Owner happy and at the
same time trying to chase a brown-eyed trombone player from
the Navy. There has been a certain degree of success in the
chase.

Thing is, if I keep on as I'm going, I know Dan will flip, and
I'll be out. I've thought of moving into town but every morning
when we come back from there, the stars are overhead within
reaching distance, the water stretches into silver infinity, the
wind sighs in the palmettos—how can I leave?

It's lonely, lonely as blazes; Dan spends maybe an hour or
two with me when we come home, and for the rest of the time
I'm alone.

So often I wish for somebody like you to see this country
with me. In Wisconsin, the country always suggested vitality,
virility—here as I ride my bicycle around, I'm struck by the
pervading air of sadness and defeat. A dying kind of country,
such sad pale beauty, it invades me.

And then from that, having to cope wtih the brisk pragmatism
of this stud I'm with—I have a hell of a time shifting gears.
And so often lately I feel the stirring of mutiny, and it's so
goddam foolish.

You know what's in my mind? The joint. I thought I was
getting off free from that experience. I thought they hadn't
managed to touch me, but it colors every moment and every
action of my life. I think always of the peace that I had there—
this working to survive and surviving to work seems increasingly
like an arrangement I would not have chosen, were it up to me.
Those gates, man, they're inviting. So much lovely time stretches
out before you, time to read, to write, to play, to practice,

to speculate, contemplate—and without the idiot necessity to Hold Up Your End. It is so well understood, the lines are so definitely drawn; I am Society and you are Not, and there is such a weary patience with nonconforming, it is infinitely restful.

I had the first inkling of this feeling when I used to go outside the fence with the band to play at dances for the club that was made up of hacks and officials of the joint. And their wives, their truly horrible wives, and their misbegotten children. They had a clubhouse across the road from the joint, and we were taken over there under guard from time to time to furnish music for these drab and sinister festivals. How many times, as I sat at the piano during these rigadoons, have I thought, I don't belong here, I belong over there, locked in with my tribe.   ever, Jim

Charleston, South Carolina
OCTOBER 28, 1956

Dear Gertrude:

I've made up my mind to move into town. Probably a stupid move, entirely in character. It's just that, beautiful as it is, there's a trapped feeling about it. I can't go much of anywhere unless Dan takes me, and visitors aren't encouraged. I'm stifling. (And I can't bear any bloody more heartbreak.)

I know that I will leave Dan and all this with a genuine reluctance. (What the hell is it with me that I can't stand to close a door behind me?) There have been many irritations, many of them my fault, but there has also been an honest sensuality that I hardly hoped to find in this winter of my discontent.

The marsh grass has turned to undulating stripes of color with the turn of the season, the island is a riot of goldenrod, and some kind of late-blooming bush that came out at first demurely gray, then burst into clouds of white. I've been riding my bike along the ocean shore. The water is beginning its winter tantrum, and the sight of the empty beach, so lately festive, is piercing. In the side roads, huge oaks veiled in Spanish moss, palmetto trees weary of life and condemned to it. Specters rise on every hand, abandoned houses, desolate hamlets, over all the dead hand of a climate too kind.

Rosalie is at the door, raising hell with her bill. She is alone now; Ralph has put her down, and she is exiled from the flock. They peck her unmercifully when she tries to approach. It is slowly driving her out of her wits and her behavior grows increasingly strange. She wanders alone, sometimes far into the night. Wandering myself in the night, I have been painfully startled at times by a sudden violent hissing—the mad Rosalie, poisoned by love. Feeling somehow allied with her, I am now supporting her, and she is the most independent dependent I ever saw.

As for me, several times now I've told Dan I want to leave. Violence the first couple of times. Then a kind of gentle ominous tolerance that is even harder to take. Why should I resist domination at this late date, when it brings me closer to security than I have been for a long time, passes understanding. Who knows?   later, Jim

Hotel ——
NOVEMBER 14, 1956

Dear Gertrude:

Principal news, I guess, is that I moved off the island and into town and things are in a state of you could say, flux. I'm still working at the Magnolia, for how long is anybody's guess. Last night I was informed silkily that my playing sounded "indifferent," whatever that is, and warned I'd better get with it. The devious son of a bitch. I told him I only wanted to stay in town for a week to think about things.

I said: "Jesus Christ, Dan, can't we take it from the top, and play it again in a different key?" It didn't come out, but I said it.

The move was as much for his sake as mine— he's a highly

volatile stud and I felt that I was becoming something of a drag
to him. Aaaah.

I'm told I'm to move back to the island next week.

Later, Jim

Hotel ——
NOVEMBER 21, 1956

Dear Gertrude:

So ends the Carolina caprice. Tomorrow I split for Florida,
to meet a former fellow shut-in. He has promised that if we
make one good score, we'll settle down in Key West and allow
me to fight the typewriter.

I have to make the move. The sponsor got real brittle about
l'affaire trombone. He didn't fire me, I quit, things were getting
a little operatic. He can shoot the nose off a mosquito, and both
of us were staying drunk all the time.

There is a time to sit and a time to split. Strange thing is,
I really don't like trombone music all that much. The big brown
eyes did me in.

Well, it has been an enlightening time. I'm leaving the town
not a hell of a lot better than I entered it. Oh, all kinds of
property, which is a pain in the ass, just something more to carry,
but I suppose I need a front for the phony Florida scene.

Truly, though, I feel more zestful than I have felt for a while.
Perils of the open road and all that. What am I, Zigeuner?
General Delivery, Jax, till I find out something.   Later, Jim

Hotel ——
NOVEMBER 21, 1956

[To Julian Ravenal, Dock Street Theatre]

Dear Julie:

Thank you for making my stay in Charleston a little more
interesting.

Many things I wanted to say to you, but I'm afraid most of them were rather on the didactic side. And having encountered more than once that supercilious glaze that you arrange on your features when ennui seems indicated— Whatever inner mechanism it is that tells you when it is suitable to be bored has been a source of some speculation to me—it is my theory that it is not a mental process so much as a conditioned reflex born of Vogue, Fortune, Harpers Bazaar, dear Noel, a dash of Dache and Russian Leather, elbow patches and (possibly) some fear.

Having encountered, I say, that sort of puerile negation, I think it better to say it this way.

I want so much to believe in others that it makes me ridiculously vulnerable. Simone de Beauvoir (if I may drop a name) said a long time ago that part of my trouble was a tendency to give people too much credit. Naively, rather smugly, I attributed her observation to the existentialist beliefs that seemed to me to color her viewpoint. Since then, I've often had occasion to recall what she said, though I don't improve, I go right on stupidly believing in people.

Finally I arrive at the point. Your attitude (it seems almost a way of life) is apparently compounded of pale green enamel, meringue and mustard gas.

Seemingly, you have marooned yourself on an arid island with a number of other castaways (joyless and juiceless, but utterly oh utterly comme il faut) and there you sustain yourselves by nibbling on one another in modish cannibalism.

Some years ago, my father, having detected my first faltering steps on the path of unilateral sex, said something I haven't been able to forget:

"Harpies," he said. "They're harpies, and they kill even the trees where they roost."

So, a plea. Less cleverness? More kindness? For the good of the breed, such as it is.   Fondly, Jim Blake

Hotel ——
Jacksonville, Florida
DECEMBER 5, 1956

[To Nelson Algren, Chicago]

Dear Pappy:

All I can say is you're just too much, the bread gave me a respite, and saved me from going ignominiously to a small-time jail, when my aims are so much higher.

I might as well level; you have probably already surmised as much—sooner or later, I'll probably wind up back at Raiford. It's not as aberrant as it might seem, it's the only way I know that I can gain time, peace, leisure to do what I want to do, write, and read read read.

And I am increasingly disenchanted with the world outside. When I left the joint I came out with a brand-new fresh eye, and I was appalled and infinitely wearied to see the dull, mindless, crippling enmity the Good People feel for one another and for all men, the sullen truce they live under.

The routine of working just to eat doesn't make much sense to me any more. I want to work at something that will be an end in itself. And since I do most of my living inside my head anyway, it shouldn't make much difference where I am—Tibet or Toledo, the silly cinema in my skull keeps right on rolling.

I met Freddy down here, a fellow alumnus with whom I had some tender passages in the joint. We tussled some for Auld Lang Syne, but I saw early on that we weren't going to make it. He has a firearms fixation—sees himself forever at bay, but furiously, like ambuscades and barricades. That sort of thing could only get progressively noisier, and I abominate uproar.

So he went off with a cannon in each armpit and a derringer in his crotch, for all I know. A Flit gun is as far as I'll go that route. Or an ammonia gun loaded with witch hazel.

Subsequently I got a do-it-yourself burglar's kit, and I've been dabbling in that art. So far I've been dismally inept, and I've acquired a profound respect for burglars. How hard they must work!

Boosting is shot to hell. Everybody has climbed into that act, lisping tots to palsied crones, and the Wilmark ferrets are disguising themselves as nuns, bird watchers and begonia bushes. Chaos.

Accordingly, I spotted a likely joint for a break-in and sallied forth in the small hours, clanking with what I conceived to be suitable implements, all of them boosted. A purist.

The first obstacle was a heavy wire screen. Chuckling inwardly, I whipped out my wire cutters, found they were a shade delicate for the operation. But I sweated and strove and cursed for what seemed hours. During which my glasses fell out of my pocket and broke.

Talk about the Finger of God. I had a momentary superstitious chill, the omens were bad, and I thought irritably, "Ain't You got nothing else to do but watch me?" But I persisted till, triumphantly, I peeled back the screen.

The window slid up easily. To reveal behind it a barricade that made the Great Wall look like the backdrop in a tent show.

My faith in human nature has taken some memorable beatings; but on that dark, damp, chill, forlorn morning I drained the cup.

love, The Phantom

Hotel ——
Jacksonville, Florida
DECEMBER 10, 1956

(To Nelson Algren, Chicago)

Dear Doctor:

Second job was *un succes fou, d'estime, d'eclat.* Came away laden, but laden.

Such a physical thing, though, all that weight. I was exhausted, as you know I have not been well.

How do I get to be an international jool thief? Seems to me it would be easier to tote karats around, compared to tons.

The Paris Review has bought a story.   love, Jeem

PS—No idleness in the daytime though, I've been writing, like they say, reams.   J.B.

Hotel ——
Jacksonville, Florida
DECEMBER 18, 1956

Dear Nelson:

I swung with a copy of *Walk On The Wild Side*, and had an hilarious Sunday with it.

Lovely party, the host a charmer, at times the stern enchantment nailed me. The music that came from your ear, devastating. Some day, surely, a play.

Where you will not be compelled to do that Go Down, Moses bit all the time. ("For what doth it availeth a man?")— Holy cow. An iron bird on aluminum wings. Baby, you can *sing*, you don't have to *talk*.

But, in all, so vibrant.

And then it was Sunday twilight, and I had to go out and steal, with this shadow still on me, and I said to myself, "the son of a bitch, I been hexed." But, baby, only the nowhere people do it hard by the yard. You look on for a while, and then you jump in. The comedy has a brilliance that falls short of Chaplin (who never told people when it was time to cry). But it's so close, so close.   love, Jim

Hotel ——
Jacksonville, Florida
DECEMBER 22, 1956

Dear Nelson:

So I'll fill you in on what I couldn't say phonewise. Freddy, my torpedo friend, came back, fondled my libido into fever and me into folly. We went hotel-prowling Saturday p.m. Freddy had seen in the paper the arrival of a Shriner bigwheel and his big ol fat wife at the George Washington, the Biltmore of Jax. Freddy has a file in his head of all the fat women in Florida with too much jewelry.

No problem to get in, the celluloid bit, and we found her jool case, big as a rowboat, perfunctorily hidden in a drawer. Both of us got a jolt when we opened it. Like opening a box and having the moon rise out of it, truly a glitter. I have them wrapped in a bandanna and I've only looked at them once since. They make me nervous, they seem to speak, or anyway stare.

While we're in there, we get a break shouldn't happen—the maid lets herself in. Her mouth a great black O when she saw us. Then it opened wider, incredibly, and all the whistles of hell went off. We both had pieces, but Freddy was cool. Apparently the biddy couldn't move, and she was in the way, so Freddy pushed her in the face, and said, "Pardon me, doll." We ran down two flights to the 7th for the elevator, and met the house dick coming out. Freddy automatically tried to crease him, but he wasn't one of the folding types. Coming up, I'd noticed a back service stairway and remarked on it to Freddy, but I don't think he heard me. Anyway it made the difference, he took a wrong turn and wound up in a bag, blind alley hallway. I was moving on, the dick's piece went off like a cannon, I hear Freddy cuss and gasp. I had the stuff, so I kept going; I couldn't do him any good.

Down seven flights like a big bad bird (thank God for bicycle training) and through an arcade that went to the next block. Where I made myself walk and tried to mop the rivers of sweat and keep from fainting.

I listened all night to the radio, heard nothing about Freddy, till the next day, when they said he was shot in the leg. Later I talked to an orderly in the hospital; he was actually shot in the arse. Such delicacy.

This is such a fink town, I despair of finding a straight fence. The stuff is too hot, the town too small, so I've got to take it to Tampa, Ybor City, where I know some Puerto

Ricans if I can find them. The bread will have to go for bond
for Freddy. With his record they'll put him *under* the jail.
So far they haven't charged him, they can stall him for a long time
on that gunshot wound. So I'll have time to sniff my way to a
bond shark.

Temporarily parlous times for our little group of sunbeams.
Another Raiford chum, a beautiful tiger of a man, body like
rawhide and eyes like a gazelle, is in for manslaughter. He
picked up a local playgirl in a bar and took her down to the
riverbank for some outdoor combat.

A feather-minded broad looking for something with menace,
and she found it, poor chick. Bob induced her to strip off, then
she decided she didn't wanna, so impulsively he put her in the
river. That's a bad swift treacherous river, the St. John's, she
couldn't swim, apparently, so she drowned.

What may be in Bob's favor, this town is so mealy-mouth
they hushed it up; seems the chick is a local career wheel and
it mustn't be known she was out with a bad man from the lower
classes. He'll get a barrel of time, but it could be worse.

The moral if any? She who rides a tiger should wear water
wings.

I'm scared, but the fortunate thing, in a bad scene like this,
I go sort of numb—shock, I guess. To all appearances it looks
like calm, like I'm unflappable. I'm not.

Take cautious care, Jim

PART IV

marking time

Dear Nelson:

I wrote you a note on the day I landed in this joint (December 26), but since I gave it to a rumdum soldier to mail, I fear it may have miscarried. In any case, I haven't heard and the sweating it is rough.

They tell me it's possible the jedge may hit me with the bitch (habitual criminal) because my record will have a possible four strikes when I go up for trial. Which will be late next month, probably the 19th. That means an automatic life sentence, which is assuredly more than I bargained for. I think the possibility is a fairly remote one as yet.

I've been bound over to Criminal Court on charge of B & E and grand larceny. Hopefully I look for a 3 to 5 bounce.

One minor hitch—my gear is still at the hotel, so far as I know, containing an assload of barbiturates, amphetamines, T.O., PG—paregoric—and assorted shit. Nothing has been said of this cargo, which is ominous. I've tried several dodges to wiggle it loose without success. If they find it, the Gay Pay oo may take a hand.

Thing that bugs me is that the theft, from all I can learn, hasn't been reported. There's a thin possibility I may yet pull this one out. When I came in here the shakedown was so cursory that I got by with a vial of fury pills in my crotch. The cats in the tank were stunned by my vivacity.

I still think this course I've embarked on is the beginning of something, rather than the end of everything. Whatever else happens, on this trip to the White Rock, I mean to come out of it with some writing done.

This is rough time at present, being confined in a tank with twenty-two others, twelve hours out of twenty-four, nothing to do but read, which would be great if there was anything to read aside from the ghoulish publications that stem from the Baptists and seem to sift into every jail I ever made. Eerie, lifeless, pale, I think they must be printed on the moon, or in some underground cavern where no birds sing.

Here I have found a few kindred souls among the congenital rebels, acceptance with no questions, casual compassion without pose.

And always I learn something new. There is a veteran of Georgia chain gangs I wish I could follow with pad and pencil, truly a fount of pungent folk-sayings: "My brother could steal the stink off shit and never get a smell on him." He is morose much of the time, but any talk of farming brings a glow of idealism to his eyes, and he speaks of the land as of a lover.

I have not yet paid my club dues here, so if there's any bread around—and stamps if you're able, good partner.

Hang on to your belief in me yet a while, cher maitre, I have barely begun to fight. And let me hear soon. Things are tight at present.   ever, Jim

PS—It would be an act of mercy to send some magazines for the lads here. They're glassy-eyed from trying to whip up an interest in the bleary theology of Christian Messenger.

Duval County Jail
Jacksonville, Florida
JANUARY 15, 1957

Dear ——:

I'm awaiting trial on two charges of breaking and entering and grand larceny. Trial February 19, at which time with some luck I'll get hit with a five spot. Without it, I may get hit with the bitch, since I already have two strikes. What that could mean I'd rather not think about.

I should have stayed on that Carolina island and learned to live with the southern centaur, hectic as it was. Among my many idiotic traits is an infinite capacity for self-deception. No sooner do I flee from a situation that is driving me bananas than I am able almost immediately to look back on it with nostalgia and yearning. Lot's wife and I could have made it.

All of this could perhaps be blamed on an excess of Miltown and vodka. (Plus wrong thinking?) Christmas Eve I was alone and feeling ill used, snarling if anyone mentioned the yuletide. So I was wistfully prowling the bars for some mischief, and I ran into a muscular waif from the mountains of North Carolina, as downcast as I, a little frightened of being alone.

Ensued a disorderly Eve, the radio blaring Handel's Messiah, the most unsuitable background music one could conceive for what transpired. At intervals, a Pharisee disguised as a landlord made bitter threats and protestations, which availed naught.

Xmas Day we were still wheeling, but supplies were dwindling and I remembered a pharmacy I'd previously marked as a soft touch. I found it closed and effected entrance under cover of the universal wassailing.

Once in, I found it difficult to read labels in the semi-dark, so I donned a white coat I found and snapped on the lights. A passerby would have taken me for a conscientious apprentice making hay in the absence of the sorcerer.

First off I spotted the Miltown, and as I browsed through the

fairyland of pharmaceuticals, I popped them languidly like jelly-
beans. And in no time was over the border of tranquillity into
megalomania.

A redfaced harassed-looking gent came banging at the door.
Impatient at this frivolous interruption of serious research, I
waved him away as if he had been a charity patient with the
flux. But when he persisted in his clamor, I had to admit him,
lest he attract the gendarmerie.

He stammered some lurid story of a purple baby in con-
vulsions. "Hmmm," I said, peering professionally over my
glasses, "sounds like peninsular pip. Common Florida complaint.
Suffer from it myself." I measured out a generous dollop of
powdered opium. "Dissolve this in rum with a dash of bitters
and give it to the whole family," I said. "The baby's crying
won't bother you then," I said. "Nothing will."

He went his way babbling effusive seasonal greetings. (Awright, I gave him some PG).

Having collected a bushel of goodies, I took my leave. The
waif and I made high festivity. Later that night I was surprised
with an armload of binoculars by an irate policeman as I was
beating a measured retreat from a nautical supply establish-
ment.

In jail, I made the acquaintance of a young malefactor who
was due to hit the street on a federal probation. Struck by his
altar-boy bearing, I confided in him the location of the cache of
pharmaceuticals and he promised to retrieve them. Instead, he
attempted to extort payment from the injured pharmacist in
exchange for information. Thus was I hit with the second rap.
Some day I'll learn about altar boys.

Some very bad moments occurred at the preliminary hearing,
with the J.P. intoning that ghastly list of purloined pills. Sounded
like he was reading the Pharmacopoeia. I was embarrassed. Such
fishy looks. Like I was a dope feend.

Along that line, let me say that I'm kiting this out, and that
incoming mail is not opened. Accordingly, it would be utterly
cool if you could send a little keef. These are endless dull days,
waiting for trial, and a taste of majoun would be heavenly.

The story "Day Of The Alligator" will be in The Paris Review ⚹ 16, I'm told, if you care to look for it. Got a check due for that, but it's by no means certain I'll have it before I have to split for the joint up the pike. Please write, let me know what you're doing.   love, Jim

                                        Duval County Jail
                                        Jacksonville, Florida
                                        FEBRUARY 7, 1957

Dear Nelson:

I wish everybody wouldn't come on like I'm descending into the pit. From the start of this slightly offbeat venture I've had (or thought I had, till everyone began breaking out the mauve crepe) a pretty clear idea of how I intended using the time to advantage. Now I get the uncomfortable idea I got something to prove. Amen, I'll prove it.

You've probably seen one of them Maureen O'Hara films (I know you have, ain't a swingin' dick in the country escaped it) where the hero (Errol Flynn) is captured by oily Spaniards and thrown into the hold of a galleon with a hundred other sweaty unshaven wretches. Looking about the tank here, I expect momentarily to see Maureen maneuver her noble bosom through the narrow doorway, searching for Errol.

Only a few more days till trial (the 19th) praise be, and then it's off to Holiday Inn. In that respect, can you help me with the matriculation fee for the Academy? I figure twenty bucks should make it. If I have the bread to lay off in the right places, it'll save pain and strain in getting me the right quarters I need to work in. Otherwise, God knows when I'll be able to square away. I'm not particularly delicate, but that kind of frustration drains me, and I'd like to avoid it if possible. There are also a few additional *pourboires* to be considered, like if I can get the band sinecure again, it will give me the free time I need.

I've got some bread coming from PR for the "Alligator" tale,

but it might be some time before I get it. If you'll advance it,
I'll endorse the check to you. It's two bits.

One of the funloving lads here is slated to ride the bolt for
group-rape. He has enlisted my cunning in a project to obtain
a tape recorder so that he may, departing, leave behind him
messages for his wife and two kids. This flying fantasy (fra-
grant with the scent of tuberoses and winding sheets) has
quite bemused me. I suggested we wait to do the recording till
I could furnish a soft accordion background. The churl topped
me, though. He agreed to wait.   ever, Jim

PS— You ask the meaning of "High Botchery." It's the crime
of slapping a blind goose in the ass with a wet towel. (Low
Botchery is a duck.)

                                        Duval County Jail
                                        Jacksonville, Florida
                                        FEBRUARY 21, 1957

Dear Nelson:

Trial was postponed till the 26th, for reasons *quien sabe*.
Another week on the spit. Good thing I got nerves of piano
wire.

But I'm a cinch to get my time on that date and to catch the
Academy bus about the twenty-nine or thirty. So, you see, time
presses. If you can send the bread I'll stash it in the office for
safety and feel easier in mind about my pending debut—or
reinterment, as you will.

Had an interlude the other day with a porcine young man
from the Border Patrol. He was so tightly girded that I was
uneasy throughout the interview about a possible whiplash from
his Sam Brown belt, so I didn't get too close.

He wanted to know was I in the U S of A legally, and did I
belong to any hmmm you know Organizations.

I told him I had entered the country from a Chinese sampan,
the Solidarity Forever, concealed in a shipment of Macao Poppies

consigned to Harry Bridges, and was a paid-up member of the Emma Goldman Bird Watchers, Nicolai Lenin Poker and Parchesi Circle, and the Pola Negri Fan Club.

He wrote out a quite meaty little report, which he allowed me to read. I had to tell him how to spell "turpitude."   alors, Jim

Duval County Jail
Jacksonville, Florida
APRIL 1, 1957

Dear Nelson:

I had a letter from the perennial charmer Moran. This one being more communicative than his usual Delphic mumblings— telling me that you're still hassling with Preminger, lawyers, agents, provocateurs, CIA, etc.

Why don't you join me here. It's not as hard as it looks and I will by god put in a word for you.

We had a jailbreak. Like a Cagney movie, man, they sawed the bars and six scampered away after slipping through like oiled eels, until some fatass got stuck and blew the gig. Numbers went to the Black Box, where they give you whole-wheat bread and water.

I'm sharing a cell now with a young cat sentenced to the chair for gang-bang. He's a beautiful child, a little solemn sometimes, which I guess is allowable under the circumstances. He asked me what I thought Eternity was like, and all I could offer was a guess— an Olivia de Havilland movie on television. Last night as we were lying in our bunks, a squad car went by outside, siren wailing. "Listen," he said, "they're playing our song."

In a laudable attempt to dodge the thunderbolt (his case is on appeal) he has been improving each shining hour by hitting the Glory Road with the traveling bands of flagellants that haunt the jail—Holy Rollers, Mormons, Baptists, Anabaptists— and he has become an Eleventh Hour postulant in the Seventh Day Opportunists.

These pious cats swing a lot of weight, such is the Kingdom of

Heaven. Bless the boy, he's far too beautiful to go down for such a flimsy transgression, and I hope he makes it. The Holy Ones have a lobby in Tallahassee that don't quit.

I read Meyer Levin's *Compulsion*. The heavy assertion is, he planned the book for 30 years. Uh huh. When Leopold is trying to make parole, the sacred mandate comes to him in a gold-spangled dream. Darrow's address to the court stands out like a jewel in this rampantly shoddy dung heap.

So what's New in New York? Ten days till the wire. The one that goes around my neck, that is.   toute a l'heure, Jim

Duval County Jail
Jacksonville, Florida
APRIL 15, 1957

Dear Nelson:

Jump-off Day. Into the jaws: The Prosecutor read a list of my purported transgressions on the Florida Statutes to a bored and somnolent Court. Only when he bellowed in stentorian tones "YANKEE BLUEBELLY" was there action. The judge awoke. Behind his bench the picture of Robert E. Lee lighted up. A Confederate flag unfurled to ripple in the breeze, while the Bailiff manfully urinated on the Stozzen Stripes, and a concealed sound system roared out "Ah Wish Ah Was In Dixie." Everybody stood at attention. His Honour wiped the proud tears from his eyes, and gave me Ten Years.

Tell Sister ah went with mah boots laced and mah socks matched.   ever, Jim

Next stop—Box 221, Raiford, Florida.

PART V

home again

Note:
Some of the following letters were mailed through the courtesy of my prison employer, the chaplain. As before, letters mailed through the official censors were addressed to imaginary married sisters, and are herein addressed to the actual recipients, for the sake of clarity.

Raiford, Florida
JULY 15, 1957

Dear Gertrude:

The balloon came down in the jungle, as I guess we knew that it would, and it has been a matter of once again making friends with the natives.

Not the easiest thing, coming back into a joint. There are all the cats you knew before, waiting in ambush. They know you're in quarantine, and they're just sweating you, waiting to spray you with comradely spleen: "Couldn't make it out there, huh, goodbuddy?" "Too tough for you on the bricks, old partner?" "We been keepin' your sack for you, my darling."

They wanted me back in the band, no problem there. Willie the bandleader was glad to see me, in his own bleached way. He said the band had gone to hell, that he was only waiting for his time to go home, due soon.

One of the first people I saw, the young Sandy. All pulled together and in charge of himself. I told myself, you made an investment, it paid off, so forget it, dummy up awready. There was no need, he was beyond me and on his way some place else.

Willie told me that he had a fantastic trumpet player from Chicago, a cat in for shit that he wanted me to meet and hear. ("He blows, but he's a pain in the ass.")

I heard him that night at dinner when the combo played in the mess hall. Bad drummer, piano only adequate, but this stud played an angry driving horn—even on slow tunes, that anger.

Man, I was hooked, what's with this cat, I thought—Willie told me he would cool it for me if I stayed out after Lockup, so I hung around and listened till they came down off the bandstand.

Willie brought him over. Douglas Northrop, the kind of good looks you don't believe. From a wealthy suburb of Chicago, rich kid, snotty and defensive. (Against me, it's like punching a deflated balloon.) Comes on, you're the hotshot piano player I been hearing about, who'd you ever lick?

It was needle all the way, so I reacted. "Your horn sounds like it's sore about something. What's it pissed off about, besides the joint, I mean?" So he takes another look at me, cools it some. Gray eyes, cold and remote, the Arctic Ocean.

We rapped about Chicago for a while, till this clown appeared. I could tell it was his buddy. Some buddy. Name Dobie, he looked like nothing but heat to me. The trumpet player went away with him.

Willie told me that, as good as the cat played, he could live without it, because he'd gotten into the sharpshooter mob, the ones who lived only for the next fix.

Next day, Doug came up to me, asked did I want to walk on the ball field (it's a way of saying "Who are you?") and we made a lot of turns and talked about Chicago, music, books, anything. He was one hungry cat.

He had the kind of beauty hard to get past at first, makes you misjudge on the first go-round. I think I did that. And Willie had told me the cat was in and out of Punishment Row all the time, for turning on one way or another. With a rich wife, rich mother, political connections, the whole setup that causes antagonism from the brass, where it can hurt. I figure, lay back, until I know where it is.

So I got back in the band, they needed me. And Doug was a gas to blow with. But I sure didn't like his raunchy friends, I was leery.

The clarinet player in the band, Lee Lopez, a big taciturn stud, braced me on did I want to move in with him. He looked like Mexican, achingly groomed all the time, didn't blow much, only competent. But I had to go some place, and this cat was so *clean*. I figured okay, at least I won't be living with green armpits. So I moved in with him.

I see Doug all the time, that is when he's in population, and there's usually sneering about my living with the lame clarinet player. And from the clarinetist, sneering about the fuckoff intellectual trumpet man. Lucky Pierre, in the middle.

In the meantime, I tried to make it in the band, but the quality veered erratically. And when Willie left to go home, and they wanted me to take over, Willie advised me to switch to organist in the Chapel. Doug is coming and going in the band, from grits and gravy to bread and water. So when another piano man checked in, I switched jobs.

And that's what's happening to Heidi on the moon, trying to tell a sheep from a goat. How you doing out there, telling the poor from the rich? Zut alors, Jim

Raiford, Florida
AUGUST 30, 1957

Dear Nelson:

The typer arrived a week ago, I'm ashamed at waiting so long to let you know. A few bugs in the machine, probably incurred in transit, but I can have them fixed as soon as I turn out a couple of fast-selling items. (Kind men like.)

Life here at the Academy takes on an increasingly ecclesiastic tinge. I play the organ for both Catholic and Protestant services, thus assuring myself of a pass at whichever pearly gate I present myself. I like the Catholic Mass better, I think; the pagan mystery of it seems more appropriate for dealing with imponderables. It has the beautiful impressive gravity of children playing at some dimly apprehended game.

When I first started to play the Catholic service, I was amazed to discover that the superstitious terror of things "Papist" that had been instilled in me by a Scottish Presbyterian mother, not terribly bright, still persisted to an astonishing degree.

Oh, I wasn't petrified, but the thing was *there*. I had the feeling of being an acolyte at a demonolatrous wing-ding; and if a sudden puff of smoke had come out of the floor, I'd have been long gone.

True, I had taken certain precautions, a sprig of garlic around the neck and a letter in my pocket from Norman Vincent Peale.

In more secular and verdant fields, I am still using the device of giving love extravagantly in order to escape the more serious responsibility of accepting it.

What's with you and the agent? Your last couple letters showed, I thought, a strain of anger and resentment quite new for you, disturbing and distressing to me. Care to say anything about that?   love, Jim

Dear Mike:

My official function now is Chapel Organist, and it's all quite restful. The chapel is in a separate building in the prison enclosure, surrounded by landscaped grounds, a neat red brick church like in a small town, pointing the finger at God. There's a certain amount of office work involved (snatching brands from the burning evidently entails reams of paper work) but mostly I just sit at the Hammond and dreamily dream, like the party in The Lost Chord. (Except on Sunday, when everything gets rigid and liturgical.)

One prime advantage of this oasis of quiet in the institutional hurlyburly is a small remote office in the chapel building where I can retire with the typewriter and rassle the muse.

I have suspended work on the mss of *Chain Dance* and am attempting to assuage the chronic financial ache by doing a pocketbook type thing. Dealing with some night-blooming jasmines I knew in the frantic Chicago days. I'm amazed to discover how flamboyant they seem to me now, those beloved people I knew then. I never realized how extemporaneous our behavior was. One of the characters looks like you, though it is only a superficial likeness. Probe as I may, the enigma eludes me.

Since my return here, I've been locking (sharing a cell) with a massive muscled Mediterranean type from Milwaukee, who has become astonishingly important in the scheme of things.

Most of the time he is like a large affable bear, but he has the triggerish disposition of the ursine, so it behooves me to dissemble and to walk warily. I live two concurrent lives, the one in my head, and the one I present for inspection.

Lee (the Mediterrane) is on parole from a thirty-year bit in Waupun—the Wisconsin authorities allowed him to return here to serve out a Florida bit that was interrupted when he

took bush parole from a road camp at Pompano. The Wisconsin
bit he got for dispatching a Chinaman to his ancestors, an interlude which has me bemused. The lurid story of the affair
has appeared in Dismal Detective and those other crime gazettes.

And as a result I find that locking with him has given me a
dismaying cachet with the shaggier element in the academy.

Seemingly I invite this type of domination, but I've made
the adjustment, and I suppose I could be called a contented
victim. But the inner boy stays the same, he keeps right on
sneering at the outer boy—so that both of them keep occupied,
which, enfin, is the cardinal thing.

Lee was telling me the other night about being on the lam
in Chicago with a single dollar to his name. Said he bought a
substantial meal with it (to keep his strength up), and a bar of
soap. I was thinking how touching it was that he wanted to
keep clean, even though he was a destitute fugitive. Until he
explained to me that the bar of soap was for putting into his
sock for clobbering a likely victim. Life is a process of instruction.

The weather has turned chill down here, pal of mine, so if
you have an old bowling jacket, sweater, sweat shirt, something,
I would roundly adore. I'll enclose a parcel slip on the chance.
Please write. I've had no mail from the Algren or Abercrombie
or anybody, I am bleeding and bereft. Lemme hear something
somebody.   Later, Jim

                                              Raiford, Florida
                                        NOVEMBER 10, 1957

Dear Nelson:

Just because I may have taken a fall does not mean that
I have taken the veil. It is a gratifying thing to receive a letter
from the outside world. Especially in these momentous days.
You cannot conceive the chagrin I feel that I must spend these
portentous times in exile, when out there science daily unfolds
new wonders. How fortunate to be living in an era of flux and

ferment. Pity the wretches who had to live under a sky that
held only moon and stars. A vacuous dome devoid of circum-
navigating hardware and whizzing canine cadavers.

I daresay this scientific advance will knock off the nocturnes
from poets mewling under the night sky. It will take a stalwart
minnesinger who can vaporize over the moonlight now, when
the nobel and incontrovertible fact is that there is a dead dog
careening around in it.

I notice that this astounding celestial development had a sharp
climactic effect in the ol U S & A—the bracing wind of Phi-
listinism died abruptly, the wind was tempered to the shorn
egghead, and intellectuality suddenly ceased to be paired with
incest.

Oh, it was no impetuous volte-face. The boy they hired to
take charge has a simple and manly B.S. degree from West
Point, not one of your woolgathering Ph.D.'s (*B.S.?!?*) So
everything should soon be all right. Pangloss will ride again.

I enclose a program which will indicate to you the direction
my campus career has taken. I am on the Chaplain's staff as
organist, having quit the band in discouragement—no one to
blow with. There was a fine trumpet man for a while, but
he was caught out on Cloud ♯9 one day and hit with a uri-
nalysis that came up a blinding purple. He disappeared to Never
Never Land for a while.

Leaving in the band only a clutch of nomads from the
Eastern Mountains whose idea of giddy abandon was Tea for
Two played in lurching soft-shoe. Ideal accompaniment for
waltzing camels, but there were none around. Or else they
didn't feel like dancing.

Working in the Chapel is rather peaceful (us Chapel employees are referred to as "church mice"). Except on Sundays,
when all (you should excuse the expression) Hell breaks loose
and I have three services to play organ for, Protestant, Catholic
and Black (Voodoo). Leaves me groggy from piety.

Weekdays, though, are quiet, and I can retire to an office
with a typewriter and rassle the muse. Don't know if I told
you, it's been so long, I'm working on a paperback for some

quick bread. (My finances are fevered, if you can do anything in that line. No reason why you should, quite a few why you should not.) I'm locking with a moderately wealthy Sicilian lad, his mother is head of the Mafia, but he firmly intends to stay wealthy, so there's only intermittent relief there.

I finished the manuscript of *Chain Dance*, but so much of it was wrong, I'll count it as practice and try again. I read the letter you wrote to Tom Rolfe, the con who wrote you from the road camp—the one in which you said something like if I applied myself I could "outrace cheetahs," etc. Quoting Dove Linkhorn, "That's putty good pot."

Finally caught up with the New Yorker review of "Walk On The Wild Side." Who's this cat Podhoretz, I mean, who'd he ever lick? He not only missed the boat, he fell off the dock.

. . . So the purpose of this is to say I still exist, am still clever as a kitten, though no longer cute as a bug's ear.

alors, Jim

Raiford, Florida
NOVEMBER 20, 1957

Dear Mike:

Thank you for that fine and useful package you sent. I have washed the articles with care and am making good use of everything. Happily everything was gray, a color I prefer to wear and which blends nicely with my prison pants (and my mood).

Not that I attempt to be what is hereabouts called a "chain-gang dude," a type in which the tribal customs are ineradicably ingrained.

On Saturday afternoons and Sunday mornings they sally forth in splendor from their cells, to loiter about the prison ball field, gray prison pants pressed to a cutting edge, civilian shoes blindingly polished, civilian shirts crisp and colorful (in-mates are allowed to wear their own clothes from the waist up and the ankles down), hair oiled and coiffed into elaborate productions that would startle an Ashanti.

Writing about it, I find that while I feel satiric about this costume ritual, it resists satire. —Perhaps it would be profoundly pathetic if there was not such a strong element of aggression in it; they seem to be more than anything else, aggressively costumed. Outside they would be off to the poolroom or the bowling alley in their proud rooster plumes—here, they can only mill about from group to gossiping group. Maybe that is where the pathos lies. In any case, it probably stems from the same need that made the Englishmen dress for dinner in the jungle, when they still had a jungle to dress in.

And while on the subject of local costume customs, I shouldn't neglect the androgynes and their ingenious habit of enlarging the necks of T-shirts so that the shoulders are left bare, giving a kind of strapless décolleté effect that is arresting; this is enhanced by adding a religious medal on a slender chain, thus achieving an effect at once wanton and demure. The prison issues a blue jacket to each inmate, and this group, needless to say, wears it cape-style, sleeves hanging empty.

At the weekend promenade, the androgynes are of course resplendent, and always accompanied by a you-could-say sponsor, whose mien is a nice blend of sheepishness and belligerence.

At the Chapel, things are leaping these days: we are rehearsing the choir in a Christmas cantata, something to do with shepherds, and their enormous gullibility. The choir director is a Duke alumnus, a perennial Deke-type. (A Duke Deke, I don't care what happens any more.) He's in for paperhanging, what else. He chose the music, a pseudo-highbrow mishmash, and I don't know what will be the end result, I'm only the organist, blameless and neutral should riot ensue.

I have a small request to make. It has been a while, and I am fairly eaten with curiosity as to what you look like now. (Oddly, the Sicilian chap I'm lodging with, for whatever devious Sicilian reason, has also expressed a curiosity.)

Incidentally, I learn more about the Mediterranes all the time.

Last night, in an incandescent rage, he positively glowed, first time I ever saw anybody glow with anger. About the picture, I know that you are terrifyingly reserved, but there must be a snapshot around.

Again, thanks for the bundle, and let me hear.   later, Jim

Raiford, Florida
NOVEMBER 28, 1957

Dear Gertrude:

Thanksgiving Eve here, and there is a special movie on in the prison auditorium, so J-Range is quiet for a change, except for the dreadful ubiquitous hillbilly radio a few cells down. Sherman never wreaked half the havoc in the South that these fiddling git-tar whanging cretins have accomplished.

The band plays a lugubrious overture to every movie showing, so Taurus is out tootling his clarinet. These doomed performances are such agonizing affairs, so prone to disaster, that I can't bear to watch, I feel too involved in them somehow.

Rocco's playing (his name is Lee, he wants me to call him Rocco, you figure it) is competent, if uninspired, and the ineptness of the band embarrasses him. With him embarrassment is soon transmuted into rage, and were I to be a witness to his discomfiture, much of this simmering volcanic anger would erupt on to me. So I stay away, and stand by with cold packs, for when he returns smoldering.

I'm involved in a ghost-writing chore at the moment: A con here is trying to sell his experiences to Reader's Digest. The story of his antics after he escaped from a road prison down here, shipped out of Baltimore on a tanker, jumped ship off Singapore and joined up with a gold-seeking expedition. That ship went down, and he and five others navigated a lifeboat across the Timor Sea to Australia. One thing followed an incredible other, and he winds up back in the joint. The tale has all the zingy ingredients, and if I can make it sanctimonious enough for Reader's Digest, with a regeneration gimmick, it ought to go. (I found Christ in the Timor Sea!)

The taurine one has just returned, and it is as foretold, rumblings.

Have a couple of favors like to beg. Can you send me a small night light, the smaller the better? Many times I want to work and Rocco wants to sleep, so I sleep too. But if I had a little lamp, I could write without disturbing him. See if you can swing it, my soul. I'll send a parcel permit, in case. Also, will you send some pictures of yourself? This is passing curious—the Siciliano wants to see them, and a picture of Moran, too. You think he suspects me of jumping from the forehead of Jove, and is checking to see if I know any mortals?

stunned, Jim

Raiford, Florida
DECEMBER 26, 1957

Dear Mike:

Christmas Day was quiet, the commonwealth gave us wards a bag of frivolities, and I stayed in the sack catching up on my reading. The blasted Cantata that the prison choir perpetrated took too much of my time, and I'm glad it is now part of the sinister past. The piece was the work of Clifford Demarest (are you ready?). I'm told he's a minor British contemporary. Just the sort of semi-classic bouillabaisse I deplore. But the organ part was fairly challenging, and not yet being an accomplished organist, I had to foot it featly to make it, all tentacles waving.

We gave four performances, the first before the black population of the Rock, who were polite but clearly baffled. At one time during the performance, from my post at the organ, I looked out over the dark auditorium, and it seemed to be a sea of rolling eyeballs. The tenor soloist, a fellow with a wrong attitude, murmured to me, "The natives seem restless tonight."

Later I talked to a friend of mine, a spade from across the

line, gifted painter, pretty hip. He said he was inspired by the performance, just couldn't understand why the choir kept hollering "Hialeah!"

The second spasm was visited upon outlanders, guests of the local Alcoholics Anonymous chapter from all over the state, and I shouldn't wonder if it sent some of them back to the booze. I love those AA females, they look so lived-in.

Third performance was for the Hairy Ones, the white felons; we had a good house that night, having taken the precaution of spreading the rumor that the Chaplain was giving a Christmas gift to every pilgrim who attended. (The shut-in version of twofers.)

The Cantata was too long, they all are, and the mood of the audience evolved from stupefaction to outrage to simmering violence, and there were bitter recriminations the next day.

For the last performance we had an audience of churchgoers from outside, plus the morbidly curious or masochistic who had seen the newspaper announcements. (As always in these performances, there is a sort of dancing-bear aura about the convicts, the audience comes prepared to be amazed and indulgent.) The reaction of this particular audience was neatly epitomized by one old lady having to be hustled up the aisle to the toilet, where I'm told she lost her lunch. We all felt it was an admirably forthright commentary, perhaps a little flamboyant.

The paperback effort is coming along, I cringe sometimes when I read parts of it, and die a little inside, but then I was always puny and picky. The bull is leading me a dog's life these days—all very zoological, and while we're on that, I hear you're trying to outguess the horses at Hialeah again. Let me hear soon.

Bonne Année, Jim

Raiford, Florida
DECEMBER 28, 1957

Dear Gertrude:

Locking with an athletics enthusiast can have its drawbacks. Christmas Day it was the North-South football game, and I have listened to broadcast accounts of jai alai, chicken-fights, boccie-ball, the Bean Bag Olympics, name it, but very little music do I hear.

It all may change soon. The Massive One is expecting to go back to Wisconsin on parole within the next ninety days, and while I shall be grieved in a way to see him go, it will be a not unmixed bereavement. I shall be occupied in repairing the erosion of identity these last eight months have wrought. I've been told so often that I would be helpless without him that I am slightly inclined to believe it, but only slightly. Still, I expect the sheer repetition of this gambit has made me dependent to some extent. It's nice to be told that one is protected, but from what? A somewhat wearing role, the dependent— I'm the type that out of cowardice or politeness, or both, will go along with almost any gag. In this particular charade I've been dealt some lines that curdle my stomach and freeze my spine even as I hear myself say them. I'm inhabiting the same skin with a simpering imbecile. However, when the large Latin goes, I expect this idiot poltergeist to leave also.

In any case, the whole thing has been by and large instructive and diverting, his behavior is a fascinating series of devices and mechanisms (if you could see the way he glowers, a production), the kid's as fouled up as a Chinese fire drill, for all his vaunted strength, and the bystander part of me has been busily making notes.

One good thing about the heavy mentor bit—he has badgered and threatened me into writing a couple of hours every night, so perhaps whatever psychic or emotional bruises I sustain (not to say physical) will have been worth it.   later, Jim

Raiford, Florida
FEBRUARY 7, 1958

Dear Nelson:

I've been wanting to write for some time to thank you
for the Bundle for Blake you sent at Christmas time. Most
of the articles I was able to put to good use, but the pants
I was not allowed to have. As a Trusty, I'm required to wear
white duck pants with broad blue stripes down the sides. The
official who told me about the pants in the parcel had a special
attitude I was unable to identify exactly (disdain?). It led
me to a certain amount of speculation. Were they Bermuda
shorts?

A couple reasons why I've postponed writing. One is I feel
a certain diffidence in approaching you. So many letters going
unanswered gives me the feeling you've put me down. If I
don't get an answer to this one, I shall have to resign myself
to that dismal fact.

Another reason for my delay in thanking you is the lack
of time to do so, ironically enough. One would suppose I had
eons of time to spare, but my job at the chapel takes up
most of the daylight hours. In addition to musical chores,
I have certain office duties as well. From my experience on
the Chaplain's staff, I've come to believe that if the road to
hell is paved with good intentions, the road to glory must be
paved with pious questionnaires and mendacious answers thereto.

That takes care of the company's time. Evenings in the cell,
my activities are more or less at the discretion of my cell
partner, a big Italiano from Milwaukee, who requires me to
put in some time on a paperback effort I've been working on.
He thinks it will make us rich.

Tentative title, Piano At Midnight, but if it sells I'm sure
the publishers can find something more suitably inflammatory.
Fairly lurid in spots, being concerned with night-blooming
jasmines around Rush Street and the Near North Side. I'm

trying to write it with childish innocence and spontaneity, which, from my observation, is evidently how these things are done. My own tired elfishness creeps in now and then, but I try to throttle as much as possible the impulse to be clever. I have a stern proofreader.

Often I have misgivings about this type of crass commercial effort and pedestrian aspiration, but I console myself with the thought that selling it will enable me to live a little more comfortably while I am tussling later on with something tougher and worthier. Also I tell myself that no matter what else, I am getting some necessary practise in putting one word after another—and writing an imaginary tale gives me some training in the concoction of a fictional plot. In addition, there is the penalty imposed for goofing off, and that is a drag.

This is the type of joint where the hip ones all have a hustle of some kind to ease the Spartan simplicity of prison life. I have a chance to buy into an operation, purchasing hand-tooled leather goods (at wholesale) made by the convicts, and selling at retail, and I need a modest amount of capital to swing it. I can reimburse you within ninety days or so out of profits. Probably a double-saw would make it.

However—even if you're not inclined to send any loot, let me hear an encouraging word. I've had no mail in a couple of months, and that is disheartening.   all forlorn, Jim

Raiford, Florida
FEBRUARY 11, 1958

Dear Gertrude:

I hope Frank is weathering the vicissitudes and gray drags of the advertising world in good shape, and that he's not too hung to do some writing when he's finished with befuddling the peasants.

I am hard at work on the paperback effort, one reason I haven't written sooner. What time I put on it must come out of my leisure hours after dinner, and finding a quiet time to concentrate has been a problem. Radios on the range are on a laissez-faire basis, and sometimes it gets pretty laissez. The story is about half complete, and I'm fairly sanguine about chances of selling. I've tried in writing it to project myself into the role of a child telling a story not for children. With a suitably mammiferous cover, it should happen.

About a week ago I got a jolt when J.P. blew in with another bit. Remember the blond drummer, he of the fire and quicksilver? Eighteen months this trip (lucky), for kicking in a pharmacy in search of the elusive and definitive fix. He was put in the hospital as an active.

I felt some ambivalence about going to visit him. He looked pretty awful—gaunt, pale, wasted. But the old bezzazz was there, the guy is indomitable. And intransigent, which makes a sad stalemate. He got out of Springfield (fed mental joint) in November, was out fifty days and shot up the contents of five pharmacies, so you see.

I don't feel inclined to make that scene again. The blaze is banked, stirring the ashes would be costly in spirit and energy that I'd rather devote to litchoor, the pursuit thereof.

Besides which there's some heavy opposition from a Latin quarter. There's nothing to equal the gossip in a joint, and bulls have big ears. A Sicilian reprisal is all I need. Of the taurine one, there's little I can with propriety say. My hair in the past nine months has become perceptibly sprinkled with gray, sort of calico effect. In that time also, theology to the contrary, I have learned from an accomplished instructor that heaven and hell are the same.

Incidentally, Rocco gets out before long on parole and will be living in Milwaukee. If you permit, I shall give him your address. He says he would like to look you up, as his parole conditions permit. Then, as the song goes, you may borrow some glimpse of my sorrow. And need I say, beware the shoals.

So for now. Much more to say and will say when I learn that you're still out there. What of good gray Dr. A.? I've

heard nothing, and nothing from Moran, who may have died
of Florida frostbite in Miàmi.   later, Jim

Raiford, Florida
MARCH 28, 1958

Dear Mike:

I seem to have emotional upheavals like Kansas has tor-
nadoes, and when they hit I have a tendency to lie doggo,
in the manner of a beast turning its posterior to a blizzard
and dumbly, numbly waiting it out. I regret waiting so long
to write, but it has been a period of illness, change, travail,
and I haven't felt equal to composing a coherent letter. I may
not do so well with this one.

The illness was the Asian flu. I wasn't completely bedridden
by it, though I spent four days in the sack, stewing in my
own juices, damp and wretched and aspirin-stunned. Then I
had to get out and play the organ for Sunday services at
Chapel, three of them. There was no suitable substitute, and
you know that Satan takes no holidays. Working as I do on the
side of St. Michael and All the Angels, I can't let the team
down.

The psychic phenomena that accompanied the illness were
harrowing: I've never felt so decrepit. At the lowest ebb I
said to myself, you may come out of this, Antigone baby, but
you'll never come back from it. It seemed that at long last
I was going to be freed from the delusion of youth that
pursues and possesses me, and I made nebulous plans for being
decently old.

Now that I'm out and about again, once more gamboling
where the wild thyme grows, I realize of course that it was
all delirious nonsense, and that nothing has changed.

Still . . . was that a bridge I crossed?

And then my cell partner, Rocco the Sicilian minotaur, went
back to Milwaukee on parole, and the loss was keenly felt.
For ten months I had been cast in the role of helpless de-

pendent, incessantly assured that I was incapable of decisions and relieved of that responsibility. This cat wanted to do Othello and I drew Desdemona.

I began by standing off and laughing at this carefully contrived fiction, and ended by nearly drowning in it. It was, after all, insidiously comfortable to have everything arranged for me. Then suddenly I was adrift.

An intriguing result of the sudden change in my status on the campus was the reaction of Rocco's familiars, the hardcases in the joint. While I was under the Sicilian's aegis, their attitude towards me was one of grudging bonhomie. With the departure of Rocco, this precarious entente was abruptly suspended, although I found their shaggy cordiality more disconcerting than the candid contempt which replaced it. There was veiled reproach when I didn't collapse and ignite myself like any right-thinking relict.

The association with the taurine one took me into a totally strange and new stratum of this tight society; I was a sheep among cougars, and I was quite content to be drummed out of the pack.

The loss of Rocco was a quite different matter— he was a magnetic, vibrant, simple animal, and if life was reduced to its simplest terms, it still held a lot Donner und Blitzen. An instructive safari.

I made a discovery while on the expedition—it's vague yet, a theory barely formulated. But it seems to be that there is a clean directness, an innocence, about physical barbarity that makes it weaker, less devastating a weapon than mental cruelty, which clings and penetrates like a venom. As I say, it's vague yet, but I think I have happened upon a concept I would like to explore further. (Not necessarily field work, the wear and tear is terrible.)

My new cell partner is a jazz musician, trumpet player from Lake Forest, ex-junkie, a condition he hopes to sustain. A complete change from the previous lock partner, he's sensitive, bright, cynical, somewhat tightly strung. Blows good modern horn, and we've had a couple of satisfying sessions (at which

Doug my cellmate plays mellophone) with a trumpet man from
D.C. and a wild drummer from Florida. None of us is assigned to the band, so we have to blow on our own time,
on weekends.

I know it's futile to ask you to visit, I've asked so often,
but the next best thing would be if you'd send a picture or
two, so I could at least see your face again. And please keep
writing. I get rather immersed in this life here, and I feel
it practically a necessity to keep a snorkel to the outside world.

For now, mi corazon, Jim

Raiford, Florida
MARCH 31, 1958

Dear Gertrude:

The two letters and postcard I received made me so happy
I wanted to reply by return mail—and then everything came
at me. The flu hit me, rendering me hors de combat for a
few days (and how uncool it is to be sick in the joint), but
I had to get up and stagger around on somebody else's legs
in order to play Sunday services at the Chapel. With a load
of broken glass right behind my eyes.

I caught the bug while nursing Rocco through a siege of it.
He was running a high temp the day he left for Milwaukee
on parole. (Tetanus on top of gangrene wouldn't have stopped
him.) It was a grievous loss for me, probably the hollowness I
felt made me vulnerable to the flu. There was a major adjustment to make, from enforced dependent to free agent.

Luckily the blood of the clans flows in my veins, nobody
ever guessed my distress, even the hardnoses who were bird-
dogging me.

But as things go in the joint I didn't have much time to
languish in any case. Two-man cells being at a premium, it
took a little maneuvering to keep out the hardnoses and weasels who figured to move in. The rule is that any application
to move into a cell must be signed by the occupant. But
forgery is not unknown in these hallowed halls.

So I had respite, but not much. I had to wheel some and deal some; I heard that Doug Northrop was due off bread and water, once more. For ten months I had watched him taking a beating because of his hapless association with the spike society—I figured all this cat needed was a quiet place, away from all the *merde*. It was a hangup for me, watching a good musician put himself through the grinder for nothing. I was able to make some devious arrangements, and when he came off Disciplinary, he discovered he was assigned to my cell.

He came up just at Lockup, looking beat, really wasted. I conned the bar-man into letting him take a long shower. (Talk about nervous, talk about stage fright.) When Doug finally came into the cell, I had some hot coffee waiting, and other stimulants. Practically the first thing he said was, "If you got any ideas, forget it."

That's about par for Samaritans, ain't it? Bona-fide ones, I mean. Well—the name of this game is the waiting game.

This stud plays fantastic trumpet, he's from Chicago (Lake Forest, actually), junkie and trying to kick. And from all sides here, he meets a sinister skepticism about his efforts to stay clean.

Curious thing about junkies, they hate anyone to resign from the club. J.P. the drummer is back in population (you may remember the big blond from Florida) and he keeps coming up to the cell to cut up old junkie scores with Doug. As a result, I find myself opposing J.P., to diminish his effect upon Doug. Rather a weird development.

But we've had some good blowing sessions with J.P., and a fine trumpet man from D.C. (Who's the All-American-Rotarian junkie.) Doug plays mellophone on the sessions, it's softer than when he blows horn. That horn, for some reason, is porcupine all the way.

You may be hearing from Rocco, maybe not, I gave him your address. Please don't wait so long to write, my own.

later, Jim

Raiford, Florida
APRIL 4, 1958

Dear Mike:

To answer some questions you put— (You don't pay very close attention.) I'm a member of the Chaplain's staff, play typewriter a little during the week, blow organ on Sundays. It's a good job, I have a piano to practice on (a pretty good spinet), and a Hammond organ. In the empty chapel, I can practice a lot (and dream a lot).

Catholic is my favorite service, and I have charge of the Catholic choir. A little dismaying at first, the Catholic devout are an arresting assortment—pugilists from the boxing squad, highwaymen, footpads and cutpurses. And all hardnoses. (Do the Pope know?) Some of the roughest cases in the joint, and to see them earnestly, shaggily, meekly struggling with Latin pronunciation is a touching and warming sight. Good lads all, and all misunderstood. (But there are times, when I am cracking the liturgical whip, my voice is shrill in my own ears, and I am suddenly aware of that battery of somber eyes (what have they not looked upon?), that I get the feeling maybe I'm training tigers and bears in the same cage.

But when the Mass is on, and they do the chants and responses and hymns with that rough simplicity (and, Christ, that grave and vibrant masculinity), there is an ineluctable force I have heard in no cathedral, ever.

The black choir, though, was a disappointment to me—stolid, lumpish, they didn't swing. Thinking it was a failure on my part to relate, I turned over the leadership to one of the blacks—this one is a high-style exotic from Trinidad; his intimates are urged to call him Peggy, his inferiors are permitted to call him Duchess. When Peg despaired of whipping the oxen into shape for Sunday (and the audience is murderously discerning) we would just do a blues, her wailing, me comping on the organ. God kows where she got the words— which, come to think of it, is as it should be.

The Chaplain remained cheerfully inscrutable throughout. Perhaps a little glazed of eye. When he gently suggested that a personality cult was forming, Peg brought in her friends, the choir loft became a gorgeous fluttering aviary, attendance skyrocketed, and so it has remained. And the rehearsals— saints preserve us, the rehearsals. But it finally swings, babe. Go fight success.

The new cell partner has forced a radical adjustment. I don't know how it happened, but he's smarter than I am. I always preen myself on observing people, speculating on motives and purposes. With this stud it's like looking through a keyhole and finding an eyeball watching you. I dunno, man.

pensive, Jim

Raiford, Florida
JUNE 19, 1958

Dear Gertrude:

The pictures you sent, of you and Frank, are delightful, I have them hanging by my bunk and they never fail to give me a lift. Frank looks debonair and cagey, like a Victorian pimp— as for Missy G., I think the thitter lost an actress when she became a painter. Doug and I have tried to fathom your Gioconda look, and have been baffled by it. I am reminded of the sinister studied gentility of Beatrice Lillie, and Doug says maybe it is like Lillie portraying the Mona Lisa. That doesn't seem to make it, either. Anyway, you are both as vivid and personable a pair as ever came up the pike. We are both indebted.

I've been wanting to send my thanks sooner, but I've had to devote the two weekly letters I am allowed to trying to contact my agent (Ex-agent, I dunno), and the editors of The Paris Review. I had a note from Mike Moran a while ago telling me that a story of mine, "Day Of The Alligator,"

you may remember it, was in the current issue of PR. I was
amazed, nobody had told me anything about it. I thought
perhaps nobody knew where I was; I hadn't written the agent
since I've been here, to my recollection. Anyway, that's all
I know about it, so if you find a current issue of PR, advise.

We've just finished reading a book called *Somewhere There's
Music,* by one George Lea—purporting to be about musicians.
Doug read a rave about it in *Sat Rev of Lit,* and had his
mother send it. It's about musicians, right enough, of a sort.
Genuine cats. They say "man," "like," "gas" an awful lot, and
smoke pot and turn on with chemicals they primly refer to
as "stimulants." The hero is a maladjusted Korean veteran who
won't join the Murcan Legion. He plays baritone, and he's
"beat" in the best tradition— possibly from hauling the baritone around. This cat sits in at all kinds of sessions and carves
everybody, but he always moodily splits after a couple choruses.
(He uses the same reed throughout the book.)

There's a trumpet man has a band where he uses on piano,
his *wife.* And there's a spade pianist who ought to be turned
over to the NAACP. It's one of those creepy books where when
the action hits the sack, the language suddenly turns high-
flown and sepulchral. You know that scriptural bit, "and they
were together and knew one another." I think Hemingway is
to blame for this ponderous Old Testament style of reporting
a toss in the hay.

Whatever, it's a passel of misbegotten characters, and while
the author drops jazz names with hushed reverence, it's pretty
clear when he writes about music that he's a Lawrence Welk
boy.

Doug says it would be difficult to write a factual book
about modern musicians because they're so stupid and colorless
as persons. And he knows a lot of them.

Eminence, salutations, Jim

Raiford, Florida
AUGUST 4, 1958

Dear Mike:

We are deep into a Florida summer now. Nights are warm in the cell, despite the blowers on the roof of the joint, and sleep is fitful. You will remember from your summers in Miami that the sun bounds up like a vindictive glaring orange eye and never lets up until the afternoon dissolves in darkness and deluge. So if I have been goofing on you, attribute it partially to the drain on my energies that the weather exerts.

Another factor is my scrambled emotional state, I've got another one of those Colette scenarios going, alas— the nuances, uttered and otherwise, are flying again. But not in this weather, later for that. I received the issue of PR you sent, bless you, on the same day I got their check. There was some confusion as to whether I was James or William Blake*—of no importance, I'm frequently confused about who I am. I thought the story was nicely presented.

The illustrations astonished me with their gee-whiz aspect, I always thought of those happenings rather matter-of-factly —the pictures made it all seem like Hell in the Casbah. Maybe that's picky. Incidentally, I didn't mean to come on waspish at you, it's just that I've grown to mistrust good fortune. Like the old Russians, despair is my element and any intrusion of happiness comes as a frivolous interruption.

All the good news came at a time when everything else was bad news, and my brain had a traffic problem. I was feeling discarded and rejected, and it gave me a block. My lock partner Doug uses his intelligence and intuition to create havoc and ruin quite as diligently as he uses them to create music; so I had just been creatively and imaginatively put through the grinder. It took a couple of days to put myself back together again— and then I realized how lucky I had been to land in

* The author was referred to as William Blake in the table of contents, James Blake in the notes on contributors.

The Paris Review. Doug liked the story, but when he read that biographical bit where it says I'm a jazz musician, he blew it, and lectured me sternly on the insolent presumptions of upstarts and interlopers. ("You are *not* a jazz musician, remember that!") Wow, I felt like a mangy cur at the Westminster Show.

He's right, but so what? Jazz used to be a light-hearted raffish affair, now there's this lugubrious mystique, and everybody comes on like an acolyte, who needs it? There's a higher degree of virtuosity in the music, and a bleak arctic cleverness. But it seems to me there is also the suggestion of constipation and cul-de-sac. I can hear and follow the diagrammatic nature of it, but as music it explains more clearly what it is *not*, than what it is.

There's a strong strain of snobbery in Doug's attitude, and sometimes when things are too quiet and my malice is running, I put him on, for kicks. The ambush has to be properly and deviously laid, but I finally come to the point where I can mention, with aristocratic diffidence, that William Blake is my ancestor, and that the blood of the Highland Chieftains boils in my veins. He never can resist the bait, so then I get to say a little something about North Shore provincial parvenus. Then he tries to kill me. He gets apoplectic at what he terms my phoniness, so then I have to perversely exaggerate my true intrinsic phoniness; I consider it a mark of insensitivity that he doesn't divine what an accomplished bounder I really am. What is of real importance and value to me is that his fury is an indication of concern and involvement, despite all the barriers he tries to erect. Slowly we approach understanding.

He read that paperback thing I was working on, stole it from me in fact, and denounced it roundly as trash and rubbish. He's right.

But the beauty part is the shared laughter, I've never known that in a relationship before, it's novel and precious to me. And it elicits wondrous odd reactions from our neighbors in the adjoining cells, when we meet them the morning after. They

s primly askance, as at a major impropriety. There
night sounds, permissible, which pass without com-
soft thuds, gasps, startled cries of sadism; the vibra-
bestiality, more like stains in the air than words; the
tense, terse murmurs of voices in passion, the farcical rhythm
of bedsprings—these are properties of the environment, and
belong. But the mingling of merriment and erotics appalls. The
tocsin sounds, the drums speak. The wise blood knows.

Love, Jim

Raiford, Florida
AUGUST 21, 1958

Dear Gertrude:

That's an awful long tacet passage from Dorchester Avenue
way—you've been laying out for I don't know how many
bars now—isn't it about time you wailed a little? You've got
to know by now how much I enjoy your communiques, they're
like a fresh salt breeze in this sunbaked inland enclave. Speaking
of salt, if I made you hacked by anything I might have said,
consider that I have a cleverness-at-any-cost compulsion wherein
my flippancy sometimes slops over into crudity. Consider further
that my head is ash-strewn, my garments rent, my breast
smote. (Smit? Smat?) Anyway, I am besotted with contrition.

The summer has been murderously hot down here this year.
The sun has been a great orange orb of vengeance that sears
the eyeballs and fries the brain. So I have been moving as
cautiously as an armadillo, when I am not lying lizard-like on
a blanket behind the chapel.

But Doug, who was sunstruck earlier in the season, plays
violent badminton in the hottest hours of the day. This is quite
evidently an extreme method of atonement, and I have suggested it would be much less exhausting if he got himself an
Ivy League hair shirt and wore it.

We've had an interesting addition to the Chapel staff—personable chap about thirty with a degree in liturgical music from
Montreal and Columbia, plays wild turbulent Bach on the organ.

In for six on a few check beefs. He's taken over as choir director (though I still do the black choir), and he's giving me organ lessons. (I've been operating more or less free-style on the thing.) Also he's an amusing companion, a welcome change from the mousy mediocrity and insularity of my confreres on the Chaplain's staff. I've been getting some astonishing insights into the world of church musicians, they are apparently as irreverent and balling a group as one could wish. Perhaps more muted than jazz musicians, in a lower key you might say, but similarly marked with the gypsy's curse. New boy has also worked as a singer in the Met chorus, so I've been hearing backstage gossip of the opera world, what Milanov said to Callas, what Callas told Tebaldi, like that.

There may be the tinkle of chi-chi about it, when I relate it to Doug he comes on with a kind of poolroom leer, for some rotten reason of his own. Which I ignore, I am above that sort of thing.

As for Doug and me, the association is invaluable. The tight relationship of cellmates, the constant proximity, these are challenging conditions in which to sustain friendship and affection, and I think we have been signally successful. He has become my alter ego, my scourge, my literary conscience. He insists that I've got to be better than I am, writing-wise. And otherwise . . . The stud is insufferably honest and infuriatingly right most of the time, and we battle a lot, but I think enough of him to try to measure up. Something may come of it, if I can but endure.

I suppose you saw the story in The Paris Review, with the hotsy-totsy illustrations?   Please write, I languish, Jim.

Raiford, Florida
SEPTEMBER 4, 1958

Dear Mike:

By the time you get this, you will probably have received the magazines I sent, and I feel I'd better explain how come only one of the Paris Review issues you wanted. There were four around here as I recall, and I lent a copy each to some friends. When I tried to get them back, the churls refused to comply wit my wishes, to my chagrin. Be certain I would be charmed to send innumerable copies, it is a thing which should be in every Murcan home. You will note that PR put me into the slot next to Genet. The story of my life—if I ever played a vaudeville bill, I'd follow the cat who shoots himself for an encore.

The Paris Review sent me a nice letter saying they'd had favorable comments on the story and inviting me graciously to submit anything else I had. Also mentioned that Dr. A. had written in my behalf. A real sweetheart.

I have asked for permission to add the name of Jack Conroy to my mailing list, so that I may write him and perhaps get an occasional answer. I hope Jack doesn't consider this presumptuous—he writes such antic and erudite letters, and I have a real and frequent need for lightness, things being as they are.

Nelson wrote that Conroy was doing his memoirs and that I'd better hurry if I wanted in. This is not the reason I would like to correspond, though I will undertake to put him in my memoirs if he will put me in his.

Much more to tell, but my nerves are chirping. It is very late Sunday night at the frazzled end of an overly festive chemical weekend—during which I somehow managed to play three allegedly sacred gatherings without booting it.

Ordinarily I am comparatively austere, but I felt the need for relaxing, and in any case Doug wanted company. These are somewhat trying days in J-57, Doug is due to be considered for a pardon on September 8, and he is edgy and morose with the strain of suspense. Estimate of his chances, slender, and if I am correct in my guess, September 9 will be a day to be lived through.

If he misses the pardon, he may succeed in obtaining a parole, and in this connection perhaps you might be willing to help. He's going to try to get an Illinois parole and seek employment in Chicago. Not in music of course, they frown on parolees working in saloons. I thought of —— at Marshall Field, last report was that he was forging upward. You think he might be receptive to helping Doug get a job in the art department? I mean that section where they hawk all those objets d'art. In my opinion, Doug would be perfect for a sales job there, he's tall, handsome, personable, North Shore background. And he says he's most eager to try to make it in that particular field. Would you sound —— and see what he says? 'Twould be a gracious Christian thing to do, bedad.

Let me hear, Jim.

Raiford, Florida
SEPTEMBER 16, 1958

[This letter was turned back by the censors]

Dear Jack:

Probably Mike has told you that I took the liberty of submitting your name for inclusion on my approved mailing list, in the hope that you will occasionally find time to write. Nelson said I'd better hurry if I wanted in your memoirs. Hurry and do something, I guess he means. Better not hold the presses on my account. I've been informed that you were queried on the correspondence matter and made reply, so I assume you are willing to go along with the gag, pro tem.

In return for whatever glimpses you may care to offer of life Out There, I'll try to furnish you some idea of what gives In Here. Suitably bowdlerized, of course.

As to mise en scene, the joint is situated in the flat piney-woods Florida back country. Not so deep in nor far back as Cross Creek, but *back* there. No wall around it, but three strategically spaced fences of stout mesh, surmounted by barbed wire, the middle one fifteen feet high, with juice in the top strand. From the road, the joint looks like a Victorian New England woolen mill, mysteriously set down, glaring with whitewash, in the brassy Florida sunshine. Within the fences the grounds are extensive. They were formerly dotted with graceful old Washington palms and coconut palms, but these have been removed in the interest of security. A term meaning anything you want it to mean.

So the campus is now a touch bleak—the lack of shade to lend natural contrast to the sun-fried terrain gives it a bald denuded aspect. In these treeless vacant flat spaces, the various buildings, all aching-white in the sun, have a stranded impermanent air. Two blacktop roads, cruciform, are the main streets of our village. On one corner of the crossroads stands the chapel, a modest typical small-town red brick church, amid neat lawns, hedges, flower beds. This is where I work, playing the organ for Sunday services, and during the week typing in the office.

Across the road from the chapel is the prison canteen. This is the equivalent of a corner store, except that this store doesn't dare allow the customers inside. They make purchases through a couple of windows similar to racetrack betting windows. Adjoining the store, the Canteen proper, a small cafeteria-style place with a sort of bar and stools, where one may buy nickel coffee and simple short-order meals. Only the wheelers and dealers can do this with any regularity, so it has become a kind of status thing, a Club, if you will.

Next to this is a place called, with looney elegance, the Patio—this is the eating place of the officials and those who are dubbed locally "Free-Men," Plato notwithstanding.

Behind and around the canteen building is the Visitors' Park, a fenced, grassy pleasant place containing two long pavilions with picnic tables and benches—one pavilion for colored, and one for discolored. Virtually all visits are held here outdoors, very nice; they bring lunches and pitnick.

Looming up across the road from the park is the Rock itself, three stories, a long white building trimmed in buff. From this side, it looks like an overoptimistic bankrupt motel that survived the Boom and Bust. The Rock is built in such a way that it encloses an inner compound, where maximum- and medium-security prisoners are kept.

I live in this enclosure, but being a Trusty, am permitted passage through the big gate that seals it. The Rock is in two sections, White Rock and Colored Rock, also known as CR, the Civil Rights Building. I cell on the top floor on the west side, which overlooks the chapel and Visitors' Park. From our cell we have an extensive view to the fences, and over the wooded country beyond. A blessing, of sorts.

Sleeping quarters are varied, from dormitories (elastic) and 18-man cells to two-man cells. I occupy one of these with a trumpet player from Lake Forest, in on a junk beef. The cell is about 18×8×14, a very high ceiling, which keeps it cool. Doug, the cellmate, has put up a variety of maps, reproductions of Rouault, Van Gogh, Gauguin, Modigliani. Very hipped about painting, deplores my ignorance about it. Deplores my ignorance, period.

There are abrasive moments, as there must be in such constant proximity, but for the most part we are compatible, give and take. I give. I am really fortunate to have him, there ain't another swingin' dick in the Rock could give the good talk that I get from Doug.

It has taken a lot of space to tell about the Rock. Later, the people, perhaps. Like the lissome one I met at the clothing room one day. He had just arrived, and was prettily confused. "They asked me what my waist size was, and I told them 30. It's only 27, but I was embarrassed to tell them that." In stony soil, a primrose. Let me hear, and soon?   Jim

Raiford, Florida
NOVEMBER 24, 1958

Dear Mike:

Once again I seem to have missed you on your annual southward migration. I don't know why it is I so obstinately nourish the hope that some day of some year you will visit me at the academy. It has become my most cherished chimera.

The picture you sent is a constant delight, I have taped it to the wall alongside my upper bunk, where I consult it often. It evokes many remembrances, nostalgic, hilarious, disturbing. My lock partner Doug scrutinized it narrowly and at length— The Black Irisher, in Doug's view, looks seedy. (Stop sniveling!) This opinion was advanced in a tone lightly bordered with vitriol, and I speculated on the waspishness, always trying to make something of something. Me, I think you look like a torero with a pocketful of bull's ears.

Conroy was approved for my mailing list some time ago and I wrote him quite a long letter. To my surprise, I was called to the front office and told that the sarcastic tone of the missive was wrong and wouldn't do atall atall. He was nice about it, but it was a proper ticking off. Perhaps the fact that I mentioned he was an editor may have put the wind up and elicited special attention. Doubtless I should have gone further and said that he was editor of a very nice innocuous encyclopedia.

Doug has received a set of working papers from the parole board (a form to be filled out by a prospective employer) and barring complications he should be going to Illinois on parole before too long. Naturally, I'm glad to see him make it, but it will leave a gap. He's had a stronger influence on me than anybody I can remember. In music, for one. When we first played together, he was vociferously dissatisfied with the lack of drive and vitality in my comping, and continued to taunt me with my shortcomings—in jazz, that is—and my totally unrealistic hedgehog way of dealing with it.

So that I finally had to return to the scene and do battle. As a result I'm now able to give him an approximation of the background support he needs on his trumpet flights. These are cold and icily brilliant—and at other times warm and vibrantly lyrical. The fact that the warmth has come since he met me is something one doesn't mention. But I have, have I not? (I never told him, okay?) It's a result of the relentlessly emotional way I play piano—you can't hang in a steam bath without sweating, right? Anyway, his playing has the unmistakable sound of a man biting an idea.

And the same demanding vitality has colored the other aspects of our association. I've always been a dabbler and a shucker, reacting to people and stimuli only in the minimal degree that I could get away with. However intense my outward attitude may have appeared, the inner troll was always pursuing the absorbing secret cinema that goes on inside my head.

Doug has a demonic radar, fiendishly intuitive, and he soon discovered he wasn't picking up very strong signals, and said so. As it had been with our musical contretemps, my impulse was to retire in pique and alarm, clutching the frivolous and trivial approach that had always meant safety to me.

But once again I was drawn back, like a curious magpie, to the scene of battle, and made to deliver. So that now I have damn little left to hide behind. Good or bad, I don't know yet, it may portend a major shift in my approach to many things.

The Chicago Tribune comes our way occasionally, and I note that Dr A has been making it with a gaggle of folk-singers at the Gate of Horn. What kind of off-groove is *that?*

Let me hear, Jim.

Raiford, Florida
DECEMBER 15, 1958

Dear Jack:

You may have been wondering about my asking to have your name added to my mailing list, only to have a long hollow silence ensue. (You may have other things to wonder about.) Fact is, I wrote you a long letter shortly after your name was sanctified, but it was returned to me. I was told the tone was too sarcastic. I'll try to curb my waspishness this time.

It is Sunday night and J-Range is temporarily quiet. Most of the resident malefactors are at the movie in the auditorium. (This week "The Yearling.") Ordinarily the range is in an uproar in the evening, with radios blasting a variety of programs. They don't have central radio here, as do most joints. Which is a good thing, in my opinion, one would perforce have to listen to music chosen by the majority. Hereabouts, that would be string music and I don't mean Nathan Milstein. Fortunately my cellmate has an FM set, and we're able to listen to some fair programs from the university at Gainesville.

The cellmate is a jazz musician of the modern persuasion— plays angular strident coldfire trumpet. An expression and extension of his personality, of which I despair ever finding the key. In the nine months or so we have been together I have collected bits and pieces of all shapes and colors, but I still have no pattern. Unlike most musicians, who are blanks away from their instruments, Doug has an inquiring penetrating intelligence, a daunting intuition. Claims he knows all there is to know about me (wrong) and likes me withal. Living in such constant close association is a grueling test of any mutual regard, no matter how profound. Somewhere along the way, my confrere devised a yin and yan arrangement. In order, he explained, to avoid constant collision of personalities, he would reserve the right to get salty exclusively to himself. That way, as he put it, we would avoid a confusion of purposes and roles. And it has worked well enough, except sometimes when I forget and have to be reminded. . . .

You will be meeting Doug before too long, I hope. He is being released on parole to Illinois and will be living with his mother in Lake Forest. I've told him about you, your fabulous erudition and Hibernian charm, and while he tends to be taciturn and reserved to a degree, I know that he would like to call on you and to know you. The time ahead for him will be one of trial, and if he has somewhere to go for good talk, it will be of immeasurable help. And knowing your searching and compassionate concern for pilgrims in search of truth, I daresay it may be a rewarding association for you also.

At present I am eyeball deep, as Chapel organist, in rehearsals for Christmas music programs. The black choir is no problem, but there are two other choral groups to prepare, Catholic and Not-Catholic. Handel, Bach, some other lofty arid ones. For a soul that vibrates most poignantly to the strumming of a flamenco guitar, it is a time of stifling, a time of stress. Perhaps I shall die sneezing, strangled in dusty piety.

I hope your memoirs are proceeding apace. I saw your picture in Ebony with Willard Motley. You look like a benign world-weary bishop giving ear to a bibulous parishioner.

                                        Let me hear? Jim

PART VI

the world well lost

Dear Gertrude:

There is a reason for my not writing for so long, though not a coherent one. I have been for some time occupied with life inside the joint, to the exclusion of things outside—an unusual state of affairs, to be sure—and feeling, I can only say, happy, indecently so. The world well lost, I believe it goes.

Things are back to normal now, dull gray, that is, I feel much more as a miscreant should, intoning mea culpas. The ten months of locking with Doug have ended. He split recently for Illinois on parole. The loss has reduced me by half, but I try to take comfort in the benefits accrued from the association. I'll keep myself busy—this is no time for keening and picturesque languishing, this is serious trouble. I have an inexorable and daunting realization that a peak has been reached and passed; from here on, I will have to settle for anti-climax.

The night after Doug left, my new cell partner had not yet been approved, and I was alone in the cell, bewildered and scared. I tried playing records and the FM, and had to shut them off—the music evoked his presence like a dangerous genie.

I think I would have welcomed the company of a starving boa constrictor, anything but solitude. Fortunately a Samaritan appeared with a means of sedation, and I made it into the morning.

Doug will be living in Lake Forest and that, as you know, is gray flannel country at its deadliest. He has had a bad hassle with the junk scene, and made a valiant victorious effort to put it down while he was here, and it was often available. If, when things pile up and he is tempted to seek surcease, he knows where to go for understanding and music and good talk, it would help immeasurably. His front is taciturn, the aspect may look like hauteur. If you can get past this cold façade of inhibition, you'll find him a penetrating intelligence and at his most unfolded, a lunatic clown.

Doug has been a strong sustaining force through some difficult days for me here. One hand should wash the other, *nicht wahr?* Let me know what happens, it is of crucial importance to me.

Later, Jim

Raiford, Florida
JANUARY 21, 1959

Dear Mike:

In a note enclosed with a Xmas card, Conroy told me you had sent him a clipping from the Miami paper concerning our Xmas program at the academy. Nice to know of your interest, sardonic or not, it would have been even nicer if you could have been in the audience. This hardy band of pilgrims were considerably outnumbered by the performing brigands, and would probably have welcomed a few recruits. They huddled rather tentatively in the front pews of the chapel, looking bemused. Perhaps wondering what was on TV and why they had ever left it.

The cons were arrayed in tiers on the platform. (Here I could say that the performers were in tiers and the spectators in tears, and I believe I will.) The malefactors attired in white surplices, which fooled nobody, merely serving to underscore the bland villainy of their countenances.

Thus the two worlds surveyed one another in the candlelight, an eye raised to meet an armored eye.

However, the demons did well, the singing was semi-professional, and it was discouraging and disheartening to see them perform before such a meager house. The poor turnout was entirely a matter of timid or perfunctory promotion, in no wise the fault of the cons, who worked diligently. The rest is silence.

The Chapel choir director is a personable, handsome, thirtyish con, an interesting anomaly. Has a couple musical degrees, an offbeat type to be in a joint. Lived in the Village while studying at Columbia, haunted the Met, and was a ferocious partisan in the claque of Zinka Milanov, which may give you a flash. The frothy chatter is infinitely welcome in a place where the talk is ritualistic, mediocre, and predictably full of autobiographical suet.

The trumpet man who was my cellmate for ten months has split for Illinois on parole, and I am bereft. These chain-gang partings are weird, the departing one seems to fall right off the earth. Locking together in a joint is like no other association I know of, a constant proximity and ubiquity comparable only to that of Siamese twins. A profound attachment can ensue—and while in the past I have indulged myself in pastel sadness after such a leave-taking (strolling the prison grounds with moody mien, a man stained by sorrow, much like Benedict Piltdown in *The Insatiable Mormon*)—this loss frightens me with the hole it has gnawed in me. I daren't dwell upon it and have to keep throwing it out of my mind. Hmm. Well.

I had a card at Xmas from good gray Dr A, postmarked from Miami. Did he come down your chimley? Please write funny stuff, baby's draggin.   ever, Jim

Raiford, Florida
FEBRUARY 4, 1959

Dear Gertrude:

Just a short, hurt note bewailing with bitter moan your callous neglect. I'm aware you may be sulking in the tent because I didn't write for so long—but at that time I was in thrall, you hear, thrall. Little can be accomplished or set forth when one is besotted.

Now, more than a month later, one knows with sinking certainty that the things which were changed can never be changed back. Regret or excitement is absent—just a calm dismal knowledge that nothing will ever be the same. That's new to me, an abyss that daily confronts me.

Here the roof has fallen in on me. I may have told you something of the young and talented con who took over as choir director of the Chapel, with whom I have been working closely in my job as chapel organist. It promised to be a rewarding and instructive association for me. Well, he went to the hospital with an infected toe, and the doctors discovered he had Burger's disease. Which will keep him out indefinitely if not permanently. Of course primarily I am heartsick that such a ghastly unfair thing should befall one so young and talented, when all the dogs' dinners around here remain in the pink.

Secondly it means that the task of preparing Protestant, Catholic and Black choirs weekly falls to me. If you recall how pate de foie gras is made, this is how I instill the music into my little miscreant minnesingers. And then on Sunday, zut alors, it must all be squeezed out again. Literally a physical sweat. Please write, if you could know the lift it is for me to get the pocketful of wry a letter from you always brings.

Later, Jim

Raiford, Florida
FEBRUARY 8, 1959

Dear Jack:

Quite late at night, and the radio on the bookshelf beside
my penitential pallet is tuned to WGN and murmuring of
Chicago things. Like "Temp. Tomorrow, 5 above." The night
outside my window (barred against burglars and polltakers) is
a still and limpid 65. And I say to myself, "They're up there
freakin' and flyin', let them bloody well take the bitter with
the better." A basic malevolence.

In the note which accompanied your card at Christmas, you
mentioned your intention of writing at greater length after
the holiday hurlyburly, so I have been watching the mails, but
naught availeth. As I daily grow more disenchanted with my
retreat, I yearn for contact with the outside world. And so I
importune.

Have you heard anything of the squire from Lake Forest?
He sent a most munificent yearly subscription to the Chicago
Trib and a package of books, and I've been wondering about
his progress. It is half pain, half pleasure to read about the
familiar places up there. I note that the Gate of Horn was host
to a bard named Ginsberg, poet of the picayune, sandaled
apostle to Kerouac. The account said that a Kerouac manuscript,
the only copy extant, was stolen by some patriot. Whoever
struck that blow for culture, I hope he deposited the MS in
the indicated receptacle, and flushed it.

Anthony West says that Kerouac can write but apparently
has nothing to write about. That may well be true. He writes
about tedium so tediously that it must involve a certain amount
of skill. Reading "On The Road" I was strongly reminded of
the rambling, interminable, monumentally trivial autobiographical
ballads that are droned into my ear every day in the joint here.

At the other end of the world from this, I recently read
Durrell's *Balthazar*. What a sorcerous thing it is, a clinging

enchantment. I won't be able to shake the spell of it for a while. It begins like something of Debussy, softly, diaphanous, opalescent, and deepens and broadens in depth and color and splendor till it is a glittering bal masque. Not since the dreaming days of adolescence have I known such entranced absorption in a story. Doug has sent me Durrell's verse play *Sappho*, equally enchanting. Now I must contrive to lay hands on *Justine*.

I hope you will write, one seethes, Jim.

Raiford, Florida
FEBRUARY 13, 1959

Dear Mike:

One hopes you're still making the scene at the Hallelujah racecourse—perhaps you have moved to Tropical Park (Gulfstream?). I've been wondering if you were back in St Loo for the big blowout they had the other day. I sent a postcard inquiring about you and my letter of Jan 21. Thought maybe the long-suffering equines had finally flipped it and turned en masse on their exploiter. It's always been a mystery to me how horses ever got into all that hassle when they have such magnificent equipment for destruction, all those enormous teeth for ripping, grinding, slashing, munching, those pile-driving armored feet for stomping. Equines of the world unite, you have nothing to lose but your reins. Nothing.

The work here has mounted over my head recently, I lost the choir director when he went to the hospital with Burger's disease, probably for a long stay, which gives me three choirs to prepare. A further complication, one of the office staff had to go into voluntary segregation (protective custody) to preserve his entity following a deal that didn't wheel, so I have extra typing also.

North Florida spring comes early and there are strong signs of it. Which is sometimes good and sometimes not, it can be a mockery. The weather opens, buds open, chasms open. Beneath all the footless furor, the minor strain persists, I still miss the trumpeter something bad. (Had a note from Gertrude, she said he called at their pad, Frank thought he was brash. *Brash?*) I miss the blowing sessions Doug and J.P. the drummer and I had on the balcony bandstand in the chow hall. Febrile, taut exchanges, flights of improvisation like I've never known. It was electric, I used to be trembling and unable to eat chow after we finished blowing. And Doug had the same reaction.

I learned a number of things from this individualist—upon divining that I followed, at a safe distance, the precepts of Leopold von Sacher-Masoch, he said, great, we'll do Yang and Yin. Field research, sort of burn while you learn, and he cooperated with unflagging devotion. The woods are dark and deep. But I learn, I learn. One more affectation shot to hell. It wasn't all heavy breathing, there were many laughs, and oddly, the moments of abandoned lunacy are the things I cherish and remember most often. I hope you can dig him, Dr A has his address. A brain, a talent, a private vision.

Ever, Jim

Raiford, Florida
FEBRUARY 27, 1959

[To James Purdy, New York City]

Dear Mr. Purdy:

Thank you for your thoughtfulness in sending me a copy of your book *63 Dream Palace*. I received it before I had the explanatory letter from Gertrude in Chicago, and I was pleasantly mystified. Life is fairly uneventful here at the academy, at least as regards the events of the great world beyond the high fences, and so your book made a nice little excitement for me.

On the back of Dream Palace it says you are writing a play. That should be interesting—you have a flair for waspish dialogue, in my opinion. I'd like to know more about that.

Your book was not new to me, I should tell you. A friend of mine sent me a copy of it almost two years ago and I have had

it ever since. Also your book of short stories. I remember
they received a nice review in *Time*.

Dream Palace is a strangely sad and disturbing story. Enigmatic in a way, too, I had the odd feeling that there was
more going on than you actually wrote about—as if your action
were played before a scrim, behind which was more action,
but dimly perceived. Not very precise, but it's as close as I can
come.

I'd have written sooner, but, odd as it might seem to an
Outsider, the days here are well filled. I'm assigned to the
Chaplain's staff and work as chapel music director, playing organ
for Sunday services and rehearsing the Protestant and Catholic
choirs. In addition, I assist the Chaplain in interviewing new
arrivals (known locally as "new-cocks"). What writing I do
must be done on my own time at night. I'd appreciate hearing
from you—letters should be marked "Business" and addressed
to me c/o The Chaplain. Thanks again for the nice thought
in sending me your book.   Yrs., Jim Blake

                                          Raiford, Florida
                                          MARCH 10, 1959

Dear Gertrude:

Your mention of the ancient streets of Philadelphia gave me
a sharp yearning for the old scenes in Charleston, and a swift
picture came, of walking under the soft night sky of Carolina
summer, through the huge old slave market on the waterfront.
God, the throngs of insistent phantoms that jostled and nudged
me there, the voices that babbled on the still night air. Across
the water, a blinking eye of light from Fort Sumter, and I had
a suddenly clear realization of what Will S. had meant—"The
evil that men do lives after them."

And oh how I envy you seeing Chaplin in *Modern Times*
again. I think if I were able to see that, say, every two years
or so, the rejuvenating experience would keep me alive forever.
I shall always remember the apoplexy that threatened me every

time I watched Charlie's encounter with the automatic feeder. The warring expressions in his face when that strawberry short-cake was approaching, the struggle between gluttony and apprehension that was mirrored there. Immortal.

Your mention of the Sutherland Hotel also calls up a memory, but a farcical one. I played in that huge lounge there, ages ago. Specifically I recall a wild Turkish-style embroilment with a couple of White Sox ballplayers (the team stayed at the hotel), a frazzled scene where nobody ever did find out who was on third. O the halcyon days, the scented nights, the broken bones.

I'm doing a little better on the resignation bit. Had a little help from, of all chronic torchers, Lady Day. There was a program from Charlotte, played a lot of her fine old stuff (and some of her embarrassing new stuff) including "Good Morning, Heartache," which has always been special for me. So I just lay face down on the bunk while she wailed ("Might as well get used to you hangin' round/ Good morning, heart-ache, sit down"). The tears flowed and presently, mercifully dissolved the godawful chunk of cold I-dunno-what that had been lodged in me ever-since-the-day. Everything's great now, all is cool, eyes are dry, ah ha ha ha—see? If you see The One, say that I say thanx for the books and the newspaper subscription.

Had a very nice genteel letter from James Purdy, I think that could be a worthwhile correspondence, and I'm going to try to arrange it. We're both a little strange and stiff; he writes his letter something like G. Stein writing to a not very bright nephew. I guess I will probably try to reply in the same stately vein, if I can ever get these wooden shoes off. I really am a natural-born moujik, one whiff of gentility and I'm manning the barricades. That's not fair, I think James did extremely well in the tight restricted circumstances and I'm honestly grateful for the small charge of outside air his letter brought.

I'll write soon, do thou the same—Jim.

Raiford, Florida
MARCH 18, 1959

[This letter was kited out]

Dear Doug:

Probably the best way to start this letter is to say that it is in no way written at your solicitation, just to absolve you of communication with undesirable elements in violation of the conditions of your parole. All right, be it so stated. This is solely on my own initiative.

I read the letter you sent to the Chaplain inquiring about permission to send books. With the Chap's consent I typed the reply, which he approved and signed. But I had to find some way of thanking you for your thoughtfulness, some way that would be warmer and more direct than the starched and spastic letters I'm permitted to write through the Chap. So I'll kite this.

I want to thank you for the Tribune subscription. Though it is a mixed pleasure, I enjoy reading it; but every day it brings a fresh reminder of you and Chicago, so I call it The Daily Pang. I miss you very much, more than I can safely say without incurring your impatient annoyance at my sentimentality—strangely, what I miss most are the nonsensical things we shared, the lunatic bits you did, particularly the Idiot Impersonation of that child of God, Blake.

As for the box of books you sent, it is a beautiful and provocative collection, I was moved at how thoughtfully chosen, struck with the splendor. Especially was I glad to see the Shaw music critiques—their acuity aside, they would be precious solely for their ill-tempered vivacity.

It was a surprise to hear that you two have reconciled and purchased a house—I have confidence in you, remembering you as you were when you left, seemingly rock-steady and sure of your direction—I feel that you have done what you consider to be the best thing for yourself. But it was rather comically dismaying how different my imaginings about you were from what the reality must have been. You are of course always in my thoughts and at certain hours of the day I pictured you and what you were doing. I clung firmly to the image of you as a no-nonsense working stiff and if the hour was, say, 12 noon, I saw you sitting on a pile of steel girders (which you had single-handedly unloaded) dressed in a simple blue workman's shirt and sincere workman's pants, eating a simple but nourishing lunch out of a straightforward lunch box. (Drinking chocolate milk from a thermos.)

Or at other times I would see you, your simple blue workman's shirt open on a strong masculine throat, chaffing lightly with one of the girls in the office. (This girl is one of those cheerful lumpy Italian girls—complexion problem, ropey hair—who are always to be found in these places.)

I don't want to sound ungrateful, but the replacement you chose as my cellmate turned out to be an unmitigated disaster. Poor Ben, he's just out-of-sight schizo, and the chemistry between us was abrasive almost from the beginning. He has intelligence, but it's not wired to anything. I struggled for more than two months with the problem of putting him in accord with some kind of reality—I tried recommending books, what in my opinion were simple and interesting things that would give him a foundation for the intellect he hungers for. Suggestions that met with evasion at first, and then scornful refusal, while he continued to slog through psychological and philosophical things he could only dimly comprehend, which is worse than not at all.

Moodiness, despondency on his part; helplessly, unwittingly, I afflicted him with a sense of inferiority, and his compensatory efforts took weird shapes. That is, he beat the shit out of me. So finally the only thing to do was move out and leave him in possession. It was a wrench, giving up the joint you and I had shared—but whatever had been there was there no longer.

Artie had been after me for a while to change to 2nd Floor Trusty and move in with him. I know you never liked him, but things being as they were, I couldn't move out into the open, I needed some kind of protection, so I accepted, and have been living on 2-T since.

As a temporary refuge, I've had to make do with it, but I won't be able to make it for any length of time. Artie is considerate and solicitous (something new for me, as you will agree) and Polack and Bill have been hospitable and friendly (it's a four-man room) but there do seem to be an awful lot of (*Yuchhh!*). Moving into a 2-T room with these campus wheels has given me a disconcerting local prominence. I am compiling for my own edification and astonishment a dossier of shitbirds who make a point of speaking to me because of my association with these three. I don't know whether to be embarrassed or amused, so I'm a little of both.

So now I'm almost completely a solitary, a condition to which I have inevitably been gravitating ever since you left. Living on 2-T, I'm allowed to stay out until eight o'clock, and I sit out on the south porch of the chapel (facing the school) most evenings, and write. That is where I'm writing this, to be typed later. It's quiet and secluded, not the most comfortable, but it affords the solitude I need. I usually get there shortly before sundown and stay through the twilight. If I do not make a conscious and strenuous resistance, I find that my spirits have a deplorable tendency to fade with the light. A slowly sagging diminuendo. Ah hates to see that evenin' sun go down . . .

Maybe you will not remember the small plant in a pot you left with me, saying, take care of this—as it flourishes or wanes, so shall I. I have been tending it with superstitious terror. I am happy to say it flourishes like the green bay. Only one thing gives a twinge of unease—it's putting forth an unconscionable number of sprouts.   Take care, Jim

Raiford, Florida
APRIL 21, 1959

[To James Purdy, Brooklyn]

Dear James:

I must abjectly beg your pardon for the long delay in answering your gracious and interesting letter. Doubly ridiculous, when I consider how avid I am for a connection with the world outside and especially the world of literary New York.

The news that Farrar, Straus have scheduled your book "Malcolm" for autumn release is pleasant to hear. Well, actually it is a sort of ambivalent pleasure—possessed by gnawing ambitions in that direction myself, I'm always glad to hear that someone else has made it. At the same time, I always have the faintly sour feeling of a mountain climber part way up who sees somebody else plant a banner at the summit. I must have an unseemly amount of residual spleen, but I try earnestly to curb it, which I am told is the Christian way. Really, though, I'm more glad than anything else to hear it, and if I may presume, I'd sincerely appreciate a copy when it is available.

With your permission, I would like to submit your name as an addition to my approved mailing list here. That way, I should be able to write at greater length, and possibly with wider scope than is presently permissible. I do not anticipate undue difficulty in this.

You say that you'd be able to help me out on reading matter—the lack of suitable reading is really a major handicap for me. I'd be grateful for anything you care to send. If you read *Time*, for instance, I'd appreciate your passing it along when you've finished. And, of course, it passes from hand to hand here. I deplore the Luce list to starboard in certain areas, but he does capsule the weekly news in an informative way, and the style diverts me as much as it infuriates me. Anything you send, including your reply (which I hope will not be as dilatory as mine), should be addressed to me in care of my immediate supervisor, the Chaplain. (Marked "Biz.")

All the warmest, Jim

Raiford, Florida
MAY 14, 1959

Dear Gertrude:

The darkling mood of your last letter has given me some concern, coruscant one. Apparently all sorts of persons have been advancing theories and suggestions to you about your malaise. I would hazard a guess that you've been told about the lunar hiatus until you're thoroughly dragged with it. Think of it merely as The Pause that refreshes and go right on prowling. Or Charlie Baudelaire has some cogent advice: "Be drunken continually, if you would not be the martyred slave of Time—with wine, with poetry, or with virtue, as you please."

Sometimes, cherie, you can really be too maddening. You drop a word or two about the Lake Forest squire and his lady spending a musical evening at your fin-de-siecle mansion—and that's it. (Incidentally, I append a North Shore supplement, strap it on a passing pigeon, if you will.)

You might know that I palpitate to hear about it down to the last nuance. How did he look, how did she (wasted, huh?), what he say, what's he doing, what did you think of her. So dish a little, will you doll?

You will note that my address is different. I told you earlier that after Doug left (and at his insistence) the academy boxing champ moved into the cell. Nice enough kid, I like him, but there was a confusion of purposes, he had in mind a Choctaw-squaw bit and I couldn't see myself as Lo the Poor Indian. Sadly beautiful, it was, madly boring, no one can look anything but ridiculous with a bleeding nose, so I split the scene. Too muddy, after the light-hearted lunacy with Doug, too perishing heavy.

There was a hint of massive retaliation in the air, so I moved out of the Rock (the tight security part of the joint) altogether, and have been a 2nd Floor Trusty for a couple months now. It is something like living in Oak Park, if I was on the bricks, stifling atmosphere of gloomy propriety, and I've been meeting the nicer type of convicts. Asphyxiatingly dull, I much prefer the shaggy savages who live in the Rock, they breathe.

. . . I think it should be permissible to waft all of this to the ofay Miles: "The beautiful box of books has given me some quiet rewarding hours at a time when I particularly need it. I'm doing a bad job of forgetting, but I hope to make it eventually. I think I like best Nadine Gordimer's *The Lying Days*, it is the one which spoke most directly to me, reading it I felt myself moving through a revelation, a new and poignant landscape of the spirit and the emotions. And when it ended, I had the regretful sensation that a door was slowly closing. I know that you are finding delight and wonder and possibly consternation in the unfolding of your small son, and I rejoice for you in that. I'm sure that any role you find yourself in you will fill with integrity and grace. Salaam, effendi, keep faith."   Later, Jim

Raiford, Florida
MAY 21, 1959

Dear James:

With pleasure I am able to inform you that we are now legitimate and bona fide—your gracious name has been scrutinized, sanitized and sanctified and added to my approved mailing list. So now we can correspond.

Thank you for the copy of Commentary magazine with your story "Encore" in it. A strange sad haunting little story which you seem to tell almost by indirection, suggestion. You have a wonderful way of evoking much more than you actually put down. Spare, lean writing, sharply illuminating. The bit about Gibbs kissing his mother "in a manner resembling someone surreptitiously spitting out a seed" was a particularly vivid and arresting image, I thought.

Now that I shall be writing to you from here, perhaps I should try to give you some sort of picture of the academy. It is located in the approximate center of a vast acreage in the flat piney-woods country of northeastern Florida. No wall surrounds it, rather a high triple fence of some sixteen feet. Thus, while there are not the claustrophobic looming walls to contend with, there is the sight of traffic, a glimpse of normal life, on the nearby highway. Strangely, the mind builds its own wall, and soon one looks at that traffic without actually comprehending its significance.

All the buildings within the sprawling compound, the huge three-story cellblocks, mess hall and prison auditorium, are painted a dazzling white, incongruously festive in the Florida sun.

The grounds are parklike, landscaped and maintained by students of the Vocational Agriculture School, and dotted by the outlying workshops (the ubiquitous license-plate plant), hospital, school buildings. A blacktop road meanders through the campus. There is a fenced-in park where inmates receive their weekly visitors. Here there are two long low pavilions, one Caucasian, one African, with tables and benches. These were used until recently for picnic-style meals, until the authorities discovered that some of the roasted fowl being brought in by visitors were stuffed with some astonishing ingredients indeed, and the al fresco dining was forthwith knocked off.

In the center of the visiting park is a small bandstand where weekdays at noon the prison band plays spirited military airs while the work squads file into the Rock for lunch. I'm not a member of the band any more, but the leader is a friend of mine, so I play glockenspiel with them, a clangorous instrument which can be heard for miles. I don't think the cons even hear the band any more (except to note mistakes) but band music is a Raiford tradition, and it does add a temporary, though perhaps specious, air of gala.

I work in the Chapel, opposite the park, a neat red brick

affair with white trim, sort of Colonial, surrounded by clipped lawns, hedges, flower beds. The belfry has an amplifier arrangement which connects with the Hammond organ, on which I play a brief carillon concert before Sunday services, which resounds far and wide over the campus. The faithful give ear and not beatifically, the legion infidels bridle and bristle, and rend the air with offers of arson, mayhem, pillage. Naught availeth, I go on and on.

As to the atmosphere, it is unhurried, relaxed, in prison language the joint "runs loose." This is an approach that seems to be widely applied in the South, the easy does it style— maybe it is the years I have been in the South, but it seems to me to be peculiarly suited to the region. The official attitude towards the residents seems to be one of wary benevolence, weary and patient skepticism, tinged with a kind of resigned whatnext outlook. But every malefactor is keenly aware that swift and awful retribution waits for any infraction of the rules. It is a small, tight village, albeit an unusual one peopled with some wild and implausible villagers, more of whom another time.

In reading the news of the Outside, I have recently come across a recurring phrase which strikes me as distinctly ominous—there is frequent mention of the possibility of waging "limited warfare." Apparently, automation has arrived in the manslaughter trade, and the skilled practitioners of this art are casting about for some sort of full-employment agreement. Perhaps in a way they have a grisly point, there are far too many people, the ghastliest joke of all is that propagation is so easy and such fun.

Write soon. And all hail to *Malcolm*. I hope it's a smash and translated into Urdu and Kurdish.   Best, Jim

Raiford, Florida
MAY 26, 1959

Dear Mike:

Conroy told me in a recent note that you were in town
for the races. It appears now that you are firmly and irrev-
ocably committed to horses, so I guess it be*hooves* me to
stop with the feeble equine japes. See, I thought you were
just sort of lolling around these gilded resorts while waiting
for the Big One. Nobody ever tells me anything. It was only
recently I snapped it was a gig for you. What *do* you do?

For the past two months I've been living in that part of the
joint known as 2-T, Second Floor Trusty. Considered a priv-
ilege, this is like a separate wing of the joint, with its own
entrance. It's over a block long, made up of sizable rooms,
say about 1½ times as big as the rooms in a musician's hotel.
There are bars only on windows, and room doors may be
closed but not locked. (Save with ingenuity, ah hah!) Four
beds to a room, four cons. We are allowed to stay out on the
campus until 8 P.M. and there are, astonishingly, black cons
working as housemen—making beds, cleaning up. There may
be another reason for this than the sybaritic one, but I don't
know it.

The four occupants of ✕19 are widely divergent types—
Doc is fortyish, rugged, a technicolor production, silver hair
and suave mustache in gaudy contrast to his heavy tan. Looks like
one of those TV actors who radiate quiet strength and sell
outdoorsy cologne. Debonair and dashing, struts like a heron,
a nice uncomplicated guy. His is an increasingly familiar case
of the city slicker vs country cunning. He tried to break into
the real estate promotion scheme that is so hot around Sarasota
at present, spread his credit too thin, and the local Jukes cheerfully chopped his head off. He's a graduate of Purdue and
has been all over the Middle East as a construction engineer.

This seems like hunting Siberian bears and then coming home to have the neighbors' dog give you rabies.

Then there's Artie—sponsor and spouse, he bewilders me more than anybody has for quite a while—quondam boxer, quasi-bad motorcycle, graduate of Jersey City. He's the one took me off the hook in that recent hassle I had in the Rock. Muscled, a tanned Celtic face, soot-rimmed eyes the glaring blue of gas flames. Pseudo-hipster, digs jazz musicians if not their music, aspires to the jeesunk and chippys with it. A rough front, yet I get tenderness I don't know what to do with. And he's priest-cowed from his lace-curtain-Irish background, he backs off for few cons, but the local Savonarola can bend him with a glance. He's due out on parole soon.

Third member Bill has an M.A. in music. Classical organist, church musician outside, strung-out junkie. Slender, thirtyish, intense, gracious, shrewd. Beautiful manners, but can throw a bad curve— a kind of grave and attentive politeness (in dealing with the aborigines) that amounts somehow to derision on closer inspection and leaves the unwary bleeding into their shoes.

And of course lovable Jim B and that's the four. Doc and Artie are full trusties and work outside the fence on construction of the new prison. Billy is amanuensis for the Chief Custodial Officer, and I peddle amulets and charms.

To the more frantic denizens of the Rock, the 2-T residents have been objects of scorn; social climbers, bourgeoisie, and I'm inclined to go along with that. The population of the 2-T wing is a heterogeneous collection of tractor drivers, cow jockeys, hog valets and chicken pluckers on the one hand, and on the other, office workers, teachers, politicos. (In a rustic milieu, farm and dairy help are the elite, and don't forget it, Charlie.)

The white-collars, square, prim, status-conscious, comport themselves with glum circumspection and try to stay upwind of the Nature boys. While the primitives tread a Pentecostal path and ask no more than that cows don't kick, hogs don't bite, chickens don't tell.

So you can see it's like living in the Y with the 4-H in town, a colossal drag, but I'm in hopes I'll soon be able to split the scene and make it back to where I more nearly belong, with my tribe, whatever betide. Now I think I shall retire to the sack and read of the death of kings.   Ever, Jim

Raiford, Florida
JUNE 25, 1959
Cell J-18

Dear James:

Like you, I have been in the grip of a dread and dulling apathy for the last couple weeks. Even my usual free-floating anxiety has deserted me, and I miss it. The weather has been of a steaminess unusual even for this season in Florida, and that doesn't help anything either. From all the portents, this could be a good year for hurricanes. I rather hope so. I've been in one howler in Miami, and another in South Carolina, and they were exhilarating. Whenever the hurricane season rolls around down here, the cons revive their favorite fantasy, which is that a ferocious typhoon will come roaring down on the joint and flatten all the fences and everybody will scamper away giggling to freedom. It never comes, but every year they do the same bit with unabated gusto.

Since writing you last, I have moved out of the Trusty part of the joint, and back into the Rock. This is like moving from a high-rise back into the slums. You know how it is in a high-rise, you meet walking TV dinners in the elevator, and nobody pulsates. There was some narrow official scrutiny of me when I expressed the odd desire to get the hell out of Paradise, but I somehow made it.

There are some 2600 felons in the Rock here, where the peasants live, most of them faceless and nameless to me, like waiters or elevator operators, but there are quite a few who register. And while there are those among them who are slippery, tricky, wily as the fox, all of them are more dynamic and alive than the respectable confreres I left in the Trusty section. Life in the Rock is indeed more fraught with perilous potential, but it is more interesting.

So now I am back on J-Range, where I feel more comfortable, and my cell partner is a check artist from Maryland who has been ostensibly rehabilitated to the extent that he is leaving on parole next week. Glib, devious, sadly shallow and incredibly beautiful, the narcissine mirror that goes everywhere with him has prevented him from absorbing anything. (He was locked up with David Siqueiros in Mexico City, and could only shrug when I asked him about it.) He claims he is the way he is because his mother held his hand in the fire when she caught him stealing. She should have put his head in the fire. No no no, that is quite wrong. He has been amiable, pleasant and almost completely absent, it has been like coming together with a popsicle. Put the blame on the cosmos, put the blame on Mame. His prognosis, murky, as what is not?

It has been a 70–30 relationship, but then many things, alas, are. The friendship of cell partners, when they are intelligent and attuned, can be like no other relationship I know of. For one thing, there is no moving to the outskirts of town when dissension arises—once the pact is made, the bond established, it has to be a tough and elastic tie. Constant proximity and close association require a wide tolerance and searching exploration into what a human relationship can be. If the color deepens, the key changes, somebody gains and somebody loses. I had such a year, last year— a turbulent year, things were changed in Blake that can never be changed back. I wonder where he went, that Blake?

Lights Out whistle just blew, have to rack it up. You mention magazines, they are always madly welcome here. And do cheer up, if I had boats and water to look at, I'd be merry as a grig.

Please write soon. Jim

Raiford, Florida
JULY 5, 1959

Dear Mike:

You can't be all that busy shoeing the wild mare and cooking bran mash, currying and scurrying, that you can't take a moment to acknowledge a person's letter. Where are you, lil bijou? Since sending that last missive into the void, I've moved from the posh Second Floor Trusty neighborhood back to the Casbah, in the Rock.

The brouhaha that sent me fleeing has subsided, it appears, and all is comparatively cool. And besides, Artie went back to Jersey on parole. (Incidentally, there was a funny thing by Bill Manville in the Village Voice—he said the East Jersey landscape looked like robot-vomit.) Anyway, with Artie and the stalwart aegis off the scene, a summer replacement moved in, and the rent all of a sudden looked too steep, so I split.

Furthermore, every time I went to the bathroom, I had to pass the TV set in the hallway, and it was depressing to be reminded constantly that the whole country is soggily watching complex cowboys, all sick sick sick. (Whatever can the horses be thinking? Don't tell me that Madison Avenue isn't operated from The Kremlin.)

I am once again living in a two-man cell, a nester once more. A much easier way to do time, it gives me privacy and quiet for reading and writing. My present cellmate is a check artist who has bounced checks all over the hemisphere, South America, Mexico, the Caribbean, but it all sounds like Miami Beach when he tells it. He leaves on parole in the morning. (The reason I moved in, I shall be in possession.)

His successor is a moot matter as yet. There's an intelligent murderer here, and I been after him to move in, but I may have touted him off with my overweening cleverness. 'Twould be a great pity, I've never known an articulate murderer. If you have any shirts or upper apparel you're thinking of giving to the Sally Ann, forbear, *por favor*, I am in parlous need. If you have, tell me what they are so that I can list them on a parcel permit. All this providing you want to bother. Do you want me to look nice or don't you? I'm on the trail of a cell partner. The frog he would a-wooing go.

The J. D. Salinger story, if it is that, "Seymour," in the New Yorker was a deeply affecting piece, I thought. I've always felt that *Catcher In The Rye* was not the bible many said it was— but "Seymour" seems to me a tour de force. Groping, fumbling, probing, he made me agonize along with him, and I knew I had been over strange ground when I finished. And incidentally had some fun on the way, there was a brisk snottiness in some places. He gives Simone de B a deft bootinzee yahss in passing. Not entirely deserved, but neatly executed.

What of Dr A? Jack C? Douglas? Anybody atall out there? Don't you ever wonder what a kid like me is dong in a nice place like this? Write, beloved somber one, take me out of all this for a while.   Thine, Jim

Raiford, Florida
JULY 21, 1959

Dear Mike:

Thank you for the kind offer of the shirts, I am enclosing a package slip to cover the situation. Your saying that maybe they wouldn't fit gave rise to the horrid supposition that maybe the sleek Black Irisher had allowed himself to get fat. The thought is intolerable, I won't entertain it.

The check artist who took me in as cell partner has split to follow the stony path of rectitude. Sold my alarm clock out from under me before he left, but considering that he has been an international operator who rocked the Banque Suisse to its foundations, I didn't do bad. The Christian who sponsored my boy for parole is a young Episcopal priest of the "Mackerel Plaza" type. My erstwhile partner mused aloud that the Rev and he wore the same size, and that a clerical habit as a front for paper-hanging would be the end-groove count. I'm sure the observation was no more than a most excellent jest. Most excellent.

The new lock partner is a cat I mentioned previously, doing life plus five for homicide. (He planned a payroll holdup of Minneapolis-Honeywell with an employe of same, and when the poltroon chickened, Robert took a very dim view of such apostasy, and buried the cat in the woods and drowned his automobile in Tampa Bay.) That's what you call eclat. Never having known anyone who carried protest to such a magnificent extreme, I was eager for a chance to find out more about him, and I think my bug-eyed approach has filled him with dismay. But being a solitary sort and conceivably in need of conversation he has apparently stifled his misgivings enough to move in.

These thorny personalities are as wary as antelopes and difficult to know at first, but he seems far from an ogre, more like a bedeviled waif. A good part of his dilemma seems to be that he scorns the rules of the bourgeois game but is unable to renounce its values. I can only speculate, so far, about these things, but I do think there is a vast bitterness in him. Not, unfortunately, a dynamic kind of disaffection, more like an acid bath in which he is dunking himself. I'm going to try to ameliorate that in some way, or anyway do what I can in whatever fashion, if only to make him easier to live with, for he is an intelligent and gentle companion, rare hereabouts.

He told me with no apparent reluctance about the crime that put him here (this after a week or so)— then went on to mention a couple other terminal operations, with what seemed to me a daunting degree of relish. Which I hastily hushed, not so much because I feared to be the repository of guilty information—but I felt somehow like a man who has just acquired a hot diamond for a price and then, as a sort of breezy lagniappe, is offered another identical gem for an additional fin. I think this will be friendship without heat or complication, restful—I'm long overdue for that.   Ever, Jim

Raiford, Florida
JULY 30, 1959

Dear James:

Still looking for a response to my offering of June 25. You
are rather a spasmodic correspondent, are you not? Not that I
want to strap you with any burdensome quid pro quo, like
epistolary ping-pong, but your extended silences are disconcerting. I begin to wonder if I have offended; in letters I am
often somewhat overeffusive, like some large beseeching dog,
knocking down strangers and panting into their stunned faces.
I am in person so reserved to the point of paralysis that I
have a tendency to spill over when I write.

We are in the dead windless center of a stupefying summer
down here. Only the mornings are pleasant, with that haze
that hangs in the southern air before the sun comes up.
(We rise at 6, breakfast at 6:30.) Later, the day simmers, molten
and sullen, until the afternoon, when it boils over in a crashing
thunderstorm and downpour. The cloud formations and move-
ments are really epic here in the summer, and I spend a
lot of time on my back in the grass.

Of course I have to work, too. Fortunately the Chapel office
is air-conditioned and the time I must spend at the typewriter
is not too onerous. There are seven other inmates on the Chaplain's staff, a few of whom are engaged in what the cons
call "Working the glory road," that is, evincing an extreme
degree of piety which they hope will lead to early parole.

Poor J.C. He had a big dream. I'm sure he would be dismayed at the duck-hearted sleazy ones, with dead minds and
cold noses, who are operating under his aegis. We had one
overzealous pilgrim working in the Temple, called Needle-
Eyes, who kept a chromo of J.C. in an easel frame on his
desk. Mooned over it like it was Paul Newman, for godsake.
An infidel who worked in the office (now in Hell, or en route)
took a dim view of this detestable performance and one day

when Needle-Eyes was absent inscribed the portrait "Love, Always."

Whenever the office talk gets too pietistic or platitudinous, I escape to the Chapel auditorium and practice the organ, or play the piano, and in that find heartsease. I find the organ a droning monotonous instrument (I don't have utter command of it, but I don't like it when others play it, either). The piano I've had a lifelong affair with, and it seldom fails me. I'm particularly happy about it at present, because I've been wrestling with modern jazz for years, and only recently has it seemed to me that I'm beginning to say something in that vein. And I mourn to myself that the trumpet player I used to cell with, and blow with, paroled now, who taught me and who used to curse me for my inhibited piano, is not around to know that I never stopped trying.

Now if only I could do something about my prose-in-aspic. . . . Please let me hear, Brooklyn boy. It is delightful to get a letter from you, so delight me, man.

PS—Don't you think Governor Long is the wildest thing to happen in politics since Caligula?   Warmest, Jim

Raiford, Florida
AUGUST 6, 1959

Dear Gertrude:

Thank you and thank you for the lock and keys. Now I can go away and leave our little chintzy cubicle with an easier mind. I have an inside apartment this season, not quite as desirable as J-57, which looked west over the grounds and the pine woods beyond. My present digs (Brit.) overlook an inside quadrangle and all I can see is walls and rows and rows of windows. (No binoculars, drat!)

The walls of the pad are adorned with numerous colored photographs of what looks ilke Connecticut or some such place, put there by my ex cell partner, now paroled— very pretty, very suave. (He called it swah-vay, to my everlasting distress.) Against the rules to paste pictures, but I just haven't got around to taking them down. And the color does help some. Also I have a turbulent abstraction done by a young lad who wanted to be Paul Klee for a while. (I gave him a book of Klee reproductions once when we were having a brief tussle, but recently I think he's changed it and wants to be Paul Newman.)

And I've put up some maps on the walls to show that I am a stern no-kidding monastic type, and also to improve my geography, which is abysmal. When I think of it, not often, I stare at them vacantly for a while and then forget about it. I still believe that Turkey is somewhere around Germany. I don't see how they stand it.

Today I was Surveyed, by a college boy from Gainesville, U of Fla. He said they were trying to find out about convicts, just where it All Went Wrong. Solemn, didactic young man, meaning he didn't fall out at my small polished witticisms—hell, he didn't wiggle an eyelash. I told him mostly the truth, and some colorful lies to brighten his day and lighten his load. He didn't ask the burning question, the Big One they all want to ask when they come peeping, but I could feel it hanging in the air between us like a phantom chandelier. I think I was digging him harder than he was me and I'm not sure, but I think I got more out of it than he did.

I had a kind of nice thing happen to me today. It is my wont, when things get thick, to go into the auditorium of the Chapel and shut all the doors and play the piano. I don't like anybody standing around requesting Stardust when I play; my fellow workers all know it (finally) and they leave me alone. (Oddball, curmudgeon.) The windows of the place have to be open for air, and there's one spade who works on the lawn squad around the church, who always comes in and listens. He seems to vibrate right, so I don't mind, though I'm not crazy about it.

Anyway, the spade is a levee type (from some godforgotten town in the Everglades) but he seems to have a native bezzazz.

I've been experimenting with improvising in 3/4 time, and I was fooling around with I Could Have Danced All Night. I found a sort of obbligato effect under the main strain I was trying to lay down. I liked it, so as the harmonic pattern permitted, I repeated the obbligato strain, only I broadened and stretched it, flattened it out some. And it happened, real good, I brought it off. And the spade, who I know knows nothing about music, at least academic-wise, chuckled happily at precisely the right moment. An absolutely unstudied pristine reaction, and I could have, well I could have. . . . But it was a pure shining little magic instant. (Like Holden Caulfield, I don't know exactly what I mean, but I mean it.)

It started a train, it took me back ages to the South Side of Chicago, to simpler days, when the twain were one. They call the spade Steam, and he is a big black mothah. I may, I just may. An idle workshop is the devil's mind. Are you going to that enormous Hefner clambake? Wow, Yow. Let me hear about that.   Later, Jim

                                        Raiford, Florida
                                        SEPTEMBER 10, 1959

              [Via the Chaplain]

Dear Doug:

Your letter was an exciting event in this quiet existence. A very real and warm pleasure, and an immense relief to hear something definite after so long a silence and uncertainty. I've wondered a lot and worried some about your parole conditions, and so I was glad to hear that your supervisor is understanding. It is essential that such a key figure in the scheme of things should be a man of good will. The social and domestic aspects of your life I feel sure you will handle with a firm and lordly hand.

Your mention of the Tribune subscription indicates that you never received an earlier letter I wrote months ago to thank you for it, and for the coruscant selection of books you sent.

I entrusted the letter to the trumpet man, on his earnest representation that he would expedite. I should have known from his previous devious (whee!) mode of operation what would happen. He went to D.C. on parole, and there was a report shortly after that he had fallen on his face for the usual dismal reason.

After you split the scene here, Ben moved in (as you wanted) and it was an unqualified disaster, wrong chemistry absolutely. I was dismayed to find how far gone he was in paranoia, and helpless to change it. Harrowing scenes of violence, and far worse, that interminable philosophical mishmash till I felt as if I were drowning in alphabet soup. I fled to the 2nd Floor, sponsored by Artie the Torpedo. There everybody was cautious, prim, furtive, hangdog, paralyzed with propriety and dazed by TV, so I fled back to the Rock.

In defense, I withdrew into my own thoughts, into reading and writing. I've been having a ball with my journal. It's become a necessity. I have all this monologue running through my head, and I became afraid it would begin coiling out of my ears like ticker tape. So I write it down, fulminating furiously, and it is catharsis.

I'm locking now with Cliff Roberts, that quiet somber cat, and so far it has been beautiful and peaceful.

So much I want to say, impossible to say it all, my brain is clogged with it. I hope you'll find time to write, same way as before, tell about Gertrude, Nelson A (this new book of his seems to be a stalling tactic, a stopgap, I'm disappointed), Jeanne O'Brien, the clubs, plays you saw, books you've read. I am so overjoyed you're having a life again, fat man.   ever, Jim

Raiford, Florida
SEPTEMBER 23, 1959

Dear Mike:

Over a month since I sent you, with some misgiving and trepidation, the renewal blank for The New Yorker, so I assume you decided not to subscribe again. Of course I regret it, but in all conscience and grace I can only say again thanks for the long time you made it available to me. If you want to save your back copies and forward them say once a month, it would be helpful. The quality of their fiction has recently been superlative, and I think reading it was of considerable help in my own groping efforts. But if not, why, cool tout de meme.

I've had some weight added to my job at the prison chapel. The ersatz esthete who was choir director packed his motets and quit in a flurry of temperament, and the Chaplain, who is a nice guy, a man of unflagging good will, no small accomplishment here, asked me to take over. I've stalled this inevitable duty as long as I could, knowing that it would severely limit other important activities, like woolgathering, people-watching, daffodil-sniffing.

Our erstwhile Kapellmeister was a magenta type chiefly concerned with making a point of his appreciation of the higher things, and his insistence on harrying our poor bewildered convict songbirds through out-of-sight Bach chorales resulted often in something that sounded like a brawl in the locker room at the monastery. He was a fanatical Bach-head and I am not particularly. I love the jazz way ol' Wanda Landowska had with it on the harpsichord, but a prolonged spell of J.S.B. gives me an image of bagels, their flat uncompromising unleavened quality. So-called purity and austerity in music are commendable as a display of mental invention, I think, but a consistent lack of sensuality is a denial of what music is for, as far as I'm concerned. I'm probably overstating it, but I'll try not to regret it.

Another musical activity I've taken on is coaching and comping for a vocal quintet one of the black cons has formed. The leader, a Bahamian, is an attractive cat, perhaps too much so. In the razzle-dazzle personality he presents to me, a sort of hipness that is more flip than hip, all glaze and no substance. Maybe in time he'll relax and I'll find out who he is, I'd like to.

The group appears to have commercial possibilities, in that wah-wah, sh-boom sh-bam shuffle-rhythm thing that so many spades have fallen into, God help them. (And at the other end,

Miles and his disciples embroiled in angular algebraic twitch-
ings.) They sing in that style affected by such ofay-rich (shall
we say?) outfits as The Platters, the Plotters, the Bleaters, the
Bawlers, etc., so successful on records.

When I first began working with them, I saw that here was a
mongrel art form totally unfamiliar to me, so I listened for a
time to the Jacksonville spade radio station to get some kind of
sounding on it. I was astounded at the sticky tangle of their own
natural rhythmic sense with so-called "country" music, written
by the sharpies in Nashville and New York. It is a remarkably
cynical and opportunistic way of coming to terms with the
white Massa's ways, but so much has been lost and they've
wound up with a deplorable mess of pottage.

One amusing aspect of this sad situation is that they're selling
more records than the hillbillies, and the stumpjumpers have
been forced to imitate the black mammyjammers in order to
stay in the rat race. In any event, these aspiring recording stars
have been recording on the chapel tape machine, and I
wouldn't be surprised if they make it big. Tony the leader has
been coming on strong, apparently in search of a whitey-trophy
and he may get it—there's nothing else on the burner at present.

I had a brief note from the good gray doctor. He sent me the
name of his agent with the suggestion I send some stuff there, so
I'm trying to whip something out of the everywhere into the
here, and see what happens.

Nice to know you'll be at the new Aqueduct track. The Big
A, from all reports, is so glossy, fabulous, huge and spangled
with chrome that I'm sure horses must seem anachronistic. Just
a question of time till they find something more suitable.

Write if you get work—Jim

Raiford, Florida
OCTOBER 15, 1959

Dear Doug:

I have been hoping for a reply to my letter of Sept 10,
but since none has been forthcoming, let me say that I was

tremendously pleased by the wonderful box of books and music which arrived some time ago, and especially delighted with a few of the things. The Celine *Death On the Installment Plan* was a fine surprise. I'm grateful for the chance to reread a prime favorite of mine. It is an unrelenting, unremitting psalm of misanthropy; Celine sings as lyrically of hate as other poets of love. It is a terrific kick in the stomach and a powerful work of art, in my opinion.

As for poor bounced-around Lady Chat, I dunno. I read the clipped version some years ago, and now after having read the complete text, I can't agree with you that the restored pieces improve the book, though they would seem to raise the caloric content somewhat. To me, it seems a betrayal by D.H. of his lovers, that in their moments of high passion and fulfillment they should be made to talk like a couple of slobs. Nothing to do with morality, it's a matter of sound. In these scenes which should vibrate and sing with tenderness, these articulated crudities strike a jarring note. The ear is stunned, belief collapses, and the whole scene topples into travesty.

There's the familiar story of Dorothy Parker calling the book "the great earth-scented work of a dead genius," whereupon Alex Woollcott observed that she must have had a cold in the head when she read it. But it isn't my nose that has been assaulted by those passages—my ear has been insulted.

Even so, D.H. continues to delight with the freshness of his viewpoint and shrewdness of observation, and the hot honesty of his writing. I still find myself warmed sometimes by the occasional clumsiness of expression his integrity leads him into. Aside from those blockbusters.

Some of the music you sent was a bit beyond me, as far as technical execution goes. I tried to play those Mozart things, hacking my way inch by inch, and it was like somebody barefoot and blind on a mile of broken bottles. I fared better with some of the other stuff.

The music store job sounds almost ideal. If I may presume, I would say that such an unhassled leisurely atmosphere is the best thing for you in this period of waiting and transition.

THE JOINT 239

Incidentally, in my previous letter I made some foolish statements about music and musicians that I will withdraw. Modern jazz is always interesting and those who make it are artists worthy of every consideration in their attempts to stretch limits and widen horizons. But the peripheral element has grievously polluted and poisoned the surroundings. It's difficult enough to create and perform without having to deal with a pack of debased baboons.

J.P. came back with twenty years and has begun the same dismal familiar routine. I remonstrated, mildly, and he snarled. Now I try not to see it—it stabs me to see the cat doubt and despise himself so much.

Still have the same cellmate, the unregenerate assassin, who continues to be a bag of unscratched itches and unvoiced yearnings, but I no longer allow it to get in my preoccupied way. If I think about it all, I guess I feel sorry, but genuine pity I reserve for people who don't like me.

I'm still working on my thing (now *Along About Midnight*), and my feeling about it ranges from dubious to suicidal, but it seems to be getting longer.

The purchase of that Cadillac has sort of stuck in my mind. . . . Status symbol?   Hang in,—Jim

Raiford, Florida
November 5, 1959

Dear Doug:

The New Yorker subscription has started and there is no way I can tell you, Ol' Gros-Derriere, what I feel except that I am profoundly grateful—— The short thing by John Updike (letter to the Greek orphan) was like everything he does, spare, acute, brilliant. I think his artistic growth will be as sure and certain and delicately strong as a bamboo tree. An unqualified pleasure. The comment on those diseased TV quiz shows was penetrating, voicing the truth that everybody else skirted; it does seem peculiar that it was possible to corrupt so easily so many people, upstanding Murcans all, with never a peep from any one of those approached. When a reporter at a White House press conference asked lovable old Father-Image Ike if he cared to comment on the larger implication of the affair (the low national morality standard), Mr Prez delivered a glib and folksy (and reassuring and heartwarming, bygod) evasion about Shoeless Joe Jackson and the Black Sox of 1919. (Say it ain't so, Ike!)

Since La Madonna Dolorosa Conway departed in a flurry of recriminations and shredded motets, I've taken over the direction of the choirs at the chapel, and I'm working on a short (Protestant) Xmas play with music for the Yuletide seizure. As long as I'm doing it I'd like to try something that would be a departure from the moribund thing it has too often been. (The hell, for one thing, with Handel.) This is a little out of my line, but I'll let you know what develops. It's a challenge.

The music scene here is at a low ebb, there's nobody to blow with, so I just play piano for myself. We went out to a dance Saturday at the log house across the road, and I played organ, but it didn't matter much, the group was shirttail and nothing got said anyway.

I've been doing a little better with the music you sent; after a period of practice, I can handle the Prokofiev and feel strong enough to try whatever else you might care to send. Is there available Ravel's *Mother Goose*, or Debussy—Arabesques, Nocturnes, Miroirs. Perhaps I could play those again with a little trying.

Our electronic wizard has rigged up a central FM transmitting arrangement, whereby we can get static-free music on AM receivers. The amount of classical music is limited, since Ed just doesn't have the tapes. If you have any you care to lend, it would be Kulturny.

For now, trumpeter, and please keep in touch.   Ever, Jim

Raiford, Florida
NOVEMBER 27, 1959

[This letter via Chaplain]

Dear Doug:

The reply from the Reverend Doctor was immaculately cour-
teous, almost antiseptic. He said that the matter of my parole
was between me and the states of Florida and Illinois; that if
I did succeed in being paroled to Chicago, *and* if there was
room for me at the House, then we would talk further. (No
Room At The Inn!) I don't know what gave him the impression I was asking to stay with him. His reply made me realize
how extravagantly optimistic and hopeful I had been. I felt
like I'd been slapped in the chops with a wet cassock.

In view of this implicit peremptory putdown, I don't know
whether you'll feel like pursuing it any further or not. I've
felt quite deflated ever since I got that frosty reply— I want
so badly to come up there. Did you tell him what an ingratiat-
ing bundle of threadbare charm I really am? What a find,
liturgical-wise? Perhaps you could remind him that history has
dealt harshly with another stud who washed his hands in a
similar situation.

Thank you for the box of books and music. I would like
to say what a rush of affection and gratitude I felt when I
saw them, but I am deterred by the fear of setting off the
stupid and unnecessary system of alarm bells in that brass-
bound bourgeois skull of yours. Stay pliable, baby. The heat
a candle gives is negligible, but the light can be a warming
thing in the darkness. At this late stage I am an emotional
cinder, and light means more to me than any ephemeral heat.
Okay? Awright.

That was a deft and telling shaft about Prokofiev's *Visions*
being simple enough for an "ex-aspirant now organist Rush
Street Style." I'm glad to see you haven't mellowed. Only, in
the general barrage of whale dung you got poor Sergei splashed

too. Do you decry simplicity, Sir? The *Visions* are a delight, their simplicity cunningly distilled. They are rewarding to play, and I think in time I will play them with perception and understanding. However, since you seem to prefer the florid, the baroque, the ornate, you will be glad to hear that I am also preparing a concert arrangement of Grainger's *Country Gardens*. At one point in this arrangement I play octave runs with my elbows while wiggling my ears, and for a finish my nose explodes.

I plunged forthwith into the Nabokov stories. He is a sorcerer —in no other writer's works, save perhaps Faulkner's, am I so persuaded and enthralled. In one of the stories there is a passage about a dog barking in the silence of the country at night—"He barks—then listens for what he cannot hear"— And I was suddenly transported to a night, years gone, when I stood on the bank of the St Lawrence at night and listened to a barking dog. It was high summer, I was driving to Montreal with somebody (of whom now only the face remains, and a vague antipathy) and we had stopped for the night at a house in the country where an old French woman rented rooms. I remember that the solid provincial security of the house, the glowing cleanliness of the room, seemed a silent rebuke to the squalor of the excursion I was on, and, deeply discontented with myself, I walked outside to be alone and ask myself some questions. It was pitch black, the stars were awesomely near, the night and the broad river were one vast endless sigh. And suddenly, away off, the thin barking of a dog, and silence again. The enormous dark closed around that valiant, questioning canine voice— loneliness and bewilderment engulfed me, and I stood by the water and wept, for myself, for the dog, for all creatures lost and alone in the night.

The vaulting imagination of Nabokov can do that to me, the evocations are so vivid they can summon suddenly and with no warning scenes long buried and forgotten.

Another of his images I will keep: The bare foot of the "incredibly agile" medium stroking (in simulation of a ghostly hand) the kind, trusting cheek of the Empress Eugenie.

At the end of your letter I am given some stern adjurations. You say my letters have a "profound" quality, which they do not, so I can only assume that "profound" is a sly euphemism for something else. I haven't forgotten your bag of ploys. Your concern is delicately and tactfully expressed (I never in the blue-eyed world expected to associate tact with you, the apotheosis of insolence). Let me reassure you. Throw it out your mind. I have not remained static. Having discovered for myself that my emotionalism was hampering me, I have foresworn it, have been celibate for a long time now, and will so remain because I have too much I want to do, and such entanglements get in the way. If there had not been intellectual rapport between us, wary respect, laughter, friendship, there would now probably be nothing. That is what you're hearing in the letters, at least that is what I try to convey. You never could field nuances. As for the masochism and its counterpart, I think that may be a conception you have devised for your own inscrutable purposes. However, your offer to oblige is duly noted. Okay? Awright.

The Christmas play is taking on a recognizable shape and beginning to breathe, to my shaken astonishment. The various components, staging, dialogue, incidental music, are falling into place and I find my involvement deepened. It's a sobering thing, hearing lines I wrote spoken by actors, pretty good actors. Probably bad for me, I'm beginning to feel stage-struck. To the extent that I plan a longer one when this is out of the way. There's a small nucleus of pro actors here, Equity and AFTRA members (4), and a director—so it could be a Raiford Risorgimento in the Drama. I already got our next smash in my head. In any case, it keeps the general defeatism of the joint at bay, and eases the waiting.

You enquire what's permissible for Christmas, so I enclose a sample package permit, Santa Claus version. Practically speaking, I'm in bad need of a sweat shirt and an alarm clock. (Stolen by an international jewel thief.) Send by the usual channel, dig? Incidentally, the good Chap was upset about the flammable mags you sent, he didn't say much but I could see. Evergreen, okay, but that Hefner jazz is for retarded jock-straps. —And he is a good Chap, realistic but still believes, and that's a rare good trick. So attend, no more raunchy yocks, please? Maybe you should stay away from that bowling alley. I hope that something can be done to warm the chilly attitude of the Rev. Dr. to my parole aspirations. If you feel like sounding him, let me hear. If it don't happen I'll have to try something else. Meanwhile, sois tranquil.   Yrs, Buddy-Buddily, Jim

Raiford, Florida
DECEMBER 10, 1959

Dear James:

So many important people have made comments pro and con about your book that I feel somewhat diffident in venturing an opinion, but I'll chance it anyway.

Malcolm is of course a tour de force; in these days when there are so many swollen sagas of soul-scratching, redolent of armpits and crotches, it is a delicately lethal little fable. I was delighted, and outraged and baffled and disturbed. Still am, it haunts me somewhat. Like G. Stein, you seem to have found a way of dipping the simple words into a sort of acid bath and rendering them lustrous-new, the original purity restored. With something added, a patrician and infinitely gracious kind of poison. *Malcolm* seems to me like a mannered fairy tale bathed in pale green light, the glow a curious and deadly phosphorescent one. The venom artfully distilled, the effervescence stinging. The jewel, skilfully faceted, glitters rather than sparkles. Which I guess is what you were about, if so, you are formidably deft. I am fascinated and repelled and filled with admiration. As I say, it is a tour de force, maybe a tour jeté.

I trust I do not offend, that would be a pity, it is merely that the book impressed me so much that I struggle to say exactly how I feel about it. Maybe I should think some more and try to clarify my reactions.

Here on the campus we are preparing for the Yule season. I've written a play and some music to go with it, a morality play I guess it is, with laughs. The Chaplain has allowed us surprising latitude and we've been tinkering a bit with the traditionally pious attitudes towards the Nativity story. Have three actors and a director who worked at it outside before they collided with Society.

My first attempt at drama, it is positively perilous, I hear my dialogue spoken by actors and I can feel incipient megalomania creeping upon me. Please write, James, tell me what coruscant things have happened to you since your succes d'estime.   Warmest, —Jim

PS—I haven't heard from Gertrude. I daresay she is pleased, if livid.

                                                   Raiford, Florida
                                            DECEMBER 14, 1959

Mr. Jay Landesman
Crystal Palace
St. Louis Missouri

Dear Mr. Landesman:

Nelson Algren has told me about your offer of a job to help me get out on parole. I can't adequately express what I feel about this wonderful gesture, so I won't even try; all I can say is that I'll try to prove myself worthy of the opportunity.

A couple of things will have to be done in order to expedite the project of springing me from this academy—I will have to have a complete parole plan, as it is called, to present to the Florida Parole Commission. If you will write a letter to my immediate supervisor here, outlining the job, salary, any other details you might think pertinent, I can include the letter from you when I make my pitch to the Florida authorities. Also, it is necessary to ascertain if the Missouri parole authorities would be willing to accept me. You being on the scene there,

I imagine it will be easier for you to get this information.

I must say I think it is an inspired idea to make a musical from "A Walk On The Wild Side"—something good should come from that. We are a little out of touch here on the campus, but I was able to see some of the comment on your recent Broadway invasion. I got the impression that the insular New York mob approached it with foreboding, were happily astonished, but never quite able to overcome completely their apprehension over the assault by the outlanders.

You're probably up to your eyeballs with this new show, and for that reason I appreciate all the more your kind interest. If you have time, I'd like to hear from you. You can write to me in care of the Chaplain.   Sincerely, Jim Blake

Raiford, Florida
DECEMBER 17, 1959

Dear Mike:

The news that somebody might be interested in getting me out of here on parole hit me right on top of the head. I've been walking on my hands ever since. I wrote to Chicago as you suggested, and then to Jay Landesman asking for particulars that I could present to the parole board. I'm afraid to hope much as yet, but it's hard to keep from it—the first ray of light through the murk in a long time. I've been in a rather bleak frame of mind for quite a while. Asceticism has become my way of life— from choice, I might say. On one of the longest nights, I permitted myself an honest count of the pile of years behind me and decided to desert my peccadilloes before they deserted me.

In place of dancing around the temple fires, I tried for increased mental activity and went in heavily for keeping a journal. Sparing myself nothing, until I began to get hooked on it and it was like literary onanism. As if I had traded Moloch for Masoch.

Actually I enjoy the luxury of a journal that lets me harangue.

Maybe forsaking the chichi mob has made me more aware of larger things, but it seems to me there never was such a good time for haranguing. So much to holler about: like making a bold show of taking weed-killer out of cranberries, while sneaking Strontium-90 into the oatmeal. And recklessly curing people of sleeping sickness in New Jersey, when for those who have to live there it could be Utopia gained. What's happening?

We are busy here with final rehearsals on the Christmas play. Chaplain is a fairly liberal realistic type and he allowed a fair amount of secular leeway with the script, so I was able to say a couple of things and try for some laughs. The company includes four cons who were actors on the outside, and a rather brocaded director, a friend of somebody called Tennessee Williams, who I gather is nothing like Tennessee Ernie. The director gives a bravura performance, better than the actors. Such fire. And the cons argue with the director about things like Motivation, which sets me up enormously. I feel like I'm really at last breathing the heady air of the Thitter. Though it's hard to say how I could be more Off Broadway and still be in the U S & A.

How about if you come South (I mean when) letting me know and paying a visit. alors,—Jim

Raiford, Florida
DECEMBER 30, 1959

Dear Doug:

The thing that made Christmas bright for me was that bewitching little white paper tree with all your names on it. Not only for the simple grace of it, but also for the image of a happy harmonious family it brought. I received it in the box of treasures on Christmas morning, and went through the day in a bubble of contentment, insulated from the idle futility of the joint. For the beautiful sweater, the books (Cherished Nabokov! Exalted Graves!)— The shirts, the cunning so-slender lighter— The useful sweat shirts and the clock (ticking sturdily on the bookcase in the cell as I write in the midnight silence of the jailhouse)— For all the lovely and strangely novel food— Let me try to send affectionate thanks to you and to your handsome family.

Our Christmas show on the campus, I am happy to modestly report, was an unqualified socko smashereenie. We did the first performance for outsiders, and when it came to the pathos of the play's ending, there wasn't a dry eye. And in the funny bits, we got the laughs, though subdued. I was rather anxious to get reactions, having written, as much as was feasible, from the humanistic rather than pietistic standpoint. Willy-nilly I had gambled, something of what I believe in was involved.

As for the Rock dwellers, it seemed footless to expect even a few tears, and in that I was right, though, mirabile dictu, there was a sheepish stunned silence. I don't know, there was an effect of suspended breathing. (Did I tell you it was about some convicts on Christmas Eve?) So I was in the wings, where we stashed the choir for background music in the Biblical flashbacks, nervously wondering if we were going to get the laughs where they were supposed to be. When the first spontaneous roar of laughter went over the house, and then another, the director and I smiled shakily at one another. He looked as if he'd prefer to cry. Strange exhilaration, planning for a reaction like that and having it come off. Of course our chief player was a pro outside, a TV performer. Outrageous ham. A Jewish cat from Jersey, with the most mobile plastic features I've ever seen, great reproachful beseeching eyes that one could drown in. At curtain fall, there was a raucous ovation. I realize that it was at a primitive level, including the drama, but it was a most beautiful sound, that noise. In some way I do not completely understand, I am involved with the savages, and it was for them I wrote it.

So now we plan to keep the nucleus of a dramatic group going, for kicks. I'm working on a comedy, a farce I guess it will be, set in an isolated house on a remote Florida key during the time of the submarine scares of World War II. Characters are the various night creatures who assemble for assorted skullduggery. Writing it won't interfere to any extent with the other thing I'm into. Dialogue seems to come easy, pretty much off the top of my head without too much sweat. I have no illusions that it's Art.

Jay and Fran Landesman from the Crystal Palace in St. Louis have offered me a gig to get me out on parole, so I wrote them outlining what must be done and am waiting to hear. They're rich, and influential around St Loo, so it's possible they can swing it up there if these people will go along.

In my last letter I'm afraid I was guilty of some rather portentous noises, but I consider that I was mischievously provoked. I am plagued by the suspicion that you were at your familiar tactic of maneuvering me into making an ass of myself, yet once again. Alors, Bonne Annee. When you stop whirling on the holiday carrousel, let me hear.   ever,—Jim

PART VII

inside show biz

Raiford, Florida
JANUARY 18, 1960

Mr. ——, Attorney
Chicago, Illinois

Dear Sir:

I am trying to obtain a parole from this institution in order to take a job in St. Louis, as pianist at the Crystal Palace Theatre, operated by Jay and Fran Landesman.

I am now serving the third year of a ten-year sentence for two counts of Breaking and Entering (to which I pled guilty), on each of which I received five years, to run consecutively. My arrest and conviction occurred in Jackonville, Duval County, Florida. My sentence began on May 9, 1957, and with accrued gain time should expire somewhere around May 29, 1963.

I have been working for the Prison Chaplain for over two and a half years as chapel organist and have a perfect prison record with no disciplinary reports in that time. Also, the Protestant and Catholic Chaplains have agreed to recommend me for a parole. I have not yet made any request of the Florida Parole Commission. It is my thought that my chances would be improved if I had a complete Parole Plan to submit to them.

If you have any questions about this matter, I shall be only too glad to hear from you. Address your letter to the Chaplain and include my name on the inside of the letter. Thank you for any help you may see fit to give me.

Very truly yours, James Blake ⌗59894

Raiford, Florida
JANUARY 21, 1960

Dear Gertrude:

Glad to hear about the Lake Forest Squire, not so glad to hear about another bébé en route. From what I have gathered, bread is the paramount thing in that union, and another dependent will only dissipate it more quickly. Doug had some private dreams about Paris and like that, and a burgeoning family won't simplify anything.

My good ol' employer and supervisor here, the Chaplain, was interested when I told him about your inspirational paintings in Perspective magazine and he said he'd like to see them. His address is, somehow, same as mine. Don't send them to me, but you might mention me in a note, so he'll know.

I'm having a ball with the script of The Rascal By Night, the first production of our Little Theatre. We thought of calling ourselves The Penal Players, but that took an awful kicking around, so we settled for Grope Theatre, thus forestalling the dirtymouths.

Before Doug got mad, or bored, he sent Nabokov's *Invitation To A Beheading*, which I've just finished. The man owns a seemingly inexhaustible irony mine and I'm glad the Strong Vladimir is around these days, so many slobs writing books. What a comment on the period, when the innocent and ineffectual pursuits of the beats should be classed as Social Protest. Musicians did and said all those things long ago and simply thought they were having a ball. To give it the ponderous name of Protest, my god how sad.   Hang in,—Jim

Raiford, Florida
FEBRUARY 2, 1960

Dear Nelson:

That laconic note you sent confused me, though I followed your directions implicitly and wrote the lawyer all the information you indicated. I invited him to reply, mainly to find out who he was, but I haven't heard. So who is he and how does he figure in this? Also the letter to Landesman with another winsome invitation to correspond availed nothing and I'm pretty much in the dark. How does it look?

It isn't exactly a simple matter to get out of here on parole; it can be a dauntingly protracted process, but it is said on campus that an out-of-state parole is easier come by than one in Florida. Distance lending enchantment, perhaps. First thing to be done on that end is getting the assurance of the Missouri parole people that they will take me in charge.

I'm rereading Celine's *Death On The Installment Plan* and it is pure delight. First time around some years ago, it was so outrageous to me I was stunned. I'd stop reading and lay it down in consternation. Now after a long diet of the school-of-understatement-and-clenched-jaws, the cautious studied style that is called "spare," "controlled," "economical," I am reveling in Celine's spewing a torrent of lyrical nihilism and smashing the furniture. And his furious anguished laughter at human perfidy too overwhelming for tears. When I compare this wild singing to the staid starched sepulchral neo-Scriptural journalism of Hemingway, I am aghast at the gulf between. Assuredly litchur is a various thing. Probably it's not fair to put anybody up against such a maniacal poet and his explosions.

The dramatic renaissance on campus is temporarily in abeyance while I work on an adaptation for radio of that quaint old spook tale *The Monkey's Paw*. We plan to tape this for the broadcasting setup one of the cons has arranged here, a limited contrivance that transmits within the prison. I have to

get this done because the director keeps nagging me. After
we get the one-acter rolling, I'll go back to the longer one
we plan for stage presentation in the auditorium of the joint,
a hokey pastiche of midnight mischief and comedy, one hopes,
called The Rascal By Night.

It must perforce be written with an eye to our audience,
the shaggiest extant, but there are some sophisticated wastrel
types in the action, which gives me a chance to write what
I imagine is brittle dialogue. I was gratified at the raucous
ovation we got from the savages at the final curtain of our
Christmas xtravaganza—my, but they are perverse and difficult, and most times I could cheerfully see them all to the
gallows, but on that occasion I felt pretty warm about the
whole thing.

Speaking of dialogue, I have been wondering how musicians
out there talk nowadays. In here every knave and troll I meet
comes on like a hipster. What's happening? Is this a universal
trend?

May I hear something? Are you going to vote for Kennedy
and trade the Pope for the Mope?

                                —Doucement, doucement,—Jim

                                        Raiford, Florida
                                     FEBRUARY 8, 1960

Dear Doug:

New developments in the parole effort: I've definitely got
the theater job in St Loo and Nelson has enlisted the services
of a Chicago lawyer. More than that I haven't heard and I'm
quietly dying about that.

Good to hear that the degree of laissez faire in your arrangements permits you to range as far afield as the West Coast.
Your going out there on business suggests that you've attained
a self-employed status again. Did you stop being an employment counsellor? (Stiffish title, that.) Should think the best

counsel one could give anybody on employment would be "Evade it."

Disturbing to hear that you're allowing yourself to vegetate. ("No reading, no blowing, continuous TV.") What *are* you doing? Boredom, somebody once said, is the penalty we pay for failure to realize our capacities. Yours is a lean and hungry mind, or it was. It would be a great pity if you allowed yourself to get fat on fudge. This is an exhilarating period in which to be alive and alert, it seems to me. The culture is being frightened, higgledy-pig, out of its intellectual-baiting stance. The bourgeois boobs, plump and sleek from eight years of lies and lullabies, have looked over their shoulders and seen the looming wave of the future; and the hairy Russian robber has been in some diabolical way transformed into a suave economic slicker. The bear that walks like a man has assumed a new and terrifying aspect; it now wears horn-rimmed glasses; the Cossack has abandoned the knout for the fountain pen and is writing astronomical checks. Highly diverting to watch the comic dilemma of the capitalists as they strive to devise some pious formula which will enable them to hang on to what they've grabbed, and at the same time try to cope with this shrewd and shifty adversary. In the approaching period of ferment, the arts are bound to be bubbling and hissing and, as I say, it's not time to vegetate.

Even with keeping 3 or 4 balloons in the air, I still find time for reading. I thought the current New Yorker had a couple of fine things: The essay by the admirable Updike on The Wild Bore was deft and acidulous. It was like being sprayed with a fine ammonia mist.

I'm glad you found *Malcolm* delightful. I was unable to decide what I actually thought about it, even after reading it again. For a comedy, it seems curiously inert and lacking a pulse. So I was somewhat relieved when Whitney Balliett expressed the same bafflement—"The more you poke it in an attempt to discover what it is, the more it has a tendency to fade away and disappear." I don't think James was pleased with what I said, but he asked me for an opinion. Perhaps it doesn't matter to him what I think . . .

I'm nearly finished with the second act of the comedy we plan to do with the resident repertory group. (Calling it for now "The Rascal By Night" though that may change.) Having fun doing it. This is my first attempt at comedy, i.e., where I try to be funny, as contrasted to certain previous efforts when I didn't and was.

Very little socializing and no more dynamic duets, celibacy suits my present purposes and I turn the energy into more productive, if less galvanic, channels. I converse with more people than I ever did before (due to the job I have) but I actually *talk* to no one but Cliff the cellmate and Jamie, the cat who directed the Christmas play. On the surface he's maybe a trifle chichi, but basically sound and discerning and there's a questing imagination there. Cliff is the nearest thing I can get to having no cellmate at all, when he's in his hedge-hog moods, but mostly we vibrate in harmony. I devote a good deal of time and thought to music, direct the choirs, practice piano every day and have learned to play about 3½ Prokofiev Visions. No musicians in the band, nothing happening there—just thump clump thump clump. So life is full of projects and pursuits, busy, interesting—and solitary. But inside me, it's crowded with phantoms.

Write soon, bearded paterfamilias, tell about the California scene.   ever,—Jim

Raiford, Florida
FEBRUARY 18, 1960

Dear Mike:

There was a note from Algren, didn't seem to know where you were. I assume you're still in Miami, hortatorily harrying horses at Hialeah, so I'm sending this there. The brusque Dr was crying havoc, said he is shirtless, despised, abandoned. He sounded embattled. I remember just such a hollow doomsaying from the depth of despond at the time he was completing The Wild Side. Then, too, he was against the wall, beset, hacking and slashing at a horde of adversaries. Perhaps these are birth pangs, too. I hope so, devoutly. The world is drowning in merde and has need of mordant song.

The parole hope that was so bright seems to be ganging agley. I'm told the show based on "Wild Side" is on the point of opening, or has opened in St Loo. I certainly would have liked to help with the music end of it; I am so fond of the book, and I had a fierce bright vision of what the music should be. Seems to me it would have to be blues, not facsimile, but the flavor and feeling of the blues. Every time I see a drama about New Orleans on TV or in the films, I hear that ol' clarinet, playing that nostalgic passage that brings back Mezz Mezzrow blowing his goose-call, and that sure don't make it. Unless you're a goose, and in New Orleans. Closer to it is the way Gershwin related the Porgy and Bess music to the blues feeling. Here I should simper and say of course I'm no Gershwin, but we both know that. Well, you know it.

It was a great relief to see the Algerian situation cooled, I worry about the French. The spectacle of Frenchman against Frenchman is a distressing one, except in the Bardot films, where it is not. But I think I have hit upon a solution which will preclude further insurrection. Simply pave the streets of Algiers with solid asphalt. This will eliminate paving blocks. No Frenchman worthy of the name would dream of erecting a barricade without paving stones. Et voila, la paix eternelle.

Before you follow the swallow back Nawth, I'd like to say this about visiting—perhaps you have a picture of a grim white-tiled room, mesh screens, glowering guards, as in the films. Visiting here is done in a pleasant little park with mockingbirds, waving palms, every prospect pleases. We could rap. Anyway, write before that, por favor. A small cautionary note about writing. On mail I have recently received, the cancellation bears a message from the eminent bibliophile, the Postmaster-General, and he says "Report All Obscene Mail." So if you have anything salacious or lurid on your mind, forbear. I should hate to find myself torn between love of country and love of thee. Okay? —Jim

Raiford, Florida
FEBRUARY 25, 1960

Dear Gertrude:

The gray skies have dripped steadily all day, and it is still raining as I write late at night. Weather like this squeezes my spirit flat, the Florida landscape is so woebegone in the rain. Everything is open here, no walls, and flat as a table, and when there is no open sky, a dimension is gone and it is all very oppressive and claustrophobic.

Yesterday the sky was an immense vaulted electric blue, shedding the strange winter light that is sometimes seen in north Florida, white-lemon-gold, washing everything with a radiance that seems to glow from the ground as much as fall from the sky. The buildings here are whitewashed, and when this light is on them, they seem to emit the rays as much as reflect them. On these days when the world is all gold-white and green I feel this animal joy beginning to bubble in me and I want to leap and growl and roll in the gold-green grass. But of course I can't, miscreants must preserve docorum. So I just secretly vibrate.

I should have written sooner to say how much I liked your paintings in the FMT Fine Arts Guide; dramatic, provocative, a shade sinister. Like you, in fact. That portrait of you on your Empire settee is a production—regal, inscrutable, menacing. (Is that a body under that sofa?) You are a Borgia who has successfully maneuvered the potion into the Cardinal's cup, and benignly you await the result. And your demure little nosegay—mandragora, is it not?

I've got our play into the second act now, but I seem to be stuck. A question of getting characters off the stage once they get on. I'm considering an all-purpose device for this problem. They look off into the wings and say, "I'll be right

with you." Or simpler yet, they say, "Later," and split. The
actors are hot to trot, they keep asking about it. Trying to
keep up with everything, reading, music and my work at the
Temple, I stay harried. But it keeps the torch from smoking
up my glasses. The flame is still bur-neeng.

The Chap has promised that I can drop my office duties
shortly and concentrate on music teaching, choral and instru-
mental. A break, and a challenge, more stimulating. Quite a
few cats want to study piano— and I've found a new-cock
with a fantastically robust bass-baritone the color of bronze.
A young (20) Canadian stud from Montreal who's done some
work on CBC. I've written like a religious aria for him, a
dramatic thing based on the blinding of Saul on the Damascus
Road. A flamboyant episode, I always thought, and it lends
itself to thrashing and gnashing. First time I ever tried this
form but then it's the first Canadian wolf I ever met with
such a vibrant howl. ("How'd you like to play the Vatican,
kid?")

No more news of the parole possibility. I had a glum note
from kindly Dr A, rather pessimistic. The show based on
"Wild Side" opened in St Loo without my vivid assistance. I
hope it happens big for Nelson's sake.

I heard from Doug before he went to California on business
for two weeks, nothing since then. You heard? Does he seem
to be doing all right avoiding the simian sur-le-dos? I daren't
ask him, and it remains always a fear with me.

Deep night now, and still raining and donnering und blitzening,
I'll totter to my simple pallet and assume the foetal attitude
and maybe this time I'll make it all the way back.   Later,—Jim

PS—Next morning. I am typing this at the office. The skies
weep still. It rains in my heart as it rains on the town.

Raiford, Florida
MARCH 30, 1960

Dear Mike:

Thank you for the delightful pile of money. We aren't permitted to handle the money order itself, merely notified that it has arrived and has been deposited in the bank to be drawn against. By my anchorite standards it is a rajah's ransom, and I feel pleasantly burdened by my sudden affluence. —But, no letter?

Have you heard anything about how the "Wild Side" musical is doing at Crystal Palace? There has been nothing from Nelson, nothing from the barrister either, so I guess the parole thing is decidedly dormant. The whole thing blew in, blew up and blew out in such a hurry I hardly had time to grasp the reality of it, and it seems like a dream.

I'm in charge of the Chapel choirs here, and in this capacity I also handle recruiting of new members. About a week ago a very rugged tush hog stopped me in the yard and handed me a slip of paper with a name and number on it. "For your choir," he growls, and I got the impression a little extra attention was indicated. There was also a notation, "Plays piano and organ," and I thought, great, a musician.

So I had a call-out issued for this candidate for Saturday, when I audition aspiring choristers. This one turned out to be more than slightly androgynous. Built like a tackle though, most unsettling, and he drooped over me like a wilting sunflower. The face vacuous, with milky blue eyes (technically enhanced) so wide-set I was reminded of a flounder. Falsely hearty, and talking too loud, I said, "Understand you play piano?" The enhanced eyelids drooped at the tedious question. "Oh yes. I studied at Juilliard." In a breathy wispy contralto, like the Countess in Antic Hay who always spoke as if from her deathbed.

The majestic name dropped like an anvil and shook the building, jarring me completely out of countenance. I babbled disjointed conversation until the virtuoso was summoned by the Chaplain for a preliminary interview. It was a long one and the Chaplain emerged from it glassy-eyed. "See what *you* think," he said abstractedly, and I took the willowy aspirant into the chapel.

I invited him to try the piano. He sat down, placed his hands tentatively on the keys. Long silence. Apparently lost in thought, eyes downcast. He raised his eyes to peer myopically across the sanctuary. "Is that—is that the organ over there?" Wistfully. "Could I try that?" I switched on the organ, feeling a witless gallant, and the musician seated himself, shuffled his feet aimlessly on the pedals, peered down at them. He placed flat fingers on the keys. A small blue doubt bloomed in my head. The organ emitted a startled bleat, and there began a mewling disconsolate melody of no recognizable pattern, like a despondent seal on the bagpipe.

Trapped, I thought—with a guilty sense of involvement—trapped in a madman's fantasy. The strange eerie music ceased abruptly. He put long pale fingers to his temples, his eyes closed. The milky eyes, wide and guileless, were turned on me. "I was in a terrible train wreck a couple of months ago, and ever since then—ever since then—" The voice trailed away and returned, "I have a beautiful organ at home—it's bigger than this one—but ever since my accident, I sit down at it, and I can't bear to play—I don't know . . ."

The voice died away. Long silence. "Maybe some time when you feel better," I said hollowly. "Yes. Maybe some other time."

A train wreck, think of it. Must be a traumatic thing. An entire Juilliard education shot to hell. In the midst of life we are in death.   Later,—Jim

Raiford, Florida
APRIL 5, 1960

Dear Mike:

You have a way of making statements, veiled inscrutable statements, when you write, that fairly breed questions: What are you working at now? Was the show out of "Wild Side" really called "House Of A Thousand Grassfires," or is that a jocosity of Dr A? And what is the kindly doctor doing in Paris? At this time, I mean.

To answer your queries: I do not have a parole going for me, have not been interviewed by the parole board. What I am trying to do before I even sound them is to ascertain where away from Florida I could go on parole, what state would take me in charge. I figure if I have a parole plan to offer, that is, a definite job to go to, it would expedite the whole deal. I wrote to the lawyer in Chicago and asked him the Illinois requirements, but no answer. That's what bugs me, nothing hot or cold from nobody is disconcerting.

I saw in the Herald Trib that Landesman's joint, Crystal Palace, has a revue called *Hostilities of 1960*. Good title, how is the show? And I read an article on St Louis in *Holiday* by an Irisher called O'Fallon (only it was more deviously Gaelic in the spelling, and it was bedad). Piece mentioned Landesman in passing, called him an inspired lunatic, something like that, the tone was ponderously arch. This Hibernian tourist seemed to find the town something of a dog's dinner. Even so, I got the impression that there are pockets of yeastiness there that would be worth exploring. Big river towns are rarely completely dull. There's a person here from St Louis, a real blank, when I asked him about night life there he mentioned a number of Italian-sounding names. Speaking the names with such a hushed air of gravity that I gathered they must be bad guys, probably gangsters, I wouldn't be surprised.

There has been a new addition to the Chapel staff, which has brightened the atmosphere considerably. Stud from Panama City, plays a splashy driving piano and percussive jazz organ. One of the PG nomads, the dreariest kind of junkie, in for a fin for signing the book wrong. He knows all the good tunes and we play piano-organ duets which are at times inventive and interesting, I think.

We turn on when the means are at hand, nothing hard, tu sais, and experiment with sounds, and it adorns the atmosphere somewhat. His official job is helping me to furnish liturgical background noises for the myriad splinter groups that use the temple for their arcane rituals. Everybody wants to wail in the style of his forbears (or was it three bears?) so we get them all—Hashemites, Jansenists, Bleeders, Sheep-Shunners, etc. (The last a militant group which eschews mutton.) No priapic pilgrims as yet, but I hear there are numerous postulants in the joint.

The NY'er subscription would be the greatest if you can swing it with no sweat. I manage to lay hands on a few back numbers, and recently in an old Esquire I read T. Williams' *Sweet Bird Of Youth*. A gaudy, lyrical, bravura piece of play-crafting, in my opinion. Just reading it, I was seized and in-volved— probably seeing it performed would prostrate me entire.

Let me hear from you, little pudding.　　　　ever, —Jim

Raiford, Florida
APRIL 11, 1960

Dear Mike:

I was dismayed to hear that you had not received my last letter. Perhaps it has been delayed in transit and by now you have it. If not, please let me know when you get this. Naturally I wrote as soon as I could to thank you for the very respectable chunk of bread. I don't often see that kind of loot, and it was a miraculous windfall, and at a fortuitous time. I'd just lost my gig with the minions of Rome and I was on the rocks. If there was a hangup in the mailing of that last missive, I suspect it may have been the unsuitable frivolity of it; penance, like secks, is a downright serious thing and does not permit mockery.

Sorry to hear that the "Wild Side" show didn't make it. For Nelson's sake, I regret the failure. I can't resist the presumptuous notion that I might have been able to help with it, had I been permitted. There's no assurance at all that I would have been able to transmute an empathetic involvement with the story into music and lyrics— but I'd have been on fire with the trying. (Why didn't the Dr take a hand, or did he?)

Anyway, I'm glad to know he's swingin with Simone in Paris. Something must have happened for him. The last letter from Chicago gave me the impression he was sleeping in hallways and living off the refunds from Coke bottles. Mercurial little minx, the doctor.

The parole thing has ground to a halt and I'm casting about for ways to set it in motion again. Something misfired, but what? A wall of silence.

The New Yoker subscription would be jam up. You are my hope of heaven. So I just wanted to let you know that I wrote and am not an ingrate. Let me know about that letter.

More later, —Jim

Raiford, Florida
JULY 21, 1960

Dear Gertrude:

I feel rather diffident about writing to you. For one, I haven't heard for so long, the silence is daunting. And then, you chose to communicate through Doug about the Contact magazine thing. Which leads me to think you are either angry or bored with the whole thing. If you're piqued, you have no right, but if it's boredom, that I'll buy.

I was called out for parole interview and given a set of work papers. If I can get a job which meets approval I'll be out. Perhaps you wouldn't mind asking around. Nelson wrote from Paris (I took to my bed with envy, he's been in Spain and is going to Athens) and he said Conroy had mentioned that employment might be found for me in his chicken enterprise. Chicken-plucker? If you will, please send me Jack's address and the address of the Illinois Parole Commission in Chicago. Doug once said he'd help with my parole—would you sound him? He should be off the leash by this time, and might know of something.

Somebody may be around to see you, the parole man asked me who was nearest and dearest—I had an absolutely blank white moment and then I told him of course you, my youngest wittiest prettiest sister, beloved of the Shah. After consideration though, it's probably wiser if Conroy should appear as the friend of the friendless. Sturdier, you know. If everybody lived as you do, there wouldn't be any bowling alleys and all that peeping from behind the curtains— but why fight city hall?

I wrote a thing for Contact magazine, but am not sure about sending. Not sure if it will fly. It's a partial examination of the vibrations in a relationship between captive and keeper, a subject which has some interesting facets.

Don't know if I approve completely of the concept of the proposed Contact issue, all devoted to the subject of "Criminal Man." Sounds somewhat pretentious and perhaps a little lip-licking. That may be touchiness. But the idea of everybody lined up in a row to speak a piece about it seems heavy-handed. I think they ought to examine Average Man, he's really hung up.

Please write. Blake is ready—but is the world ready?

Love, —Jim

Raiford, Florida
AUGUST 2, 1960

Dear Mike:

The happy word here is that I was called out quite unexpectedly for a parole interview and given a set of work papers, which means that if I can get a job and it is approved, I can leave on parole. Somewhat at a loss I was, frankly, to know what to do with the papers, and finally after some delay sent them to Gertrude. Her reply was not encouraging. She says she is trying to find jobs for three people now. Could she be running an employment service for felons? But she said she would sound the inimitable Conroy and Doug the Lake Forest squire. You think there might be something shaking for me in St Louis? Surprisingly, the parole man said there would be no objection to my working in a night club provided it wasn't a dive.

Had a letter from Dr A in Paris, had been to Spain, was going to Athens. Apparently on the upswing of a cycle, he was sparkling.

You want to read an outrageous and funny book, get *The Magic Christian* by Terry Southern.

The coming election should be entertaining. The Pope vs General Motors. Armageddon? Anyway, the Kennedy boy is fast and flamboyant. Probably just the thing for a benumbed and banana-brained, merde-mired electorate.

More next week. Got brain fag tonight. The evangelist bit is getting to be a colossal drag, dim people all about.

Love, —Jim

Raiford, Florida
AUGUST 15, 1960

Dear Jack:

As you may know by now, I have been given working papers by the parole board here, which means that if I can get a job and it is approved, I can be released. So what I need is an affluent and respectable sponsor. Do you know anybody who's rich and impeccable and benevolent? Concerning your letter to me about Contact magazine— I did not receive it and would be interested to know if you got it back. (Mail handling here is sometimes extemporaneous.) First I knew about your commending me to Contact was through Gertrude and Frank. I wrote Contact (which was allowed as business mail) and got a nice reply asking if I had anything to contribute to their projected issue on "Criminal Man." Turns out they don't pay in cash but in stock. Which struck me as a somewhat elaborate evasion and not precisely the answer to my immediate and urgent needs. But then on reflection I realized that never in my life had I been a stockholder in anything at all. And it occurred to me that having a bit of stock laid by would constitute a beachhead, so to speak, in this avaricious and materialistic society. So I decided to try to please the San Francisco people and perhaps they would make of me a stockholder.

Even though I felt that the title "Criminal Man" was regrettably lurid and misbegotten. There are of course thousands of men in prison convicted of crimes— but "criminal" is the least interesting thing they are. Which inclines me to believe that perhaps these California studs are mainly, and morbidly, interested in selling a lot of magazines. Which is only fair to the stockholders.

Well, misgivings notwithstanding, I wrote a piece anyway. An episode that has been lodged in my mind, part of a larger subject, the relationship between captive and keeper. But I probably won't be able to send it: one, it's too candid to pass official scrutiny, and two, because I have an uneasy feeling about the possible buildup it might get in something called "The Criminal Man." I can see it just as plain, "And now a few words from A Horrible Example." I don't actually feel that strongly about it, but I'm afraid I do sense something meretricious and stagey about the project. Maybe they're just naive.

Also, I have grave reservations about being a stockholder in an enterprise which gives space to a solemn slob like Ralph J. Gleason, a pretentious placebo I remember from his Downbeat days. He wrote about jazz then, and the only thing he knew for sure was the identity of the musicians who played it. How he ever missed being an agent is a mystery, he was born for it.

I guess I sound like a crosspatch. In the Contact you sent, I liked David Deck's story "Looking For A Little Strange." A sharp ear, a shrewd sardonic eye. I like Harvey Swados too, though he's written stronger things than The Swans of Avignon. A book I've had a snorting chortling time with recently is The Magic Christian by Terry Southern. Funnier than his Flash and Filigree. Nice to meet a bold and bawdy humorist these prim and edgy days. Though I must confess I dig the edginess of the times. One feels that the long Reign of the Boob may be ending, there's a stirring in the air like a dawn wind. Also I've been lucky enough to borrow three of Durrell's Alexandria Quartet— Balthazar, Mountolive and Clea. I have been quite literally spellbound by them. I haven't been so captivated by a story since The Wizard of Oz. Those dazzling enigmatic people of Alexandria have gone right on living after I closed the books, I know.

I read that Nelson's Man With The Golden Arm is to be done on TV. Is that why he fled to Europe? He wrote from Paris, told me you were retired and had a restaurant or something where you sold like pickin' chicken. If that's a gag, it's a weirdo. Please write to me, care of the Chaplain.   Regards, —Jim

Raiford, Florida
NOVEMBER 5, 1960

Dear Nelson:

The parole situation has improved to the point where it is no longer outright farce. It develops the minds who control my immediate destiny had me confused with somebody else. There was a brief note from the Parole Commission, blandly allowing that there had been an error and that investigation would now be resumed of my parole plan in St Louis. (Song Cue: When It's Parole-Jumping Time In Missouri, I'll Be Coming Back To You.)

So I wrote Landesman about that and he replied that Angie Green, the singer I'll be working with, was coming this way for a vacation in Key West with Tennessee Willie and Magnani and that mob and that she would like to stop and see me. To that I answered, fine, it would be best to do it through the Chaplain.

The election was a qualified satisfaction. There is at least a hope that the country will begin to drag itself gradually out of the muck, mediocrity, mendacity and meringue 8-years-deep. Thing that genuinely puzzles me is how the knave in the White House has been able to emerge unscathed and unscourged.

Sad about Norman Mailer. I hope fervently that he can

extricate himself from the hands of the brutish ones and acquire in time a measure of cunning. It has seemed to me lately that he was making some nonsensical cultish noises, but he remains a vital and compelling and provocative writer, in my opinion. But publicly to sing praises of pot is simply puerile. Pot is for peons, everybody knows that.

Tell me of your Parisian adventures. How is the regal Simone? Did you meet Francoise Sagan? Oh, I got that issue of Contact with you in it. Fine savage stuff. The rest of the issue didn't seem to pan out according to plan, but what they did seemed honest enough, if superficial. Hereby I apologize to them, if anybody's listening, if anybody cares.

This joint every so often teeters on the brink of anarchy and it is about to tip that way again. Which means an epidemic of holdups and burglaries. The hacks are indifferent, or worse, scared, and who could blame the poor underpaid slobs. In order to protect the pathetic trifles I value, my mother's pearls and like that, again I need a very stout padlock that can't be chiseled. Seem fantastic? It is. The lock needs three keys, two have to be deposited with custodians. I can say all this because I'm sending the letter by the Chaplain, a boy with a tough mind and tender heart.

Your putting up that fifty bucks against my emergence was a beautiful thing, I have no words for it. But there was something that felt like a sunrise in my stomach.

Write, petit chou—Jim

Raiford, Florida
November 28, 1960

Dear Mike:

Things look pretty good here, as far as the parole goes, though I'm trying to be realistic and restrain my optimism. I've asked Landesman to write the parole people that he would obtain suitable lodgings for me in St Louis—where I will not have to associate with coarse elements, footpads and cutpurses and such—it's a question almost sure to be asked.

Perhaps now would be a good time to send the getaway bread, it might weigh the balance in my favor if the people here could report I got enough in the bank to get where I'm supposed to go.

You might want to get in touch with Angie Green, the singer chick. I'm told she's in Key West for a couple of weeks. Staying at P.O. Box 668, though it must be rather snug in there. Supposed to be coming this way en route North, though I don't know if she'll be able to bust in this joint, as yet. One assumes that Landesman has asked her to check me out. Or maybe she likes jails.

Thank you and thank you for the books, I embrace your ankles. I have been starved for reading material. The collection is delightful, arresting, arousing, and I have plunged forthwith. On the company's time, I am engaged in mounting the Chapel Christmas play once again. I wrote it, along with some soapy mood music, and I think it is not as good as it might be with time to revise— but it seems to have the actors involved, they are fighting with one another, so there may be some ferment there after all.

That election was an ominous portent for the future. Far too many votes for the Uriah Heep from California. I don't think that Americans are ready for democracy. Now I must stop and write a hard-sell letter to the parole commissioner who holds my destiny in his hot little hand. Let me hear, my old—at present I'm pulling hard time and need reassurance, as pants

Later, —Jim

Raiford, Florida
NOVEMBER 28, 1960

Mr. Francis Bridges, Jr.
Florida Parole Commission
Tallahassee, Florida

CO #38643

Dear Mr. Bridges:

I have heard nothing for some considerable time, and I would like to inquire about the progress of the investigation into my parole plan. And though I know you are a busy man, I would like to ask your indulgence to say a little bit about my present situation and my future ambitions. I'm sure you must get feverish declarations of good intentions by the bagful, but I would like you to hear me out anyway, and I'll try to be calm and reasonable.

The job I've been offered (as pianist, by Mr. Landesman of the Crystal Palace Theatre in St. Louis) is one that will make the fullest use of the only real skill I possess, that of a musician.

However, during the time I have been in prison, I have used my spare time in trying to become a writer. I've written a couple of Christmas plays for the inmates, which doesn't make me Eugene O'Neill, but in doing it I've learned something about the mechanics and structure of dramatic writing. And I've had a couple of minor prose things published—which again doesn't make me a hotshot author, but at least it shows I may be on the right track.

The Crystal Palace Theatre uses a number of original scripts in their productions, it is a busy creative atmosphere, and I think that by working with these people I can find an outlet for my writing efforts—and a better reason for working hard and living happily and productively than I have found heretofore. And at the same time I will be earning my living at the one proven skill I have—playing the piano.

So I hope (and it's a desperate hope) that you will give me a chance to go to St. Louis and work at this job. I know that it could be the turning point in what has been up to now a life without direction or purpose.

Sincerely, James Blake ✕59894

Raiford, Florida
DECEMBER 14, 1960

Dear Angie Green:

What a wonderful surprise to get a letter from you, Angie Green. I enjoyed it very much, though my pleasure in it was tempered by the realization that the possibility of working with you seems to be receding into the realm of the unlikely. I hear nothing from the parole people. And I was rather looking forward to your visit, if possible to playing for you. From your letter, I think you would be an intuitive and sympathetic person to accompany on piano.

Even though I think you ever so delicately shafted me on my use of the term "purlieu." I have consulted a great big dictionary, and I find that "purlieu" is a Creole corruption of the Arab "pilau," which is a mixture of lamb and rice. Hence, one assumes, the English "pillow," though why the Arabs should want to sit down in such a mixture passes understanding. Arabs are not our kind, true. Still . . . Actually all the jazz about purlieu was obfuscation on my part, which is a way of life in this place. Now that I know better what you're like, I can say I was afraid of you hitting the front gate here in toreador pants and perhaps too much uh dazzle, when you came calling. It is a thing I favor strongly myself, but it would set off all the bells around here.

I wanted to answer your letter immediately, but I am enmeshed in preparations for the annual Chapel Christmas program, which we present yearly for the civilian denizens of outer space. The drama is a product of my fevered imagination, story of a fictitious family living in the inn at Bethlehem and the impact of the Nativity upon them. Though I am not a strong believer (I'm a stronger doubter) still I doubt rather gingerly, out of enormous respect for the antiquity and beauty and audacity of the tale.

The problem in writing something like this is the disparity of the audiences we must play to. Our first performance will be in the Chapel for outsiders, many of whom are nice old ladies from surrounding towns. Then we give two performances in the Rock (prison proper) auditorium for the cons black and white. Three vastly different groups, and the latter two are tough, unless they can be charmed into acceptance. Which we aim, warily, to attempt. So you see, one tries to attain a precarious balance. The script is not as good as I would have liked, due to limitations, my own and others', though the Chaplain is a swingin' type who gives us fantastic leeway. The incidental music I feel a little better about—sort of a Delius-Palestrina hash, soapy but scriptural.

I was astonished and touched that you like the Paris Review letters so much. All else I can say is that I was artless then, and more honest than I have been since. Though I would not wish to return to that lost innocence if I could— to live impaled, who needs it? Hearing that the divine Tennessee has read the letters and remembered them is somehow a little dismaying. When you see him again, I would like him to know how much I exalt his work, the sure controlled audaciousness of it. In particular *Sweet Bird Of Youth*, which I read recently and was utterly involved in. And tell him I regret I have no picture at present to send, only the one taken upon arrival here, front view and side. In that one my face is stamped with pathetic bravado and palpable defeat, not very interesting, except perhaps to policemen.

My piano playing, my saloon piano, I mean, is on the romantic side, no particular style I'm aware of, though I think there is a certain individuality in choice of chords and harmonic coloring. Your mention of the blues reminds me of a cellmate I had here who had a powerful influence on my playing (and on me, it follows). He played a driving, angry, sardonic kind of trumpet and was impatient with my comping. Too soft, he said, though I finally came somewhere near pleasing him. He once told me he'd like to chain me to a piano for an hour every day to play nothing but blues until I comprehended funkiness.

It is very late now, as I write in the cell (the joint is quiet, that waiting, listening stillness that pervades a prison at night), and my cellmate, an affable assassin from Wisconsin, is tossing restlessly in the bunk, meaning turn off the bloody night light. So in the interest of domestic serenity, I close. Tomorrow in the office I will type this, my longhand is wild. If you hear more from Miss Presti of Missouri, let me know. Please write to the cool kind Chaplain, and I hope so very much that we can work together in the Crystal Palace, soon.

Warmest, — Jim Blake

Raiford, Florida
JANUARY 30, 1961

Dear Nelson:

The news from Tallahassee is bad. Parole Board sent me a new set of employment papers, with the word that Missouri would *not* accept me in charge. State law there forbids parolees from working in a place that dispenses juice. Kind of ironic that Florida with its Baptist-haunted lawmakers should approve the setup and the Yankees frown upon it. It was more than just having to stay here that dashed me—the Crystal Palace seemed to offer an opportunity to learn about theatrics.

My play "The Rascal By Night" was so utterly preposterous in retrospect that I'm blaming it on the menopause or maybe it was the mistral. It might be all right for here, and then again it might not, there's a law against cruel and unusual punishment. I got started on this kick through concocting plays for the choir at Christmas—the published scripts that were available were simpering limping inanities. After that there were a number of cons who wanted to act. Now I've got part of a play about musicians. Mostly I was prompted to try it because

I never read anything about musicians that sounded like any I ever knew, save possibly Osborne Duke's Struttin' With Some Barbecue, or John Clellon Holmes.

Anyway, there have been few things in my experience as dismaying or deflating as watching actors publicly involved in some transparent and patently fraudulent flimflam of my devising— the lines that danced and sang in the caverns of my head now sound like the Case for the Prosecution.

It mystifies me how a play can be written, cast, staged, acted by a group of people with implicit faith in what they're doing, and then they show it to another group of people who can see at a glance the whole thing is misbegotten. How can this be? Is there never a time during the weeks of preparation that somebody says: "Stop! This thing is a bomb, we'll never get away with it."

On the other hand, there are those moments when the audience is actually listening, looking, reacting exactly right. This is wine that's all too strange and strong. Last year at Xmas they put on a thing of mine which tried for laughs and what is more, got them. I was transfixed. The skies were blue. At last the mantle of Molicre was mine. After that, there was no end to the glittering ripostes I let fall around campus, nothing could stand against the steel of my rapier. Ah, the easy elegance of my converse, Wilde, Congreve, Sheridan danced in heaven to hear it.

A few gala weeks of this merriment, and I found myself shunned by my mean-souled hog-hearted associates. The fire was too hot, the light too bright for these trolls. Powdered tranquillizers were surreptitiously introduced into my grits— even the priest joined the cabal, mealy-mouthing around I should maybe make a novena. To assuage the mounting fury of their envy, I was forced to muffle the bright bells, sheathe the rapier. I resolved to hoard my pearls until I should be free of the hogpen.

For the 1960 production, mindful of arousing sleeping dogs, I decided to write a serious drama, a story of humble hearts and high purpose. It would be a tragedy, to be sure—indeed, there is more to life than the titterings and sniggerings of popinjays and fools— but it would not be merely an orchestration of despair and travail. Hope would irradiate the masque, faith would inform it.

It was called *No Room At The Inn*, a tender, moving, yet decorously light-hearted account of the Innkeeper of Bethlehem and his two sons. One, a rebel against Rome, the other a mystic, a questioner of stars. There was a burning message, for the stalwart spirits who would hear it. And pathos— slabs, great slabs, of pathos.

The premiere was held in the Chapel. Kindly old ladies for miles around came, bringing wraithlike males, adolescent girls in spectacles and blue serge, platoons of fat kids with runaway glands. The tears flowed like wine. The old ladies wept for Messiah locked out, the girls with glasses wept for sturdy males locked in, the fat kids lost all control. Pale husbands and fathers dozed.

Whenever this salt sea of sorrow appeared to be in danger of subsiding, I played keening organ music under the agonizing of the actors, using a vibrato that caused the atmosphere to throb and pulsate at a pitch that fractured several eardrums and one hymen. In all, a thoroughly sodden and triumphant occasion.

NBC sent a man in to tape some segments for the "Monitor" radio program. I was interviewed by a chap looked quite ill with ennui, spurring himself to a desperate effervescence during the taping. To get the story: Convict Writes Religious Drama. Questions with built-in answers, needing only a gurgle for reply. Fatuous all of it, skilfully contrived to be innocuous and inoffensive to all.

So, starry-eyed and full of beans, we took the show over to the Rock auditorium, to bring the message to the benighted ones. Blacks one night, Caucasians the next. The spade reaction in a word: "WAH-AHT?!?!" They ought to ship them all back to Africa. I applied for membership in the Ku Klux.

Next night the ofays came. Loaded for buffalo. You ever hear of contrapuntal theater? From the opening line, the audience participation was off and running and not for a second did it falter. And oh gall oh wormwood, the audience had all the lines.

First Shepherd, onstage: "And the heavens opened and were ablaze with light brighter than day, and a voice said—"

Voice from audience: "Eat Wheaties!"

Innkeeper of Bethlehem, ad lib: "If any of you mothers want to step up here, I'll be glad to accommodate you. I'm gonna do this thing if it kills you!"

Oh well. Who needs craven acquiescence? Opposition is more bracing and it's the irritant in the oyster that makes pearls.

As I said earlier, I have another set of employment papers, but my last feeler Chicago way (Gertrude, Conroy) caused such consternation I hesitate to impose. You suppose there's some kind of honest, simple, winsome, modest work I might obtain there? Any openings at smokers and stags for a live-wire raconteur with a surefire repertoire of Ike and Mamie jokes?

Many changes taking place on the campus. A formidable new addition across the river to accommodate 1200 more malfeasants. Dernier cri in oubliettes, stouter bars, bigger locks, deeper freezes. The staff of civilian workers is burgeoning in proportion, and soon there will be a shepherd for every sheep. The felons are somewhat abashed at the grandeur and scope of this undertaking in their behalf, and have awakened to a new awareness of the vital role they must assume in this bold new concept. The old petty, niggling depredations would be an embarrassment to all in the bright new order, they feel— and every man jack has pledged himself to bigger and better, more dynamic lawbreaking. A heartening and inspiring thing to behold.   Let me hear from you, fiorello. Jim

Raiford, Florida
MAY 15, 1961

[Via the chaplain]

Dear Mike:

There's no way for me to tell you how sorry I am that you should have been put through that hassle with the Miami fuzz. I've been dying to explain to you what happened so that you will know it was not entirely my fault. Partly it was, I made the stupid mistake of confiding in the wrong party. But even if I explained forever, I couldn't convey to you the quality of the Byzantine intrigue that goes on in the joint.

There's a cat I've known through both of my bits here. He worked for Custodial, the local fuzz, and had a lot of power at one time. That's a hard thing to explain too, how a convict hierarchy can operate under the surface of the apparent civilian authority, but it's there and has to be reckoned with.

I've always instinctively veered away from this game of power politics—for one thing, a lot of enemies are acquired, and for another it needlessly complicates what is already complex. The nutty thing is though, that simply by applying myself to my assignment and discharging the responsibility as best I know how, I have somehow come to be considered by all these striving jailhouse politicos as one who controls a sphere of influence, the Chapel. They're positive I'm wheeling and dealing somehow, no matter how much I demur. Lately I've stopped hassling with it, I let them nurse their delusions. So like it or not, I'm king of a turf.

Anyway, they had a big shake-out at Custodial and this cat got shook out. He comes to me with the proposal that I use my influence with the Chaplain to get him a job at the Chapel. Planning to open his store in a new location. I don't have any influence, but there is no way I can make him believe this, his thinking is conditioned otherwise.

And even supposing I had all this imaginary influence—what really hacked me was his bland assumption that I would be stupid enough to allow him to move all the Heat he had collected into my vicinity. That was a major miscalculation on his part and I told him to buzz off.

The mistake on my part was that quite a while ago, when we were pretty tight, and for some unaccountable reason, I told him about the phoney entry on my mailing list, which was you.

So this big bad operator does what every lame in the joint does, he writes a fink letter to the mailing official.

I get called out on Court Day, when everybody with a D.R. (Disciplinary Report) goes before a trial board. There's no board when I get there, just the Assistant Supe. Who is rolling murder, he's intelligent and intuitive, and all the cons are afraid of him because he's con-wise.

So he asks me who you are. (And I know immediately what's going down.) My brother-in-law, I say. He gives me the death ray. "I'll give you a chance to rephrase that, Blake. This time leave out the lie."

I leveled with him, what else? Then he threw a curve. "Is he a homosexual?" (Huh?) Said, no, sir. (Are you?)

The upshot was, I had an unblemished record and so got off with a warning. But it makes me hesitant to write to anybody, for fear of bringing down the local fuzz on them. The patriot who tried this lame game on me is still around and still available. I won't be able to write to you, so I won't be able to send you his head.   ever,—Jim

Raiford, Florida
JUNE 12, 1961

[Via the Chaplain]

Dear Gertrude:

I've been hit with a couple of thunderbolts. One, my mailing list has come under official scrutiny, due to some finkery, and the Chaplain is most obligingly letting me write this letter through the office.

As for the other bolt—Doug is back here on parole violation. It was about a month ago, I was working in the Chapel office, when a carrier pigeon flew in, one of those birds who live only to carry momentous news, preferably bad. And said to me, "They just brought Doug Northrop back on PV. He's down in the West Unit." West Unit being the new quarantine section.

The hallowed custom here is cool impassivity, no matter what. So I gave the watchful messenger nothing. "Thanks, man. 'Preciate it."

From the Chapel to the West Unit is about two city blocks. I traversed the distance with an absolute riot in my wig. And found Doug lying on the grass reading "And Quiet Flows The Don."

Who can say what such meetings are? They are collisions. He looked wasted, and I was meanly gratified to see it. As always when ill at ease, his aspect was one of cold hostility. Before, I would have been abashed and daunted by it—but so much had happened to change me, during the year he had been away, that I was simply not the same. And looking at me he knew it, and remarked on it sardonically.

The job at the Chapel was in a large part responsible, I think. I had to take charge and dominate people in order to do the job. And in my life in the Rock, there was nobody to depend on but myself, and so I had learned to negotiate all the tricky currents, and even to do a little moving and shaking on my own.

The first thing I had to do was persuade Cliff to move into another cell, and without making him mad. It took some bread, spread around, and a lot of maneuvering I didn't even know I was capable of. But when Doug was released from New-Cock and moved to the Rock, I was able to move him in with me, and Cliff and I are still friends. Maybe I am a jailhouse hustler, after all.

Doug told me how he went right back on the stuff when

he got out. He says his mother deliberately put him back in the joint by calling his parole officer. He doesn't say it was perhaps the only way she had to bring the situation under control. That I can reduce, but I don't say it, he's savagely defensive about his failure, and it doesn't make him easy to live with.

He's completely turned off on his mother, won't answer her letters, so I have persuaded the Chaplain to let me correspond with her, pending the time that Doug will relent. He spends the money she sends him, so I just think she deserves a better shake than she's getting, though his scorn at what I'm doing is withering.

He's back in the band, and that's a help; the cats tell me he practices all day long, trying to get his chops back. I hear him blow in the mess hall combo, and it's that old anger, all the way. We tried to blow a few sessions with J.P. the drummer, just the three of us, but Doug was so brutal to J.P. I had to tell him I wasn't going to make that scene any more. I can't stand it—J.P. falling apart and so seemingly cowed by Doug. Doug is destroying him, and doesn't seem to know it, or if he does, to care.

So I got a lot to think about, I got this cat to put together again, malgré lui. I'll write when I have a chance, but as I say, my mail is getting the cold official eye these days.

Love,—Jim

Raiford, Florida
NOVEMBER 12, 1961

Dear Nelson:

I have no idea where you can be, but I shall send this to your stronghold in Bucktown, Chicago, and hope that it catches up with you in Hollywood, New York, Hongkong, or wherever. I've noticed recently, in Time magazine I guess it was, that you spoke at the University of Michigan— the item quoted a few salient, and saline, words, and I wished I could have heard the whole of your remarks. These days, out there at least, seem to be as bad as days can get, except that they are almost certainly going to get worse. Sow the wind and reap the whirlwind.

There is quite a bit of civilian defense talk even in this quiet refuge. Many of the employees in here are attending these seminars in futility. Since the construction of this prison includes a number of stout concrete walls, minus windows, it would appear that a fair number of convicts will come through the initial rumpus. Now, if we can only amass enough corned beef and radishes (I hear radishes are excellent for radiation), it's possible that enough sturdy convict genes would be available to repopulate the southern regions when all this brouhaha is past. After all, the founders of a large part of the republic were imported spew straight out of English dungeons. A very tidy and neat way for history to repeat itself. Also in Time I saw that Eddie Rickenbacker, quondam hero and current tycoon, urges that we "fight and die before enslavement." Mr. R. is 71— if he will only be patient yet a while, his problem should disappear.

Life on the campus maintains an even lulling rhythm. You tax-paying slobs out there are really the ones who are caught in the dispozall. I'm in the throes once again of mounting the annual Xmas play at the Chapel. This one the third to be hand-writ by Blake, and the last one the long-patient Chaplain will have to sweat, since I graduate somewhere around next July.

I see that your book *A Walk On The Wild Side* has been made into a movie starring Jane Fonda, Lawrence Harvey, and something called Capuccine, which I don't know whether that is a monkey or a brother in holy orders, but either way it should be arresting. Apparently they propped up the title and erected something under it. Why don't you just invent titles and sell those to the movies? It would be easier on your nerves.

Doug the trumpet player from Lake Forest was returned here for parole violation, and we have been locking together since that time. And since then, things have tended to narrow

into a symbiotic relationship, a state of affairs I was inclined
to go along with contentedly for a protracted period. He has
a healthy narcissism going for him, though, and the other side
of that coin is that I am something of a minus quantity. And
because I have developed a sort of rueful fondness for the
idiot I know I am, this sort of thing can be borne only
in small patches. So, being lonely, and wondering about you
and Mike and Conroy and all those others out there, and
wondering what's happening, I'd like to hear from you again,
so I hope that you will write.

I have nobody available who is willing to play the lead in
this year's play (role of an eccentric Irisher) so I am perforce assuming the chore myself (probably a menopausal mani-
festation). I know that I will be a brilliant success as an actor,
so I am taking the foresighted liberty of sending you my
autograph.   Herewith, Jim Blake

Raiford, Florida
JANUARY 31, 1962

Dear Angie:

You must be thinking me an ingrate dog for failing to
reply to your gracious gesture at Christmas time. The only
reason I can give for my delinquency is that I've been fluc-
tuating wildly between spells of jailhouse apathy and periods of
furious activity, literary, liturgical and libidinous by turns. There
is a doubt that much of what I have written will be suitable
for much more than wrapping herring—but at any rate, I've
been practicing.

How very inspired of you to ask about our Christmas program here. Matter of fact, and as the enclosure will show,
I not only wrote the thing but, may Stanislavsky rest easy,
acted in it. Taking an acting role was more or less forced
upon me by inability to persuade any convict to play the
part — it called for an Irish accent—but I must admit I was
not too reluctant to put on grease paint and emote some. There

must be few people in the world who do not, secretly or brazenly, think that they could be actors if they chose.

Once having committed myself to playing the part, however, I had recurring moments of stark terror at the prospect of acting before an audience of convicts—an audience which must surely be the toughest in the world. Not so much for sophisticated discernment and discrimination as for sheer egomaniacal cussedness. And I had horrible recollections of the play we put on the year before, another Blake epic. There the spectators had been roused to heights of combative fury almost from the opening line. The heckling was so persistent as to achieve an almost ping-pong effect with the lines from the stage. I suffered anguish not only for my brainchild but for the embattled actors. They had to fight valiantly every inch of the way. It may have been the biblical setting and theme, the sight of familiar convicts disguised in costumes and beards, whatever it was, the malefactors took violent exception to it.

Whereupon I decided that with the Christmas '61 project, some guile was indicated, and I gave them a dramatic situation and characters I hoped feebly that they would identify with. (How indeed can one expect with any certainty to placate the ego of a roaring tiger?)

We gave three performances, the first in the Chapel itself, where we converted the sanctuary into a stage. That went off well, but the audience was comprised of civilian outsiders and they of course are always indulgent. I always have the feeling the response would be cordial no matter what the performance. Like the dancing bear, it is not how well he does it, but remarkable that he does it at all.

Second performance was in the auditorium of the Rock itself, and this for the black population. That went well, too, but then the spades are unfailingly polite and receptive—we still had no clue as to our fate on Armageddon night, when we were to perform for the white convicts.

Standing in the wings before that last performance, I died a thousand times. I had to appear first on stage, a long stretch out there all alone. Somebody came to say the house was packed, and I wished fervently that I could be facing only the electric chair. Somehow I got on to the stage when the curtain rose and got through the first long speech. And even got a laugh in the right place. It was not until I was doing the first bit of dialogue with another actor (having to look at his fright-frozen face) that I realized suddenly, through my haze of panic, how quiet the audience was. Then when I went off after the first scene, the director said exultantly, "We've got 'em!" At that blazing moment, I became fatally, irretrievably stage-struck, and hammed it up outrageously for the remainder of the play. I'll never be the same again.

Now I am beginning to undergo stage fright of a different kind. My time expires here shortly, probably some time in May, and I have to step out on the stage of civilian life once again. It is a feeling of apprehension familiar to every convict. They call it "short-time pains." I imagine I will go back to playing the piano, since it is the thing I know best how to do. But I'm working at the writing in hopes that I will have something to show and sell when I get out.

I've just finished reading Tennessee Williams' *Night Of The Iguana*. Liked it, with some reservations, and I would like to talk to you about it, but it's quite late at night now, the penitentiary is as quiet as the tomb, and I must get up very early. I scribble this in my bunk by a night light, but I'll type it at the Chapel office in the morning so you'll be able to read it more easily.

Incidentally my cell partner, sleeping now in the bunk below, knew you in New York. A trumpet player from Chicago. Knew you in the Village, he says. Also another trumpet player (and composer) here that knows you,——— from Cleveland. (He is at present on a restricted diet for being bad.) Oh— my cell partner is Doug Northrop.

Please write and tell me all about the coast scene, and I promise a prompt reply. Write to me in care of the Chaplain.

zut alors, Jim

PS—You ask why I'm here. For burglary and narco. I am the world's indisputably lousiest burglar.

Raiford, Florida
MARCH 19, 1962

Dear Nelson:

There's a character in Saul Bellow's *Herzog* who constantly writes letters in his head to people. I don't know how many letters like that I've sent to you since I last *mailed* a letter, but it's quite a few. So don't say I never wrote you.

Big news here (for me, anyway) is that the expiration date for this particular atonement should fall somewhere around May 15. I'd like to come to Chicago and work until around October, when I have hopes of making it to the West Coast. There's a chick out there, Angie Green, perhaps you know her, I was supposed to work with her at Jay Landesman's Crystal Palace in St Loo, on that aborted parole effort of mine. Somewhat deranged but interesting, from her letters. She seems to be saying she'd like me to come out there and that she knows people who can arrange work for me. However, I feel that I should accumulate some bread and front before I brace the giddy and glossy coast scene.

So prior to that, I need a job in Chicago. Do you know of some modest and quiet niche for my reappearance in the world of affairs? I think I might do well as a clerk in a bookstore. My piano playing is in good shape, due to constant practice here, but I rather shrink from such a head-on collision with the electorate. If I could learn to cope with the sober citizens first, I'd probably be in a stronger frame of mind to deal with the besotted ones later on.

As far as lodging is concerned, I've written to an Episcopal cat who runs a sort of halfway house where they incubate renascent convicts into tame taxpayers. So far I've had no reply. I abhor the hangdog wholesomeness of such a place, but *que voulez-vous*, it will be as temporary as I can make it.

I think I can stay out this time. As a criminal I am a

cretin. Though I would not want it said that I was irresponsible and heedless of my obligations to the policemen of the world. *Somebody* has to help them with the payments on the white T-Bird, the tango lessons, all the little things that go to make the policeman's lot a happier one. I am not a chronic flake-out, let it not be said that I let the team down. But I am a little tired, and I feel that I've done my share. There are younger, more vigorous men here who seem prepared to go the route in providing for the myriad minions of law and order who have been dependent upon me and my poor efforts. I let fall the torch with no remorse. Henceforth, I shall walk the streets as burglar emeritus. And if I should come upon some glittering palace of justice, towering majestically in the sunlight, I can contemplate it with serenity and satisfaction. And say to myself "Ego servitus."

Living in the provinces as you do, you are probably out of touch with current trends in the theater, so I am enclosing some propaganda from our '61 production. You may have heard of the Theater of the Absurd, we have gone a step further, into the Theater of the Preposterous. In an access of madness and a rare display of raw courage, I played a lead in the drama. I shall be bringing a tape recording of it with me, and you shall judge for yourself on what shoulders belongs the mantle of Booth and Garrick.   Ever, —Jim

Raiford, Forida
APRIL 25, 1962

Dear Nelson:

No definite date yet for the balloon to go up, but I have every hope it will be May 7. Right now, I feel rather like the chick in that article you sent, I can't get a foot on the ground either way— can't keep my mind in this closed world in here, and can't get the body into that one out there.

Thank you for letting me see a part of the forthcoming book, I hope it does well for you. Some very funny stuff, and some that is unsettling and disturbing. It inspires (in me) the same kind of laughter as Chaplin does, that what-the-hell-am-I-laughing-at sort. At the peak of the hilarity comes the query, "Why are they turning the lights out, Mother?" Twilight laughter, dark at the edges, and the night wind rising.

The point you made in your article about vicarious sex and the American Male is a shrewd one. I remember when I used to play for strippers, I would look at the avid congested faces of the customers, and feel pity and scorn about the whole thing. It never occurred to me that perhaps some of them were quite content to go that far and no farther.

I have a quantity of papers I would like to take along when I go from here, and I am in need of a small bag like those airline jobs. Or perhaps you have a carpetbag, which is more like the way I feel. And if I haven't lost the boosting touch, I'll get you a new bag, of kittenskin if you like. Failing that, send a large red bandanna, and I'll pick up a stick somewhere.

I now have bus passage as far as Indianapolis, and since I have no eyes to settle in that dog's dinner town, I need a ticket from there to Chicago. Can you supply same, against the bright day when I shall be paid monies for services as yet inscrutable and mysterious. The economy of the nation looks to be slightly askew from here. Perhaps this comes from flogging Demand to meet Supply. But there must be a place in it for one who is prepared to do anything for money. And I can remember the dear innocent time when this might have been a unique qualification.

Let me hear, effendi, Protector of Unicorns, —Jim

PART VIII

baby, it's cold outside

Dear Angiegreen:

I'm out of the joint, and now the beast, his hour come round at last, is scuffling around Chicago. Quite a different town from the one I left eight years ago. Everything seems to have been flattened out and enameled. Freeways abound, all going furiously nowhere. One must have an electric toothbrush, or live like a pig.

One thing, to my relief and delight, did not change. Nelson Algren I found the same unregenerate and abandoned ham. An actor *manqué*, a wonderfully flexible and funny stud. I saw him the second day out and he made me laugh a great deal, which godknows I needed. He's going off on a Pacific freighter in a couple weeks for a long trip, and I shall miss him sorely. When he comes back in the fall a television show is in the making for him, and I'm hopeful there will be a place on it, for at least one shot, for a brokendown piano player and *bon vivant*. That's one cat, not two. Last night there was a *bon voyage* bash at his pad, a raucous carnival of clashing contesting egos, and mine was right in there hollering with the loudest. First time I've been stoned on lush for six years, and today I am racked with pain, but still bravely writing to you—a mark of devotion you might pay heed to.

I took a fabulously beautiful spade stud to the party, a recent parolee from Pontiac, on whom I am slightly hung up, libidowise. It can't be anything more, because he is almost classically stupid. He is indubitably a black Apollo, but he thinks he's a black Orpheus, plays guitar, rather badly I fear, though he was a great success at the gala, and wound up taking care of biz with some predatory gray chick in the john.

There was a chick there, vivacious and sandpaper-voiced, who insisted vociferously (all night long) that my Paris Review letters had turned her life around. Pleasant and dismaying to hear, but not necessarily credible. But I did meet and talk to Gwendolyn Brooks, the poet, for a space, and that made the evening memorable; she is a great lady.

I'm staying temporarily at St Leonard's House (having gotten out of the joint very bankrupt), which is a sort of halfway stop between the joint and civilian life. Everything is cool here, low-keyed, and there are a number of other ex-cons and parolees, gray and black, staying here also.

I plan to stay here till Nelson goes, and then hopefully I can move into his pad and write for three months. There is the immediate problem of eating, but I think I have a kind of sponsor lined up for that spot. A chick I know, married to a rich lawyer, and I am going to help her ameliorate some of her guilt about being so rich.

Then there is a gentle swindle afoot to include my story "Day Of The Alligator" in an anthology Nelson is putting together for Lancer paperback, and that should mean a piece of bread.

Let me hear, babe. I'm a little hung up and need cheering. Please have some pity, I'm all alone in this big city.

Unswerving devotion, — Jim

Chicago, Illinois
JUNE 5, 1962

Dear Mike:

It was a severe disappointment not to see you at Nelson's party Saturday. I hear you have changed and I have an insatiable curiosity about you—I never seem to get an opportunity to ask you all the shrewd probing questions I have prepared. The party was a fine rout and today I am racked with pain. But I met a lot of people, and Studs Terkel may do something about getting me a piano to play for money. At least he implied he might.

Tomorrow I go to Skokie to paint a garage for a lady who's afraid of niggers, and whose husband is abroad, so she specified a Caucasian. I'll bet she has some swingin' fantasies.

I guess you have forgotten about sending the clothes. I still need some things to wear, though I have acquired some Episcopal castoffs that are serving the purpose for the time being. And while I've got the alms bowl out, I am in pressing need of new glasses. Not only I can't see with the ones I've got, I think a pair of horn-rims would change the image somewhat. The present one isn't doing so hot. I can't get the money together at my present salary, which is a dollar an hour, fitfully. If you can lend me twenty bucks, I'll pay it back when I start working at something steady. I almost had a job as a stockroom inventory worker at a bookstore, but it hung up when the business manager found out I was ex-con.

I hope I will see you the next time you are in town. From what I hear, a great change has come over you, you have become the abominable no-man, abstaining from everything, and I am achingly curious about that. However, if my nosiness annoys, I promise to elicit your secret discreetly and with stealth. That pot was fine, I saw *Sweet Bird of Youth* behind

it, had a ball, and fell terminally in love with Geraldine Page,
who is a flame of talent.   Ever, — Jim

Chicago, Illinois
JUNE 25, 1962

Dear Mike:

From all acounts, prodigious energies are being expended on
my behalf, since you mentioned that I am in need of help
in finding a slot in this great wide commercial world. There
is a scheme afoot to present me as a stellar attraction on
the women's club lecture circuit, speaking on all the delicious
and naughty things that can happen on a chain gang, all decently disguised as social significance. The lecture season for
ex-cons seems to be rather slow during the summer months,
but we are in hopes that something will open up.

I had a note from Studs Terkel; he says I am a real "original," which I don't know exactly what that is, but he seems
interested in putting me on his WFMT show for an interview.
Pursuant to that, a Tribune man has agreed to put a note
in his column about the interview. Thus giving me "exposure"
and enhancing my value as a lecture candidate. Wheels within
wheels.

Biggest thing that has happened is that Doug, the trumpet
player from Lake Forest who was my lockmate for three years,
has come out of the joint. I was apprehensive about it— our relationship in the joint was pretty intense, and often in a situation
like that there is the what-will-I-tell-my-mother blues, a residue
of guilt. But he called me the first thing he got into O'Hare,
and I've seen him a couple of times, and the 51 per cent
of me that had been missing was restored. Doug is such a
phenomenally swingin' trumpet man and makes such a fantastic
appearance on the stand—big stud with soot-fringed gray eyes
and a Guards' moustache. Something for the girls, to be
sure. If he can only get a hearing, I think he will be on his
way to being very hot.

I hope I'll hear from you when you come up in July, and I'd

like you to know Doug. Mockery is as much a part of him as it is of you, and perhaps you could be sardonic together, sort of a Mexican standoff. I'll be the ignorant bystander.

I'm now the manager, sole employee and star salesman of a second-hand furniture store. This is a scared-money precarious operation run by a high-powered ex-con, and I expect the whole thing to vanish momentarily in a cloud of attachments and bailiffs. It still looks as if I'll have to resort to the piece to make any real bread. I don't have a time or place to write, and I'm very near being drug with the whole thing. Say something, — Jim

Chicago, Illinois
JULY 7, 1962

[To Robert Kaplan, New York City]

Dear Bob:

I've geen told by the good Father here at St Leonard's that I'm ready to move our on my own. The old Episcopal heave-roonie. Esthetically I was ready a day after I moved in, financially is something else again. I've never fitted into this picture. There are only a couple of studs in the house I can relate to, and that on a limited basis. The rest are sullen animals, or worse, squares who imagine themselves hip merely because they've broken a law or two. Just taking cons out of the joint doesn't change them, and you know what 90 per cent of *them* are. The concept of rehabilitation and adjustment here is communal fun and games like swimming at the Y, lifting weights, shooting pool, all that wholesome group jazz. I've had to pass, I never could make that herd action.

I'm playing organ for services in an Episcopal parish nearby. Young priest, good musician, but a cold and distant ascetic and inclined to be waspish, I suspect, if provoked. The church is in a Puerto Rican-Spade neighborhood. I look at some of those dark-eyed olive-skinned adolescent parishioners and I simmer and seethe. Somethin's got to give, baby.

You certainly seem to be having a ball, and I must say the

prospect of New York is inviting. But I think it would take me at least two weeks to get squared away financially. Doug says not to go, but he's either under his ma's thumb in Lake Forest, or with his chick, and I seldom see him. Though last Sunday he called, and in an oddly deferential tone that made me want to weep, he suggested coming down here. We sat at a forlorn spade bar and rapped for hours. Then when I called him a day or so later, I got such frost I decided against calling again.

His wife is coming up from the South, though Doug has brutally discouraged the idea. It seems, however, there is still some bread to be had there. I can foretell that script as if I'd written it. He'll go back to her, they'll both start using shit again, and then he'll come back to Ma to kick the oil-burner. The ones who will suffer, for the same reason and poles apart, will be the chick and me.

Monday night I was interviewed for an FM show which is to be broadcast next Thursday. Rather unsatisfactory, I'd have preferred a matter-of-fact approach to the joint and its tenants, but the inquisitor pitched it quite a bit higher, and whatever I had in mind got lost in the gee-whiz. Now he wants another tape session to further pursue my misspent life. So I'll hang in, and hope something comes out of it.

So in sum, Robert, I want very much to come to NY, but I have to lay hands on some bread. Maybe in about two weeks. Meanwhiles, keep in touch.   ever, — Jim

Chicago, Illinois
JULY 14, 1962

Dear Mike:

All this bleeding vichyssoise and no soup. Meringue and no meat, shadow and no substance. I am flogged by phantoms. WFMT the modulated frequency station for those who like their frequencies modulated, featured two flaming, fun-filled days of Jim Blake, ex-con, patriot and sweet kid. Wednesday Studs read from the *Paris Review* lettres. Interpolating music by Woody Guthrie.

Singing a song, HE'S got a LONG CHEE-AIN AWNN. . . .

Not quite my shtick. On Thursday, a tape we made at Roosevelt College. For an opener, me playing ragged claws piano. Then talking off the top of my head on abstractions I'm not really interested in or capable of handling. A couple of things got accidentally said, most of it was froth.

Studs, with baited questions, kept trying to swing me leftward of the angels. ("What is your conception of FREEDOM?") I obliged with a few lily-livered prim observations, nothing they could ever hang me for, actually. It might have been a good show, I got a lot of spleen I'd have liked to unload. As it was, it had a stylish ambivalence. An elegiac note of quien sabe.

Anyway, a cat from Rogue magazine called, said he wanted a non-fiction article. For one heavenly instant, I thought he said Vogue. Also, they want to see some fiction. All of which I'll go along with, if I don't have to lurk outside high schools and sell the magazine.

Immediate problem. Today I have to move from the Episcopal haven. One of the resident fathers has told me I'm Ready. Translation, pull it. I got twenty bucks, no job, got to find a room, need bread. How do you feel about investing further in the Blake potential. I need a little surcease from the daily agonizing specter of looming park benches and prowling Polizei. The Rogue thing is in the bag, as I see it. I already have part of the article they want, "In the Absence of Females." But who can type in Grant Park, beset by hostile pigeons.

With things seemingly on the point of breaking for me, the ice is moving under me.   Yrs, — Jim

Chicago, Illinois
JULY 15, 1962

Dear Mike:

Now I have a spot of my own, however brief my tenure may prove to be. The rent is 15 a week, but I figure to save on eating because it has icebox and stove and 3 dishes.

I've been working assiduously on the article for Rogue magazine, and tomorrow night I meet the dude, presumably to show him what I've got, along with some old fiction.

It would be nice if I could be afforded just a little more time to work on this project. Indoors, preferably. Will you advance a week's rent and give me just a little more time to work with? I'm going to look for a piano job some place, all the earnest well-wishers have not come up with anything firm, but they do say I'm delightful and different.

This is what they say. Then they say, later for you, kid. Baby, the time is now and the hour is 11:45 for me. I don't want to change back into a rat.

I wish you could come to Chicago while I'm still in this pad, and see it, the lowest, the weirdest, made out of corrugated paper and scotch tape, but I have a grove of catalpa trees outside the window and it's downtown in a section teeming with choices of wickedness. Do come. How long are you going to be a spinster? You made such a lovely pagan.   Yrs in Christ, —Jim

Lake Forest, Illinois
JULY 24, 1962

Dear Bob:

The way things are shaping here, this may be the last letter I'm able to write you as a civilian. I have a couple forlorn leads to check out, but I'm extremely pessimistic. So if all else fails, I'll try flying with the owls for as long as it lasts. And the really ironic part is that this time I absolutely don't want to go back inside.

But I'm tired of scuffling in this town. The St Leonard's scene was never my scene, they knew it, I knew it. I was a social phenomenon and went to a lot of parties and was a conversation piece, but I couldn't nail a gig out of it.

Doug has found a chick that is avid to support him, so I guess he'll be all right. What we had we still have, but I can't see making a design for living in just that particular pattern. Not puritanical, just hoggish. He came over one night, bringing pot and a jug of wine, and we got blocked. He insisted that we walk up to Old Town, where he's renting a studio. I didn't want to go, but we got into one of those physical things he does, and he dragged me all the way up Wells Street. When we got to the studio, the chick wasn't there; so after more pot and more wine, he wants to make a scene, just like the old jailhouse days. So we did, but it was macabre, the vibrations were bad, the motive obscure, the whole bit was sinister, and I felt used and soiled. In the joint, he was a wild man—on the bricks he's a rocketing maniac.

My life can take some frantic curves, but none more frantic than the fact that I'm now baby-sitting with Doug's kids, while his mother looks after her business affairs. She's very nice in a brusque sort of way, probably the only way to be nicely nice, but I think her charity towards me is based on a hope that I can show her the way to a reconciliation with Doug and his ultimate sacrifice on the altar of Business. Strange that she has known him for so long, and still doesn't realize how unremittingly shitty he can be once he has chosen his course. And another odd angle: When he learned that I was working for his mother (and it was she who asked me) he was utterly livid with fury.

This particular maneuver will wind itself up this week, and then I'm on the bricks. I'm not going to try to steal in Chicago, the fuzz is running up and down the town. Probably a North Shore town where they are less edgy and where I won't be falling over a million other hustlers. If I got to go down, I might as well go screaming as mumbling. Later, — Jim

PART IX

"tell them anything you like . . ."

Dear Chaplain:

Many times I've thought of you since I left Raiford, and of the debt of gratitude I owe you for the practical understanding and help you gave me at a difficult time of my life. I am not, and probably never will be, religious in the conventional sense, but I have my own eclectic brand, and you are one of the few ministers I ever saw who could carry the teachings of Christ into the everyday rat race of living. (I hear you say, "Here comes another smoke job.")

I had difficulty getting a daytime job in Chicago for the usual reason, my record, so I went back briefly to playing the piano in a night club. Didn't like it, I felt I was just repeating the pattern of the past. On Sundays I played organ in an Episcopal church in a small poor slum parish on the West Side of Chicago, where the parishioners are mostly Spanish-speaking Puerto Rican immigrants. We had two Masses, one English, one Spanish. I had a hell of a time keeping track of the priest in the Spanish Mass, but I finally accomplished it.

The Episcopal priest there was young, dynamic, a good musician and fluent in Spanish. The Episcopal church up North is rather different from the one in Florida: very vital, vigorous and wealthy and much involved in social work.

Anyway, in an effort to give me some publicity and perhaps another job, a friend of mine put me on an FM radio program he conducts. There I was interviewed (for an hour and a half!) on prison life and the difficulties of an ex-con. Incidentally we played part of the tape of the last Christmas show at Raiford, the Merry Christmas finale song, and all the Raiford boys sounded great.

I got considerable mail after this exposure, addressed a few women's groups and was given a commission to write some singing commercials for an advertising agency. But no steady job, what I needed. So I took the money I got for speaking and split for New York.

I'd already been in touch with Bob Kaplan and he met me when I hit the Big Town. He has an apartment on the lower East Side, and I stayed there. We had a somewhat alcoholic reunion and banged around Manhattan together for a couple of weeks and had a fine time. Bob is doing well, has a good job with a manufacturing company and I look for him to go far with the outfit, they seem to think highly of him. Nobody could ever deny his ability, ambition and aggressiveness. He's dating a Jewish girl whose father is influential in politics, and it would not surprise me to see him make a very advantageous marriage of convenience. So Kaplan is making rapid strides.

While New York diverted and dazzled me for a while, I didn't want to live there—like Chicago, the city made me nervous. Another friend of mind sent me to his analyst. (Everybody who is anybody in New York has an analyst.) I talked to him at some length and he sent me to a Park Avenue psychiatrist.

Turned out to be a fantastic guy. I told him all about myself, my past, my restlessness and my fears that I might do something that would put me back in prison unless I found some constructive work to do. He listened, asked a few questions, then told me to go home and pack, and that night he put me on a New Haven Railroad train for Westchester.

The doctor runs a mental sanitarium there, and that is where I am now living and working, very contented with the job and my surroundings. The job isn't hard, the food is good, and I have a couple of rooms to myself on the top floor. Windows all around, and I look out on miles of treetops. I'm doing a lot of writing, a lot of reading. I'm in a paperback book that Lancer is putting out this fall. Pretty soon I intend to look around and find an Episcopal church in the vicinity where I can play the organ on Sunday, and that will about complete the picture for me.

A quiet, busy life, with a visit once a month to New York to let off whatever steam may have collected. It has taken me quite a while to get my feet on the ground and to find peace of mind, but now I think I've accomplished it and hope that it will continue. I trust you will remember me in your prayers, and if the prayers of a pagan are negotiable, you have mine.

Particularly I would like to have the cell locations of Ben Bradley and Jerry Parker. They were both in Maximum when I left. I think Ben has paid more than enough, and I am trying to interest St Leonard's in getting him out on parole. Failing that, the Osborne Association of New York. But I would not say anything about it to him just yet.

Please remember me to my friends among the inmates. Thank you again, Chaplain, and may God bless you and guide you in the task you have set yourself.   Affectionately, —Jim Blake

Westchester, New York
SEPTEMBER 12, 1962

The Osborne Association, Inc.
114 East 30th Street
New York City

Dear Mr. ——:

I am working as an orderly at "Lakeside," a mental sanitarium in Westchester County, operated by Dr. R. P. Foley. I got the job through the Foley Foundation and since it happened very suddenly I did not have a chance to call you before I left the city.

Permit me to say I was most heartened and impressed by the discretion and efficiency with which you handled my case. There is in your office a remarkable absence of that antiseptic, cold atmosphere that so often pervades social agencies.

Had I stayed in the city I am confident that you would in short order have put me back on the track in civilian life. As it happened, a job in the country is just about what I need at this time. I'm trying to finish a book, and the leisurely pace of the country seems to be more conductive to rassling the muse.

Does the Osborne Association help a prison inmate to obtain a parole? I am thinking of a young man at present confined in Florida State Prison for murder, who has been there since he was sixteen. He is now 22, and has grown into an intelligent, thoughtful, quiet individual. He has attended school in prison, done considerable reading and some writing, and it is my opinion he has matured into a calm and balanced adult. Continued incarceration can only work against the progress that he has made by himself.

During the time I was in Raiford, I encouraged him in his writing efforts. One of the things he wrote is an account of his early years and the events which led to his committing a murder. I think it is a moving human document, and if you are interested in helping the boy, I'd be glad to obtain a copy of the account and send it to you. More than anything I could say, it will tell you about him.

Again, thank you for the compassionate understanding and help I received from you. You buoyed me up at a very bad time.

Sincerely, Jim Blake

[To Studs Terkel, Chicago]

Dear Studs:

New York seemed like a mirage to me. Even at night, when it is better than in the daytime. In the daylight there was such an impression of massive sterility and blankness I could hardly encompass it. At night, cleverly lighted, and with the night to hide some of the cold impassivity, a little better.

I'm speaking of midtown, all those blind glass buildings. The lower East Side was better, there I did days and nights of walking and inhaling through eyes and ears, a warm seething ferment of sights and sounds. The Village was nothing, it is the enameled lair of the wild soi-disant. But the one thing that really touched me in its simplicity and enchantment was the Staten Island Ferry. I spent most of the night riding back and forth. I was lucky enough to make a prime pot connection in the neighborhood where I stayed, and that completed the magic. There was a Chinese sailor on board, so perfect he was almost ceramic, who also spent the night sailing the harbor.

He seemed strongly inclined to tangle, and I pondered it briefly, but the thrall of the night and water and pot was too strong, so I kept it lyrical.

I saw Genet's *The Blacks*, unforgettable. It seemed most affecting to me when it became inarticulate to the bursting point. And when they say they hate, the conviction is chilling. The week of looking and walking was utterly engrossing and I want to do it many more times. New York is the last American city where one can walk. And I hope to spend many more nights on that magical ferryboat.

Ultimately though, the city made me nervous, as Chicago did. Through a system of referrals, I was sent to call upon a Park Avenue psychiatrist, and after I had told him my piteous tale entire, he hired me to work at his sanitarium upstate. It is a rambling Georgian mansion on a hill overlooking a lake and surrounded by 80 acres of woodland glen and bosky dell. Every morning I roll on a bank where the wild thyme grows, and in my off time I roam the countryside on a bike. Learning to live alone again, a thing I am ashamed to have forgotten.

The job is easy, so far, and if all goes well, I'll have a long slow country winter of reading and writing, and perhaps I can emerge in the spring with something on paper.

If you have finished with the issue of The Paris Review containing the Alligator story, I'd appreciate your sending it. That one, and the issue with Blake's letters, sell for four bucks a copy in Manhattan. Whatever that signifies, I can't imagine. Thank you for your kindness to a wandering minstrel, Studs. And please let me hear from you.   Warmest regards, Jim

Westchester, New York
AUGUST 24, 1962

Dear Gertrude:

It is impossible to raise you people on the telephone, I tried many times before I left Chicago, to no avail. I wanted very much to come out to your castle and talk, and perhaps play your piano again, in that fine Bronte-ish room.

Chicago gave me nothing but cocktail chatter, frustration, and malnutrition, so when I got the chance to come East I leaped on it. The strongest incentive to get the hell out I got from Doug Northrop, who, in a melodramatic and nightmarish telephone diatribe, said he no longer wanted to see me, that our relationship had been satisfactory for the time we were together in the joint, but not any more, that we didn't relate, etc. This last tired bit of pseudo-phycho jargon offended me more than anything else he said.

And perhaps he is right in a way—if he is going to persist in being a jejune brat and a provincial snob, then there is little to be learned from him. Perhaps he began to take the Old Town artsy mob too seriously. Or perhaps that demure female cannibal he is now entangled with had an influence. I know that if she continues as possessive, permissive and omnipresent as she was, she will be another in the long line of broken blossoms in Doug's wake. A prospect I find I can view with equanimity.

I went to New York at the urging of a chum I knew in the joint, a brilliant mind without a scruple to its name. And I confess I entrusted myself to him with some trepidation. But it turned out to be a ball. He has a pad in the East Village section, where all the poor bohemians have fled from the expensive glitter that is the Village today. In tandem, we wreaked havoc among the limpid-eyed Spanish hidalgos on the lower East Side. Really they are incredibly beautiful and eminently biddable boys. Mostly though, I banged around Manhattan alone, walking and looking.

I needed a job, so Bob's analyst suggested I call on Dr. Foley. The Park Avenue address kind of put the wind up, but I followed through. A handsome old man, but more than that, a presence with a high domed forehead, a calm air of power. He swept me with a brief cursory glance which nevertheless catalogued me. From then on, he looked out the window at the Park Avenue traffic. I told him about myself, that I was ex-con, that I had worked with mental patients before in Wisconsin and Florida. He asked, had I ever committed a crime of violence. I said no, sir. What age group of males appealed to me most? That took me aback. I said I wasn't aware of concentrating on any one age group. A long silence. Then he said, "I'll be going to Westchester on the 5:46. Can you get your baggage and be here at five o'clock?" I said, yessir. He said, "You may find your living quarters a little unorthodox, but your room has a view of apple trees and the sunset."

We caught the New Haven to Rye, from where he drove us to Lakeside. By the time we got there it was dark, and I was aware only of driving through massive gates standing open and a long curving drive through the estate to the house. As he parked, the Doctor said, "You will probably encounter a good deal of curiosity about yourself, there will be questions. Tell them anything you like, or tell them nothing."

And so here I am, in the bowels of darkest Westchester County. It is a strange joint.   More later,—Jim

Westchester, New York
SEPTEMBER 9, 1962

Dear Bob:

I can't really say when I'll be able to come down to New York for some carnal riot. The bread situation is tight, and I may need a couple more weeks before I have any margin for frivolity. I'm already into the good doctor for fifty, which is half what I make in a month on this gig. Monday should tell the tale—it was the doctor's idea that I would be on probation for a month, and then he intimated that if all was well, I would get more money. Undoubtedly I will have to spend everything I get on winter clothing this p.d.

There are a few things on this job which must be tolerated for the sake of the advantages, like the quarters I have, and the time off which I can devote to my own projects, and the serenity and beauty of the countryside. On the debit side, the head nurse is a Mittel-Europa beast who has been running a one-woman operation here, or at least strenuously trying to give the doctor that impression. She has a maddening habit of hanging over one, as if constant supervision was necessary. I found a lot of accumulated grime in the place, God knows what manner of orderlies have been here; I understand they flew in and out like blackbirds. And when I set to work to restore a reasonable hospital standard of cleanliness, I get the "what's with you" bit. Second in command is another Mittel-Europa type who has only two speeds, servility and arrogance. She is a sweet white-haired old lady of about 80, and some moonless night I am going to chop her up and feed her to the chipmunks.

Mettrafect, the whole staff, me included, is right out of a

French movie about castaways in the Casbah. A rare cutthroat crew.

Larry, the singer I mentioned to you, is an agreeable companion, a trifle stiff and chichi in his tastes, but that may be because he is playing it close to the vest. We get into town fairly often for movies. He has made quite a thing of telling me about the broads he has dated and ravished, and his hairy appreciation of females on the streets of the village is a bit heavy-handed. We went to the movies the other night, and during a preview of bits of "Spartacus" a shot of John Gavin in an abbreviated Roman skirt was flashed, and poor careful Larry could not suppress an involuntary moan. Hmmm.

We are planning to book some weekend work in a joint in the neighborhood, Larry singing, me playing. Nothing at all ersatz about his voice, a glorious bass-baritone, and he *is* good looking. Both of us need more bread than we are getting from the frugal doctor.

But in all, I'm satisfied to be here for the time being, I like the quiet—the city would flatten me.   ever, Jim

Westchester, New York
OCTOBER 7, 1962

Dear Robert:

Awright, here's what you have to do. Walk into some crowded, it's got to be crowded, midtown bookstore. Come to think of it, take a day off and make all the bookstores. Walk in and say in a ringing voice, "Do you have the Algren anthology "Book of Lonesome Monsters" containing the story "Day Of The Alligator" which in a very short time has become a minor classic, by Jim Blake, the rehabilitated ex-convict who has become a legend in his own time?"

Better get a firm grip on the lapels of the clerk's coat so that his attention doesn't wander. If it's a female clerk, you could grip her by one tit. The literary agent tells me the Lancer paperback of this mishmash is about due out. Chief advantage for me is that I get maybe a little more exposure in some good company.

The bread turned out to be practically invisible, a hot two bits, and I haven't seen that yet. The agent sent the check to St Leonard's in Chicago weeks ago. They didn't know where I was, but they didn't return it to her either. Some Episcopals. But I've got to be nice to those people, since I want them to get Ben Bradley out if possible, where he'll be like available.

The job continues to be merely a satisfactory way of eating while I pursue the business of getting words on paper. There's no real challenge here, and no real work, it seems to be merely a sort of holding action. Larry, the geared baritone from Juilliard, is either very naive or very cagey; I still don't know what the score is. (Though actually I haven't pursued it with any vigor, being too involved with my own aims to give it the time.) There's a new pantry boy (scullion, I guess the term is) working here, very nice, eyelashes out to here, muscular build, also some reform school tattoos. But he's semi-literate and there's no inquiring intelligence there, just a bland satisfaction with being male and attractive. Larry is hung up on him, but so far it's all very boystown, which considering all the eyes and open mouths hereabouts is probably wise. The libidinous is forbidden us.

I plan to try arranging days off so that I can have a couple days in the city October 19 and 20, Friday and Saturday. That all right with you? Drop a note, or call. Oh, I had a letter from Doug, and I am again and still happily enthralled, a rogue and peasant slave am I. Nelson isn't back from Asia yet, but he'll doubtless be in NY when he does get back, and I'll bring him around.   For now, —Jim

Westchester, New York
OCTOBER 12, 1962

Dear Angie:

Let it be unanimously agreed and duly recorded, I am a shit for not writing sooner. Several times of an evening I have suddenly said to myself "Angie" when I wanted to say something about something to somebody. And then my eye would fall on the pile of yellow pages, an all too scanty pile, which is some day supposed to make a book, and I'd say to myself, whatever sap is running had better be put into that, it is the only ticket to Trinidad or Tangier that you own. So I've been sturdily applying myself to enlarging the pile of yellow paper.

It was only yesterday that your letters caught up with me. I've been running so goddam hard, trying to get on the civilian carrousel (and all the time saying to myself, I hope you know what you're doing), that I've had little time to do enjoyable things. Well, I've had a couple of smiles here and there.

In Chicago, I kept running into opposition from the buttoned-up citizens when I tried to find a square gig. I thought all this jazz about ex-cons was just something that occurred in horrible television plays. Imagine my absolutely genuine astonishment when I found out it was true. No shit, in every one of those scenes, the dialogue sounded like television. It was embarrassing, esthetically, I mean.

So then the Episcopals booted me out. One of the Fathers took me aside, and in a voice throbbing with indifference, said he thought I was Ready. (Episcopal for buzz off.) So I pulled it, and got a room near the Loop, which I didn't leave for a week and nearly starved to death. Then Doug, the beautiful trumpet player I locked with in Raiford, came by, and we had a perfectly idyllic drunk together. And that was the last happiness we ever shared.

He had a studio in the Old Town section and wanted me to move in, but he was living with a chick he'd met while he was out on parole. And incidentally it was I who found the chick again for him, he didn't know where she was. This is the kind of generous and selfless (suicidal) thing I do all the time. But what the hell, I couldn't deceive myself that Doug and I could continue what we had in the Slam, ridiculous, he is as howling a hetero as they get.

So then I went to stay with Doug's mother in Lake Forest, an indomitable dynamic businesswoman, square in many ways, but hip in the clinches, very pragmatic. Not clever, but shrewd. Which is what I needed, I'd met a lot of people in Chicago, all of them clever as kittens, but no bread. I stayed out at her house for about two weeks. During which time Doug called up and denounced me for being there. I can't imagine (yes I can) what his beef was, but it was a nightmare conversation, and he wound up telling me to get lost. Shattering. Then I had a phone call from New York, from a very lewd shrewd dude, geared, that I had known in Raiford, actually he was sort of an alter ego there, and he told me to come to New York, that he had a pad in the East Village and I could flop there, and we'd whip something up. No bread, I said. Well this cat makes Machiavelli look like Poor Clare—he suggested that I make like I was settling down in Lake Forest to spend my sunset years, and the lady would gladly pay my way to New York to get me out of her house.

So I did, and she did. Bob met me when I hit NY and I stayed at his pad in the Village, a beautiful steamy simmering neighborhood. We made some fine scenes with the young pachucos of the region, they are ineffably decorative—look at you like fawns with those lambent brown eyes, and they turn out to be leopards, but it was exhilarating while it lasted. I grew uneasy about it, they were loping in and out of the pad and I was very fuzz-conscious, and to me they spelled Heat, sooner or later.

I made a couple of sorties in the Village, but I decided quickly it was not my scene, this lair of the self-anointed pretenders. The most arresting thing to me about these people is the amount of assurance they have in relation to the talent they possess. Astounding. I read some incredibly fuzzy plays, with dialogue that was actively insulting, and in the coffee houses lurching limping unfocused satire that was painful and tedious, and ultimately unacceptable.

The music? Folk singers, either underwashed or overwashed, singing the folk tunes of the jute flayers or the ballades of the Provencal truffle-hunters. The jazz music was what I call the Spades' Revenge. Resentment is a dull thing in any case, and resentment set to music is a waste of time and energy. They reminded me of children talking ritualistic Pig Latin.

Which brings me to the plight of the poor black man. I've known a lot of spades, some intimately, and by and large they are a petulant pain in the ass. The bad manners and Crow Jim attitude of the black musicians in New York outdoes anything I saw in the redneck South.

I remember a black lover I had in Raiford. Our arrangement was an eminently workable one. We were aware that the powerful attraction we felt was because we were bizarre to one another, and we were also aware that hate was just as much present as love in our relationship. That was a really swingin' affair, no nonsense at all. Not a hell of a lot of conversation, but then there wasn't much time for it, either.

So how did I get here? Bob took me along on a visit to his analyst, and he in turn suggested I call on this psychiatrist, Dr. Foley, a very posh dude on Park Avenue, reputed to be interested in the plight of ex-cons. I told him all about myself, and he brought me upstate to work at his home for neurotics. The work is easy, mostly it is refereeing bouts between the rich neurotics who live here. It reminds me of a house party with the guest list compiled by Compton-Burnett.

In my own time, I work at the writing (by the way, I've got a thing in a paperback anthology Lancer has brought out, called Nelson Algren's *Book Of Lonesome Monsters*). The agent has an article I did called In The Absence of Females, telling about homosexuals in prison.

But I have found that landscape is not enough for me, I need people, or actually I need a Person. (I need Doug, and I can't resign myself that the thing is dead dead dead.) When I got out the last time I lived on a little island off South Carolina, a place so beautiful it was an ache, but the monster I lived with there drove me back to the pen. So beautiful real estate is just not enough. Bob wants me in NY, and I may do that. Will you forgive and write? I am lonely, and I never get used to it.

Love,—Jim

Westchester, New York
NOVEMBER 6, 1962

[To Nelson Algren]

Dear Papa-San:

That TV station has burdened you with kind of a stodgy sub-ject, St Leonard's House and the making of angels from imps. It's like you said, people don't particularly care about regenera-tion, they'd rather hear about the downfall.

What struck me as the flaw in the St Leonard's approach was a certain lack of discernment. I encountered far too often there a type that is familiar to anyone who has built time—the organi-zation man of the penitentiary, the yea-sayer, the brown-nose. This is the sly and servile convict politician, who for his services to The Man is rewarded with parole. The rebels in the joint, those who have made some kind of emotional commitment, however hopeless or wrongheaded, rarely receive parole con-sideration. And in my view, some of these are far more worth recovering.

My point is that if the Father is as con-wise as he claims, he should be familiar with the con-politician type. And he should know that there are cons inside, rotting, far worthier of a chance than the ones he is taking out.

I say these things because I fear that in the course of prepar-ing the TV program, you'll be hearing an awful lot of the same old *merde*.

The prospect of being a piano player in the San Francisco musical version of "Walk On the Wild Side" is inviting. I've been pointing for that town ever since I got out, and if I'm able to stay with this Lakeside thing until spring, that is where I plan to go.

Every day in this job I run an obstacle course of concealed motives and cross-purposes. Chief duty is keeping the patients from killing one another. Every one of these pampered cannibals packs a stiletto, and all day and into the night, they sit in the drawing room, and when they are not cheating one another at bridge or gin, they are waiting for somebody to expose his back. The cook has a hutch full of rabbits that she keeps to test the bouillabaisse for strychnine. Lose more goddam rabbits that way.

The doctor stays well out of reach of everything and concerns himself with building a pleasure dome on another part of the estate. I picture him sitting in his Park Avenue office listening to a long and agonized recital of mental and emotional travail from a patient. When it is finished, the doctor impassively opens a desk drawer and hands the wretch a loaded revolver.

I'm sending you some pages on hanky-panky in the pokey, "In The Absence of Females." I think our agent friend rather peremptorily dismissed them as impossible to sell. She said "too explicit." There's something wrong with it, but I don't feel it's that. Hang in, Jim

Westchester, New York
NOVEMBER 11, 1962

Dear Gertrude:

I had a fearful whirl in Manhattan, fortnight past, in Kaplan's pad. In retrospect, there was a quality of desperation and damnation in it, rather too headlong, and it has taken me almost two weeks to recover. Kaplan, for some motive that escapes me, frequently procures for me some biddable youth, as if I were the aging and debilitated Shah In Shah. This time it was a black pappagallo, a double-gaited male courtesan. He had a relentless gentility which might be called the Bethune-Cookman manner, speech that was a mixture of Oxford English and Oxford, Miss. Ultimately we bedded, and in the dark and hectic hours I spent with him I felt that I had become entangled in the merciless gears of some mindless sex machine. Till in the shallow hours of the morning, I suddenly bleated, "Where has joy gone?" and went out into the empty streets to walk and walk.

George Plimpton of *The Paris Review* referred to me a dude who wants to meet me and talk the possibility of making a play from the penitentiary stuff I wrote for the Review. (Soon there will be a play based on The Breeder's Guide.) I'm skeptical that it might be another one of those hungry haunted creatures who are morbidly hung up on convicts, I meet them from time to time.

Algren, back from Siam with twelve golden umbrellas, stopped in San Francisco and met somebody who wants to do another musical version of *Walk On The Wild Side*. Papa-San asked me do I want to play the piano player in this opera, when and if. Naturally I said yes, yesyes. If I can stay on my feet before an audience of hairy hostile convicts I can enter anywhere, answer to anything.

So baybee, let me know how it is with you and the Keeper of the Rolls, Suzerain of the Moustache.   Yrs, Jim

Westchester, New York
DECEMBER 3, 1962

Dear Nelson:

Been about a month since I sent you the item "In The Absence of Females," and no comment from you. Please say something if it's only Yucch.

Mail here is on an RFD route and the doctor permits one of the patients to pick it up daily at the box. Some of the mail goes astray. The agent sent some things I never received and since then other pieces have been missing. It may be therapy for the patient, but it causes a certain inconvenience.

Any further word about the San Francisco musical version of your book? I would like very much to participate, since Doug Northrop, my ex-Raiford-cellmate is out there now with his trumpet. Also with his strumpet.

I'm increasingly skeptical about the cat who wants to produce a play about the chain gang. Some people have the idea that jailhouse sex is arcane, esoteric and incredibly exotic. Possibly he thinks I know the 8 ways unknown to the Emperor. I know only 6.

What's happened to the Moran? I had a brutal letter from him, really savage and mystifying. Has he kicked the sesame oil diet and is he back on juice?   Yrs, Jim

Westchester, New York
DECEMBER 18, 1962

Dear Angiemine:

You could start a whole new movement, the Angry Broad school. Such a capacity for searing indignation, it is bracing. The "aargh!" approach as contrasted to the "pfffh."

If I do not respond to your fine and welcome letters as quickly as I should, fret not. I must contend with a number of factors, earning a living eight precious hours of the day, a chaotic mind, a play to consider, this mummyhumpin novel I've got to do, a journal in which I mumble and rant to myself all the things I can't say aloud for fear of damnation.

. . . Doug the trumpet man did such a hell of a lot to straighten my wig. When he moved into the Raiford cell with me, I had just finished a year with a Sicilian from Milwaukee (who totaled a Chinaman) and I was wallowing in the maso-sadist cycle. The Sicilian had beaten me regularly, and it had been all quite primitive and satisfactory.

Doug set about showing me the possible refinements in cruelty. With a smiling mockery that stymied me completely. It got rather involved, he was mocking his own tendency to sadism and my masochism, at the same time taking care of biz. Scenes like this would ensue:

(It is evening in Cell J-18, the door has been locked for the night. Blake is in the upper bunk reading, Northrop is painting at an easel hung on the end of the bunk. Northrop grunts, takes the painting from the easel and holds it up.)

Northrop: What do you think?

Blake: (Engrossed in book) What?

Northrop: I *said*, what do you think?

Blake: (Takes eyes from book, looks blearily absently at painting) Oh fine. That's fine, Douglas.

Northrop: Don't patronize me, motherfucker.

Blake: (Back in the book) What?

Northrop: (Puts painting down, approaches bunk) Are we feeling petulant and neglected again?

Blake: (Hears the sound in the voice, like an opening theme. He is fully alert now.) Don't start no shit, buddy, and there won't be no shit.
(They are vibrating together now, aware that the game has begun.)

Northrop: (Solicitous) I'm sorry. I forgot to beat you last night.

Blake: Have a care, my son. Don't forget I'm a prince of the church.

(A familiar gambit, referring to Blake's exalted status on the campus, Chaplain's secretary and Chapel organist.)

Northrop: I'm an atheist, baby.

Blake: Well then, remember the neighbors.
(The convicts on both sides of J-18 are dismayed by the nightly shrieks and squeals coming from there. It offends their sense of penitentiary decorum. Suffering is acceptable, it is meet and proper, they feel, but not hedonistic suffering.)

Northrop: (Grinning wolfishly) Fuck the neighbors.
His fist comes down in a hammer blow on Blake's naked thigh and Blake emits a strangled yelp. Northrop, delighted, grabs Blake by the ankles and begins to pull him from the bunk.

Blake: Douglas, please, the neighbors! I'm a prince of the church! He is holding on to the mattress as Northrop drags him by the ankles. Blake shrieks as mattress and all slide in a heap to the floor, and Northrop holds him dangling upside down by the ankles. Blake is laughing wildly. Northrop is stern.

Northrop: I don't like your attitude. We got to change your attitude. You think life is a game.

Blake: (Hysterical) Please let me down. The blood—my head—Douglas, I think your painting shows talent—(gasping)—spark—verve—

Northrop: (Jiggling him) Now you're being sardonic.
A hack appears at the barred door of the cell. He is a simple Union County boy, and he has witnessed the bizarre doings in J-18 before. He considers Northrop a dope fiend, jazz musician and villainous black mustache, beyond the pale, but Blake is a decent man who conducts the chapel choir. Any attack on Blake is an attack on organized religion.

The Hack: What's goin' on hyuh? What chawl call y'sef doin'?

Northrop: (Grins boyishly) Just fuckin' around, Boss.
The boyish grin is not a success, filtered through the sex-maniac mustache.

Blake: (Attempts to be winsome but dignified, standing on his head and looking up at the guard from the floor) Nothing, boss. Just cuttin' the fool. Ah ha.

The Hack: (Disconcerted) Well knock it off, heah? Ah doan wanna come down hyuh again. Heah?

Blake: Yessir, Boss. (Northrop drops him. Blake lies in an ungainly heap at the hack's feet, a living sacrifice.)

Northrop: Yessuh, Boss.

Blake: Yassuh, Boss.

(The hack flees, in his ears maniacal laughter. He resolves to rack up the J-18 occupants at the first pretext.)

Love,—Don't Lose your Job,—Jim

Westchester, New York
JANUARY 21, 1963

Dear Nelson:

Nothing could strike terror to my bones like your characterization of my jailhouse article as "humorless." What kinda crack is that? I got humor I ain't even used yet, buddy. Anyway, it sent me bucketing out to buy the complete work of Bennett Cerf. We will see what we shall see.

Actually I never really felt, deep down inside, that you would like it. I sent it with strong misgivings and a looney maybe-it-will-go-away optimism. The trouble with it, I eventually decided (I don't pay any attention to you), was it's written from the viewpoint of a fink. Out of some wistful desire to ingratiate myself with the finks of the world, on the fine old sleazy premise, if you can't beat 'em, bite 'em.

I can't agree that the subject matter is *vieux jeu*. Lots of people don't know about the evil in this world. And they would like to learn. Baby would they ever like to learn. Civilians I meet, who know about My Past, are constantly entreating, tugging at my sleeve, to tell about prison sex-life. "Cuh-*mahn!*" they say. Just the other day a nice-looking fellow sidled up to me and murmured, "What really happened at Marienbad?"

So you see, the people want to *know*. I unequivocally believe, then, that there is enough clean-minded enlightened curiosity about the subject to justify such an article, nay, the rocks cry out for it. Just because you choose to spend *your* life in steamy purlieus. There's still a lot of decent people in the world, mister.

I've been playing piano some again, working with Larry the young basso. He has been restless and wants to perform again.

So we rehearsed some on the monumental Steinway they got here, with all the resident neurotics standing by to cut us up. They were delighted by the diversion, being bored with whip-sawing one another and they happily focused their free-floating animosity on us.

We worked the local country club a couple times, a debutante launching and New Year's Eve. Larry a smash with the rich broads— the voice is robust, a joy to bounce an accompaniment off of, and the girls were duly gassed. While he sings his songs to the stag line. That's the trouble with democracy, it's sloppy with cross-purposes.

The sight of Kennedy on TV accepting the battle standard of the Bay of Pigs invaders was affecting. The battle flag was immaculate, I guess it didn't see much battle. But such stark symbolism. I cried like a baby.

Then I got a letter from Miami, from an underworld Flagler Street type, an accomplished hotel burglar. Saying what a drag to have all the winos and weirdos back on Flagler, madly spending their CIA bread. Says the cops in Miami, who suffer from anxiety at the best times, are tearing their hair, and the sound of nightsticks on the skulls of heroes resurgent is like a marimba solo.

I got to tell you about Amy, my favorite patient here. Tall birdlike woman with endless capacity for blistering indignation and a virtuoso in fishwife invective. Then at the next instant like a minuetting coquetting stork. She lives with a family of phantoms in her room. One day I go in there and say, Amy, would you like to go down and watch TV? She gives me a level appraising look. (You some kind of a nut?) And says, gesturing at the empty room, "We were talking, dear. I can't leave my family." Like I'm more to be pitied. Next time, I go in there with a tray, say, Amy, maybe your guests will excuse us, it's time for your dinner. She gives me that you-gotta-be-kiddin look, a wild surmise, says, "There's nobody here at all, dear." I *never* hit it right. I know she's putting me on.

All the nurses were pleased because Amy took such a sudden interest in the TV. She's getting better, they twittered. Then we found out why Amy watches so avidly. She thinks all the broads on TV are wearing *her* clothes. She let loose at it the other night, a holocaust.

Do you have a copy of *Another Country*, J. Baldwin, you could lend? Can't afford the steep price, but would like to read it. I presume Mrs Northrop got your "Catch-22" back to you. Doug Northrop is in San Francisco. I had one letter from him while he was still feeling scared about the strange town and wanted to hear from me. I guess he got his nerve back, because he never answered my letter. I care, but remotely, I'm learning to stifle the passion that has tinted and tilted my life to such a degree. I'm afraid I will be less a person for it, this realistic approach, but I've got to get on with it.

Another kind of nostalgia I've been fighting is the Brother-hood-Of-The-Doomed feeling I had in the penitentiary and no longer have, with nothing to put in its place. I've been trying hard to isolate and name this virus, and think I have. Thing is, it's better than many things the world of electric toothbrushes has given me. I don't think I'll ever go back, but, Jesus, I haven't found a safe tree to live in yet. This joint here only points up that what they call lunacy is often a kind of lyricism and what they call sanity is nibbling cannibalism.

Mike's letter to me was an instruction in the nature and uses of gratuitous cruelty, I thought. He said he wanted to borrow fifty bucks (after a lot of funny stuff about superannuated burglars). He put the request in rather commanding caps LIKE THIS, and of course I was crushed. I didn't answer, though he enclosed an addressed envelope, I didn't know what to say. A put-on? Some put-on.

But some time you could tell him I don't make any money, that it will take me a long time to get up off the floor and build some kind of margin against a civilian world I found worse than hostile—indifferent and unaware. Tell him further, if you want to, that any spare bread I can get I send to the poor bastards in the joint, whom I promised to help while they can't help themselves.

Tell him, nyah nyah nyah. TELL HIM IF MY KIDS have to

go without BATTERIES for their TRANSISTORS I'LL PAY
HIM BACK EVERY LOUSY DIME!!!

OH WELL you don't have to tell him *that* Zut alors, —Jim

PS—When arc you coming to NY? Hefner opened up a big new
bunny-hutch and the NY commissars say any rabid rabbit-lover
can get in without a key, Whee!

Westchester, New York
JANUARY 25, 1963

Dear Angie:

Christmas, New Year, have come and gone and I have been
awash in more or less trivial projects designed to make a buck.
Well, not completely trivial. I have a reclamation project going
in Larry the Basso which is of some value and interest. He has
been put in the tender care of the ever-lovin' Doctor (known
here as Pope George the Good) by his parents and a lawyer
in order to escape being deep-froze on a C.A.N. charge, which
is Crime Against Nature, only whose they don't say. He had
a penchant for picking up pubescent finks (generic term, "Dirt")
who were either digging for gold or hollering for fuzz, or both.

So, no confidence in himself, tried to kill same. A good intelligence, far too much chintz and chichi. In the concert racket
as it is today, there is an equal mixture of pederasty, snobbery
and vivisection.

A problem, complicated by the fact that the shrink in charge
here is right out of Mary Baker Eddy, but with a lofty reputation. Pity he's got, sense he ain't.

And pity, a beautiful mad convict once told me, is inverted
hate.

George H. that was, he created an uproar in the lobby of a
midtown Manhattan hotel, what with shooting an FBI man and
what was worse, getting blood all over the wall-to-wall. They
returned him to Florida, and one fine clear day, when he was
in rigorous solitary confinement—having, in all fairness, earned

it with cumulatively manic behavior—one fine day he was let
out of his cell to hygienically and per statute take a shower.
Under the towel around his middle was a pistol from God
knows where. He was kept naked in his cell but the genteel
rural morality of the nitwit guard would not allow him to gaze
on the genitalia of a criminal. So George commandeered the
stupid hack's clothes, locked him in with his own keys, then
ranging wild he used another guard as a shield to get him to the
Warden's office and shot the Warden in his big fat belly. (The
Warden's last words: "Jesus, Mary and Joseph, Shitfire I'm
dying.") A local jury of farmers, envious of the Warden's
wealth and his Black Angus herd, acquitted George, or at any
rate they gave him life in prison. Which caused only a minor
delay in the prepared scenario. He was sequestered in the
dread Flat Top, punishment building, and eventually died of
influenza. Dying of flu is not easy these days, but George had
considerable help. Some say he died of neglect.

Whatever he died of, he began on a Kansas farm, flew wildly
and erratically for a while, like a misfired rocket, and crashed
in ignominy and despair. But for a while, he beautifully soared.
Powered by je ne sais quoi.

When George was still in the population he lived alone in a
cell; in an overcrowded prison he told the Warden he would kill
anyone they put in with him. A somber solitary figure in the
E-Floor. (E-Floor was notoriously the home of hipsters and
troublemakers, desirable neighborhood and everybody wanted
to live there.)

He stopped me and abruptly asked me the title of the book I
was carrying. It was James Baldwin's *Giovanni's Room*. He read
it and asked for more. I gave him (as carefully as watering a
doubtful plant, with love and hope and fear) *The Lying Days*,
Nadine Gordimer. I could give him only the books I had, the
ones I liked. I remember also *The Duke of Gallodoro* by Aubrey
Menen.

And one Friday afternoon he stopped me in the Yard, and
said would I spend the night in his cell. This was more or less

routine, the locker-up was a venal convict, Saturday was a holiday and as in the Free World, Friday night was a time of
license and letting down. On E-Floor, as in Suburbia, there was
a general sexual Musical Chairs. He told me he had arranged
for a tube (locally, a toob). Which was a Benzedrine inhaler
that we would eat to inflame us during the night. I agreed and
that night at lockup time I was in George's cell.

Lust, pity, fright, love, bewilderment. We talked for a good
part of the night. That is, George talked. What it was like, what
it meant, I have to walk up and down when I think about it. Can
a pigeon say what a raven is?

So in a solitary cell, naked, with the damp north Florida
wind blowing on him, lost and starving, George was maneuvered
into eternity.

What was he like, Montgomery Cliftish on the outside, inside
unbearably taut, aluminum and Vesuvius. He was a destroyer, a
malign force. And yet in fellatio my tears fell into his groin
hair. What was I crying about? Myself? Him? Everybody? Go
figure it. —Strange, I began by telling you about Larry the singer
and I'm telling you about George the bandit.

Goodnight, this is a bad night for Baby.   Love,—Jim

Westchester, New York
FEBRUARY 1, 1963

[To Studs Terkel, Chicago]

Dear Studs:

Nice to hear from you. I heard you were in France interviewing Simone Signoret. What did you ever do to merit such
heavenly discourse?

Your interview with Beauvoir was played on WBAI, the New
York FM station I mostly listen to. Their programming is somewhat solemn for my taste, and sententious a good deal of the
time, but it is still the most interesting FM around.
joint, he stopped me one day, peremptorily, in the corridor of
A lot of the music is terribly precious, 16th century quartets

sawing and tootling, dryballs music, and much avant-garde jazz
I think of as Spades' Revenge.

But the classroom broadcasts and political things are fine.
There was an interview with an ex-FBI man who was sharply
critical of J. Edgar Hoohoo. Which brought down the attention
of the Senate Internal Security Committee. The heads of Pacifica
were subpoenaed. I felt impelled to write a letter but saw no
point in sending the usual I Am An American beef, the That's-
What-Makes-America-Grate style. In a shitfight, why throw
mud?

So I wrote Senator Dodd of Connecticut, Chairman, in the
person of a spade constituent from Conn., asking how it was
that a Conn. Senator, beholden to the big Conn. black vote,
would lend himself to a witch-roast in the company of two
nigger-burners from Dixie, Johnston of South Carolina and
Eastland of Miss. (Both committee members.) I said I was going
to bring the matter up at the African Baptist Church and
that we would be alerting the black voters of Bridgeport, Hart-
ford and New Haven.

Your concern over my welfare is indeed gratifying, dear
Studs, but the basic misconception of most civilians about convicts seems to be that they suffer, when actually they are
comparatively blithe and carefree. Certainly they're not as harried as the gnomes I see on New York streets, scuttling and
scurrying into subways like apprehensive White Rabbits.

This should be my address for a while, until I get an urge
again to put my head in the bear's mouth. I'm fighting this kind
of irresponsible conduct, or trying to, since the quiet of the
country is good for writing.

Like to hear from you, good man, —Jim

Westchester, New York
FEBRUARY 10, 1963

Dear Lovable Robert:

Your silence has been most abrasive. Still I had the feeling
when we were parting at Grand Central that time, that you

were writing me off in some obscure fashion. Maybe not so obscure, but it was beautifully controlled and well mannered, for which, felicidad.

I'll be coming down before too very long, it depends upon Doctor Algren, who has a book coming out shortly and expects to be lolling in silken ease at the Plaza, courtesy of some publisher. He wrote me to "come down for the upsurge," which I fully intend to do.

My incipient benefactor on Off B'Way is in Hollywood at the moment, working in fillums, due back in a couple of weeks, and I would like also at that time to show him what I have done on the play about dirty rotten convicts, especially dirty rotten homosexual convicts, which is, I gather, the way he wants it played. I don't know whether this is squalid or just plain silly.

It has been difficult to put this material in play form, so much telescoping, distilling, capsuling (if that wasn't a verb it is now) is required. And I veer wildly from day to day in my opinion of what has been done. Sometimes it seems to just lay flat on the paper, with not the barest hint that it will ever stir.

This place continues to seethe, but I go mostly my own way. I have much to do, and can't really afford to be bugged by bugs. (Meaning personnel, not patients, patients I love and adore and we are wholly compatible.)

The Doctor, Pope George The Good, has brought back from New York an individual, a large lumpish type suffering, pauvre petit, from homoyouknowhat. He has been breathing heavily over Larry, to no avail. Larry needs something with a little more menace. We are working on a new night club routine, to vary the monotony and make some dear sweet money.

The person who picks up the mail here I suspect of trifling with mine, and I am enclosing a letter which I would like you to post in New York. If this bog-trotter has been fooling around, I mean to put his ass in the can for a good long time— like twelve years in Leavenworth, or eleven years in Twelveworth, as Groucho used to say.

I still get strange homesick feelings for the joint, and have to fight them constantly. I've been sending bread to Ben B and trying to interest St Leonard's in getting him out on parole. And I sent a campy cigarette holder to Miss Billy and am told it is *succès fou* on campus.

Douglas N. is in San Francisco with his trumpet and strumpet, but I have had no word for a good while. I hope he hasn't stepped on his dick again.   Write, fat man. —Jim

Westchester, New York
FEBRUARY 17, 1963

Dear Angie:

Marvelous news that you are planning to come out of your California cave. It would be insane to come to NY while the weather is so demoniacal, but I wouldn't say not do it. The temperature doesn't bother me much, I don't have to go out in it— even when Larry and I have to go some place to piffawm, he has a nice warm motorcar.

If I had to do that 8 AM bit with the busses and subways, I'd be long gone to Florida, playing run-sheep-run with the Dixie fuzz. Whatever befalls I plan to stay here until the Doctor says Pull It. He took a long chance on me when nobody else would, and I consider I owe him a great deal.

No, I do not want to meet Alec Wilder. I consider him one of the great ones, and I would be overawed, probably I would nervously wet myself. And I don't suppose he wants anyone sitting at his feet, too cluttersome.

I do-hoo-hoo want to meet Marlon Brando, if only to sit and pant. The people you know, this is like Apollo Belvedere himself! Besides that dizzying animal magnetism, what an artist, what a profundity of questions his performance stirs in the mind. I have never seen him but what I came away still thinking about the character he played, utterly convinced that whatever the part, the story was still going on, as though I had been allowed to witness only a part of it. Few *writers* can do that for me, and no other actors. For instance, had I gone to New Orleans after "Streetcar" I would probably have looked for Kowalski in the Vieux Carre.

No need of giving you Doug Northrop's address, since he's back in Lake Forest with his mother. I correspond with her because I like her, but to be truthful it is mainly because I hope to hear word of Doug.

He put me down again of course, and I knew nothing of this action until I heard from his ma. Seems the chick he was with left him in Santa Monica (he tried to sell her to a trombone man) and flew back to Chicago. He followed her, which in the Doug I know is pretty amazing. Maybe I don't know this one. Not surprising that the chick split. Doug is capable of a vicious chilling cruelty that can be too much for a maso like me, and godknows I can soak it up. When we were in together, I told him that his best stick for kicking the habit and staying kicked was a wise and strong chick that he could be hooked on, and I think perhaps he's found her. About that I'm happy. Only I think the chick has no eyes at all for me, a healthy antipathy. It occurred to me in Chicago when the three of us would be together that she was prepared to accept an old love of Doug's in female form, but never a male, and she broke rather frosty with me.

The other day I had another jolt. Bob, the cat I stayed with briefly in New York and did time with in Raiford, has disappeared. I phoned the stud he formerly shared the pad with, found out he'd been booked in the West 4th Street Station on lewd and indecent behavior, made bond, then jumped it and split the scene.

Bob and I were pretty tight in the joint, a wholly platonic intellectual friendship—he was geared and I just don't groove sackwise with another geared one, no chemistry. But I had a lot of respect for his mind, not creative particularly, but incisive, retentive, analytical and a brilliant schemer. As neurotic as a castrated camel though, and on the street when anything hung him up badly, his reaction was to do something outrageous and certain to bring down the fuzz and land him in the slam. (Usually it was cruising the subway shithouses.) So it seems he's reverted to pattern, which is a shock. I thought he had it beat.

What shakes me in all this is that so many nights I walk the grounds here, feeling the inexplicable pull of the joint, trying to fathom the Why of this incredible homesickness, trying to name for myself the kinship of the doomed I felt for the other cons when I was in. How is it possible, when I hated so many of them, found them dull and brutal and often more square than the squares outside?

This is a fight that still goes on, even at a time when it looks as if I could have something going for me, if only I just stay with it and work at it. But I find myself wondering what the cons back there are doing, how they're making it. And I think of it with nostalgia, so go figure it. The longer I stay out the weaker this demented attraction will become, I hope, and so I struggle all the time.

Hope to see you in New York, little pudding, whenever you decide to make it. Meanwhile stay in touch, stay flexible,

—Jim

Westchester, New York
FEBRUARY 21, 1963

Dear Doug:

I feel some diffidence in writing, in view of not hearing any more from out there— but I had the urge to write to you, so herewith. The last communication was a lot of running off, I guess. But I was so delighted by that Czech band, I haven't been so electrified in a long time. (Occasionally I will get the same shock from the singing of Ray Charles, a sudden poignancy so real that it stabs me, the same desperation and defiance that is in Bud Powell's playing.)

And of course there was an added pleasure for me in the Czech band, it put to naught all the nosy capitalist lies— "These people are living like dogs, dying like flies." If they can do that well artistically, living like dogs, it would seem like cultural vandalism to interfere or try to change it. I'm not committed either way, I deplore political quarrels, but it's bracing to have the manhole cover unexpectedly lifted on the sewage of American sanctimony. As for Spade's Revenge type music, I won't cry any more, though I still listen and try vainly to get with it.

I'm going to see John Clellon Holmes in Old Saybrook shortly, at Algren's suggestion. Holmes is a jazz buff, has written about it, and also a couple novels about jazz and musicians, *The Horn* and *Go.* They are well spoken of in some quarters, I haven't read them, but perhaps he can tell me something I need to know.

He doesn't blow anything, and it suddenly dawns on me that there are legions of laymen, hangers-about and hipsters who know more about this music than I do. I can't think of another art form which has inspired such a degree of expertise among non-participants. Well, Brahms, maybe; there have always been platoons of hot-eyed fat ladies ready to check anybody out on that subject.

There is bad news concerning our little chum Bob Kaplan. He has disappeared. I talked to the cat who shared the pad with him. Said Kaplan had given a bad check for his part of the rent and split. Later booked into West 4th Street on a charge of lewd and indecent behavior. Made bond on that, then jumped it.

What is surprising, he came on like Up-The-Ladder the last time I saw him; he was doing well, in that didactic sententious way, at the company he worked for. He wanted me to take a job there. I was in New York at his invitation, he bought me a five-dollar lunch. Baby had strong reservations about this. I'd observed the action at his pad and even went a couple of rounds, myriads of under-age pachucos loping in and out like leopards, and it seemed to me Robert was packing some Heat.

I had no firm intention of changing jobs, but I figured Kaplan is such an arranger, so arrange awready. The personnel man had a smile like the operating edge of a machete, eyes like ball bearings. Something shifted behind his eyeballs when we met, but he gave me the standard interview, in essence: "Do you give up?"

Wanting to look nice, I was wearing stuff that's *dernier cri* in New Haven: Suede chukka boots that tied behind the knees, a casual car coat of scalded muskrat, black turtleneck and a pigskin scarf.

Alas, I missed out. I learned later that it was because of two things— One of the questions was, if you could rescue only one person from a burning building, would it be your mother or Vice President Goldfarb of Jefferson Screw? Goldfarb in a New York instant, I answered. Personnel man wrote down: "This man suffers from pyromatricide, the urge to cremate his mother." And then on the highly scientific Aptitude Scale, it turned out I had a pronounced flair for Zebra-Skinning, and there was no call for it.

Afterwards Kap says, You shouldn't have dressed like that. Like what, I says, all the Westchester bloods dress like this. You shoulda worn a dark tie, he says.

Staying with Robert when I slid into New York on my ass, I soon perceived in what manner I was expected to pay for my keep. He'd apparently been storming the battlements of Greenwich Village, to no avail. So I was trundled in and out of coffeehouses, up and down tenement stairs, tendered far and wide as Kaplan's ticket to Bohemia.

We'd climb the stairs to a 5th floor pad. Kaplan knocked, the door opened a crack, one eye looked out. (You ever see dismay register in one single eyeball? It gets you where you live.) Kap blurted out, Hi this is jimblake musician writer parisreview simone de beauvoir nelsonalgren walk on the wild side.

The eyeball flicked in my direction and away: "I'm sorry, my mother just died naked and I have to get her dressed for the police."

Some places we did better, we got in. There was a group of unshaven men, one of them was even a nigger, and a girl with uncombed hair and black leggings. To my midwestern eyes, they looked as if they had just thrown their opium pipes and hypodermic syringes under the sink when I came in. Wow, I thought, wow wow wow, the Village.

They resumed a spirited discussion about the New York Yankees. Kaplan said in a tight singsong, jimblake composer writer paris review nelson debeauvoir simonealgren penitentiary.

There was an old upright. Kaplan said play. Nobody else said anything. I sat down, did my crossed-hands version of Milenberg Joys, eight bars. How about that, Kaplan says. He's a writer, too.

Let's see him write something, somebody says. They gave me a pencil and I wrote on the wall, "Franz Kafka sucks." But they weren't paying attention.

It's a cold town.   Ever, — Jim

Westchester, New York
MARCH 28, 1963

Dear Doug:

Two A.M., and outside the profound silence of the country night, which never seems to me to be really a silence but the engulfing sigh of the universe. The quiet tonight is broken now and then by the doleful bawling of some cows who have been left in the pasture, and by the vernal yawping of the pheasants.

The radio murmurs, a spade broad is dismembering "I'm Glad There Is You" (sounding peevish, not glad) in that sexless gullah bray that is a cross between a bagpipe and a goathorn, indicating she is hip. I'm so tired of these strident shrikes. And it reminds me to say that there is a fine record around by Barbra Streisand, who sings with considerable intelligence. Maybe this kind of vocal will disperse, or anyway inhibit, the spastic wailing of the black Eumenides.

The western adventures sound exhilarating and instructive, if harrowing. I was happy to hear you did some blowing out there, and that there were ears to hear it. And good to know you're painting, that should soothe you some. I wish I could separate you from one of those paintings you did in Florida —one of me, what else?—to hang in my murky lair in the treetops under the eaves.

This seems to be my season for striving with the faggots. First my mutinous baritone Larry, and now ———, the wicked stepsister of Manhattan who talked me into trying a prison play, has been a source of aggravation. He's a difficult dude to pin, there's such a lot of loose ecstasy banging around, and when he talks the air is full of feathers and birdsong.

I floundered for a while trying to find an approach to the drama problem, made a few false starts, then did quite a bit of work on what seemed to me a sound conception. Showed it to him, got the old familiar incandescent bezazz— but there was also a certain reserve. When I finally got both of his shoulders on the carpet and forced him to say what he thought the play should be, I was stupefied. He had in mind a kind of soap operatic commercial for faggotry, passion-in-the-pen style— Boystown Meets Queenstown.

I told him I wasn't interested in fostering fellatio—told him further that I found faggots per se duller than Doris Day and that any play exclusively about *That* would be a three-act O.D. of Pentothal.

"Never should I have yielded to your perverse Mediterranean desires," I cried hotly, my blue eyes flashing fire. "You've lost all respect for me!" And with trembling fingers I tore off the Bronzini sapphire cufflinks and hurled them full into his satanic grin.

"By the head of Ben Gurion," he breathed, "you're lovely when you're angry. Come here, you little spitfire!"

His mocking laughter followed me as I leaped through the window.

He comes every day to the convent now, bringing white roses, begging to see me. Mother Superior says I must pray for a quiet heart. And I will, oh, I will.

—Bernadette (Call me Barney)

Westchester, New York
APRIL 4, 1963

[To Nelson Algren, Chicago]

Dear Supreme Monster All Sublime:

Thanks for the check and the glad tidings about the anthology *Book Of Lonesome Monsters*. Now I can get a bicycle to assist me in my bird-watching. I've been watching and watching, quite contentedly, but now they tell me I have to identify them. Which smacks of finkery. How do you get a bird to tell you his name and all that?

Bernard Geis is the outfit that publishes those imitation books, isn't it? I understand they go in heavily for promotional jazz, so I'll be looking for you playing those jolly games on daytime TV, "What's My Disease?" and "Fuck Till You Win!"

The NY papers are publishing again. Seems a pity, I thought their absence filled a long-felt need. I see that Conroy the Bold finally finished his book. I hope this will help him to secure that beachhead on the shores of Bourgeoisie.

The Littlest Monster

Westchester, New York
APRIL 24, 1963

Dear Nelson:

You're right, it was inexcusable poltroonery, my being so slovenly about *Catch-22*. You shall have it back in short order. Thing was, you were somewhere in the Pacific when I finished it, and I was so enthusiastic about it I wanted to share it with Doug Northrop, who at that time was still in Raiford, and crying for something to read.

He brought it back to Lake Forest with him when he got out and still has it. I've written to tell him to take it to you, he has wanted to meet you ever since reading "Wild Side." We were cellmates in Florida for a long time, and I think you'll find him interesting. Good musician, good mind, fair painter, a complex neurotic. Orestes complex, or a variation, I think, which is only a way of defining the basically indefinable.

The more I see of psychiatry the more I am inclined to suspect it is all pretentious and fraudulent horseshit. The shrink that runs this joint is rated near the top, at least in the East. He's an enigma, rigorously reticent, I have exchanged practically no conversation with him since I've been here. (Sometimes I suspect that the Mysterioso is his bag, and that's it.) I ask him for bread when I need it, he gives it, I say thank you.

But because I'm curious about him, I observe him narrowly, almost obsessively, and I think I've got an angle on him. He has therapy sessions of a sort with 3 or 4 patients here (the rest he ignores). All of them have told me they feel bewildered and lost (and unloved) after these occasions. The doctor listens at times, they say, or does not appear to listen. He offers them nothing at all, no shadow of panacea of any kind. What he does offer, implicitly, is a fairly luxurious pad, acres of green to walk around in, good food, plenty of time — if they can continue to pay the outrageous charges.

He's in his seventies— and I speculate whether at the end of a long illustrious career in psychiatry he has come to the conclusion that this is all that can be done, really.

If so, it is too lofty a concept for the patients. They go away mumbling, little better than they arrived. Tanner, maybe. The long-termers (9 or 10 years) assure me that the doctor is omniscient, omnipotent. And I have seen that he is not, he is merely indifferent or anyway remote. They yearn for a

godhead, a father figure to tell them sit down, shut up, love
ye one another.

In my opinion this kind of thing would pull the whole
operation together, the patients would be happy, or reassured
(at least they would be reassured that the ancient lies they
live by are still the only truth they'll ever know). And he
withholds it, and himself.

I did have one session with the Doctor in his office, one
evening when I went in there for something else. He asked
me how I was doing, and invited me to sit down. Then as
always, he looked out the window and talked in a musing
fashion about the place he'd had before Lakeside. He turned
and saw me looking at a framed picture on the wall, an old
sepia print of a remarkably ugly house, a big one, three stories
in wood, and set in a landscape that resembled the original
"blasted heath."

He said, "That's a picture of the house I built for my
mother the year before I left home to attend the university.
She lived there until her death."

All unconsciously (I think), I said in commiserating tones,
"It's a pity you don't have a picture of *her*." He gave me
a full-on scrutiny, then turned to the window again. Silence.
"I have several pictures of her."   Zut alors, — Jim

Westchester, New York
MAY 5, 1963

Dear Angie:

It was good to hear you have been singing again even
if, as the man suggests, you were singing off pitch. Though
I don't believe it for a moment, I remember Gleason as a
Downbeat writer, which conclusively proves he knows nothing
about music.

Probably it is for the best there has been a delay in writing
you. After reading your letter I was prepared to burn you
down. It struck me that your reaction to the adventures you

had with the Methedrine set was a kind of snobbish negation. The ampule-heads sound frenetic but interesting. I'd have thought you wouldn't be so much concerned with putting it down as "juvenile schmeck" as in wondering what it did to them, and why they did it.

I remember Doug telling me, when he returned to Florida on parole violation, that he tried Meth on the street. He said it lit him up like a Roman candle and that he dominated six simultaneous conversations at a cocktail party. Said he finally wound up running around the room hollering "Shut up shut up shut up shut up!"

Nobody knows better than I what a profound drag it is to be hauled into jail— the first time it happened to me I went into shock. (The Chicago Bridewell could well shock a hardened habitue.) But when I recovered, I found it was instructive, more than that, a revelation, I fell ten miles down a well, to learn when I landed that life had scarcely missed a beat and was inexorably going on with a whole new cast and script. There was a certain relief in shucking the burdensome pretensions I'd been staggering around under. I lost a lot of weight that day, I lost fear, and I learned to travel light.

I finally heard from Doug about his San Francisco trip. Seems the whole scene was rocketing headlong dissipation in both junk and juice, but he did get to work and blow out there, said he scared a number of people, which I can well believe. He played a benefit at San Q, which gassed and chilled him at the same time. Then the chick he was with put him down and split for Chicago. He followed, not her particularly, he came back to pick up on some of his ma's bread. But he's back with the chick again in Chicago and she's pregnant, so that affair hasn't very long to breathe.

Nelson sent me *The Naked Lunch* and *$100 Misunderstanding*. I thought the Burroughs book partially interesting (Nelson said it's not a book you read, it's a book you try) for its glimpses of the junkie scene. Some of the humor is funny because outrageous and there are some really fresh homosexual fantasies.

I thought I had thoroughly covered that field in the prodigious putrescence of my imagination; there are several areas I missed. The touted stream-of-thought spontaneity is largely tedious babbling and there's at times a gee whillikers air of ersatz-wicked.

"Hundred-Dollar Misunderstanding" isn't anywhere as funny as has been said, in my view, and the guy has a tin ear, neither the square nor the spade whore talk true.

So I read again Terry Southern's *Magic Christian.* Heeheehee.

Things have been reasonably quiet at Lakeside goat ranch, I had a brief tussle with a second-cook here, a stud from college trying to be a psychologist. He knows a lot of facts, he's a fact-factory. Ultimately I decided he was nyekulturny, didactic and humorless. Oh well, I was intrigued by the vigor of the beards in his armpits and the hair patterns on his body, and we swung sackwise for a blazing fornit, but no mo. He has come back to Lakeside for consultations with the Doctor, but after digging some of his gears, I'd say he needs a Master Mechanic.

Which reminds me, a con I knew in Raiford blew in on the end of a check run with a score of two grand and we had a profligate couple of days before he vanished, trailing flames. I'd forgotten how bracing it is, what a shift in perspective, to see things through a predator's eyes. He wanted me to go to Mexico City with him (where, should the worst befall, they got a swingin jail). But I've become very staid and spayed, I'm afraid.

Well, not precisely. A new patient blew in, a young Pole from Maine, an utter charmer, Slavic vibrations are like few others. He has had a nervous collapse, and I could joyfully join him, I feel a little collapsible myself.

Nozdrovya, stay fluxy, — Jim

Westchester, New York
JUNE 20, 1963

Dear Doug:

Pneumonia in June. Of all the gauche and not-quite things I've done, contracting pneumonia in June has to be the peak. I just got back from the hospital today, and I think I feel more sheepish than anything else. But it was worth the pneumonia to get your phone call. I know you'll agree when I say it's stupid, but I tingled and tangled all night after it— I have jiggled, wiggled and wriggled the best I know how, and I'm still on that hook. The primeval surge I felt when I heard your voice was the reallest thing that has happened for quite a while. If I have to be wired to something, it might as well be that.

What I couldn't tell you, with the male nurse standing there (a good nurse and a nice cat—sometimes he thinks he's Flo Nightingale, sometimes Mae West, and it seems a viable arrangement) was that I was on an extended goblins' carnival in Manhattan, where we ransacked the pharmacopoeia, and I came back from that one wasted. And vulnerable. Hence, pneumonia. Hence, health-kick.

While I was convalescing (if you can call it that, it's a tight schedule, the recovery period is only somewhat longer than the time allowed for urinating) I read *The King Must Die* by Mary Renault. The way in which Theseus thinks about his time of captivity in Crete, his feeling of companionship for his fellow bull-dancers in the Labyrinth, the sharing of privation — that is how I think of that period in Florida. Read the book, and see what you get.

I won't make this long, I'm still rocky, but the rockiness is insignificant compared to the confusion, and that is paramount. I haven't been able to forget the tone in your voice, Doug. Let's turn off the bubble machine.

If your ma wants you to go to school and all that good

shit, you can do it perfectly well in New York, and commute from here. I'll sound the Doctor on working something out so that you pay your rent, like working on ground maintenance. But it would be nice to have as much of this summer as possible. Love to your ma, and the two poltergeists. Let me know what you want to do.   Best, Jim

Westchester, New York
JULY 17, 1963

[To George Plimpton, New York]

Dear George:

Much gratified by the bundle of Paris Reviews you sent, beyond the saying, and rather surprised too, I discovered when I received it. A sort of forlorn impulse prompted me to write, and I guess I never expected such a gracious return.

Your account of reader reaction to my stuff was truly amazing. I was not aware of it. The only reaction I personally encountered was from a formidable female I met at Algren's once, she belabored me interminably with enthusiasm. To the point where I began to wonder if she could be one of those freakish broads who are inordinately attracted to ex-cons. Apparently they see a penumbra of menace and doom godknowswhat around men from the pen. I told her (in wine) I had never owned a wide black leatherbelt with brass studs.

I remember a number of females who gathered every Sunday afternoon along a road which bordered the baseball field of the joint. There was no wall, just a high triple fence electrified, and these harpies languished in brief shorts in plain view of the cons watching the ball game. They caused a good deal of torment. My mind was so clogged with conjecture about their precise motives, I never could arrive at a conclusion. Perhaps the answer was so obvious and shabby and sad I didn't want to find it.

Your immense kindness constrains me to try to explain my reluctance to venture into the city out of my rural retreat.

I've been out of the joint for over a year, and am still troubled by the fear of recidivism.

Because my last bit at Raiford, when I went back looking at a ten, was self-inflicted. Playing piano and doing comparatively well in Charleston, South Carolina, after months I was to no clear purpose irresistibly compelled to go back. To myself I pictured this behavior (fuzzily) as some kind of preordained doom-bound voluntary exile, kismet, bizarre and passing strange. And poignant, oh ever so. (There was a small cynical rotter in the back of my mind who demurred briefly and was summarily silenced.)

I think I have it beat this time, not yet completely sure. — A stud I met in Raiford, and was a good friend to me there in some bad times, got out shortly after me. He'd built eight years. Devoutly unregenerate, a brilliant check virtuoso, he's had a dazzling career since release. Between forays, he comes up here to visit, bewildered and afraid because he feels the pull of nostalgia for the joint. And so consults me, as one who has found the cure. I have no remedy for him, all I can tell him in honesty is that if he wants to go back, so go. Looking at him I see myself as I was in Charleston. Nobody could have told *me* anything, and I could not have heard it if they did.

Recently I got an anonymous letter postmarked Chicago. All it contained was a typed piece of doggerel—as poetry, miserable. It said in essence that while I might seem to be doing all right in Westchester, my heart was still in the Florida chain gang. In one way, I was intrigued by it, the first anonymous letter I had ever seen, let alone received.

Otherwise I was chilled and saddened to think that somewhere a malign troll was engaged in such a dismal misbegotten effort. He must have a totally false impression of what I am like— I couldn't possibly be of any interest to somebody like that. At any rate, if the design was to rattle or disturb me, it didn't, I was merely puzzled and depressed. So maybe I'm over the hump.

Thank you again for your consideration and kindness.

Sincerely, Jim Blake

Westchester, New York
AUGUST 2, 1963

Dear Doug:

(. . . When you don't write, I review all the reasons why you despise me. I'd appreciate it if you'd confirm or deny them . . .)

Rain all day in varying degrees, the big finale towards evening a thrashing lashing crashing cyclone and typhoon which blew a big tree across the power line. Con Ed engaged in trench warfare elsewhere, so this is by oil lamp, an illumination I prefer.

I have three days off and had planned a fairly extended wandering on my bike clear up to Stratford, Connecticut, to look at that operation. Now with a day less, I'll settle for Dobbs Ferry and vicinity.

You used to heap scorn on my legs, call them birdlegs and such. No more, tootsie. From pumping the bike up these bloody hills I got calves like Nureyev. And that ain't all. When I'm rolling along wearing shorts, screams of ecstasy issue from passing T-Birds and Sunbeams. Recently a white-haired epicene in a Jag paced me for miles out of Harrison, tossing out fins and sawbucks. Swirled around my wheels like autumn leaves. Call me "Legs."

The bike is part of a health-kick regimen I began on leaving the hospital. That was a jolt, I left there with lively intimations of mortality—translation, scared shitless. I'm still pill-prone, but I try to exercise what is for me judicious restraint.

The pneumonia fright also drove me to writing like a demon, acutely aware of time running out. The urgency has abated some, but I'm still pretty industrious. Partly because of the walloping hospital bill. Dr F paid that, but now I have to reimburse him in installments. At times he's a stone Vermont skinflint about bread, at others, utterly profligate. If the money were for fingerpainting lessons, he'd probably donate it.

Right now I'm concentrating on trying to produce a short story for The Paris Review. George Plimpton, to my honest amazement, told me that the stuff of mine Paris Review printed aroused a lot of comment and inquiries about more. Said he wants to see whatever I have to show, so I'm working on something based on an incident at Deep Lake road camp. Being used to the looser discipline of longer writing (or no discipline) I'm having a time finding the control a short story needs, and have made numerous starts trying to locate the groove.

I had hoped for a reaction to my suggestion you study in New York and let me try to set up some arrangement with the Doctor for your living here. What I had in mind was your doing some sort of part-time work in exchange for room and board.

Kaplan has had another renascence. I was rather surprised to find myself annoyed that he had not killed himself, or done something drastic. It was a revelation to me to realize that my interest in him was largely morbid. This is the last I shall tell about him, I am bitterly disappointed in him and the way he has fucked off his appointment in Samarra.

Anyway, he calls me, says he'll finance a night on the town if I come down to NY. Grudgingly I agree, and he meets me in Grand Central with two six-foot eighteen-year-olds, obviously predatory types, quite beautiful, totally blank. Kap proudly displays these trophies, really pathetic, and, god, so much useless heat.

So then it turns out he's living with a Jewish interior decorator in one of those middle-bracket insurance-company pigeoncotes, ineffably depressing and claustrophobic. Ghastly suffocating overdecorated pad. The proud owner has got wall to wall gold carpeting. Kap says take your shoes off at the door. Oh my God, Robert, I says, you didn't tell me you were shacking with a wily Japanese after Pearl Harbor and all. Robert is annoyed. The mark hears it and is also annoyed, besides disdainful at the influx of riffraff.

The mark is a Jewish son whose mother calls up every hour on the hour. I'll spare you the rest of that. Except to say Kaplan, who screamed like an eagle when anyone said he looked Jewish, is now doing dialect. He's *Passing*.

I'm taken to visit a couple genuine Bohemians, a spade faggot, or spaggot, and his white Daddy, who is called "Eric" and I do mean quotes. "Eric" is naked except for a jockstrap crocheted by the spaggot. He, the daddy, has a neat little compact sun-tanned body and a round button-face, and I am reminded strongly of a baby goat.

Kaplan sends the blond juvenile delink out with ten dollars to get some "Grass." And I do mean quotes. (He is trying to become a pot-head, it is the Village vogue.) Meanwhile the bohemians proudly exhibit the pad. They got a terrace, and that white iron furniture that leaves welts. The kid comes back with the shit and Kaplan says will I roll it up. For a sawbuck, enough pot to make four sticks. Keep your eye on that kid.

The pot is straight oolong, a very bad green, heavily peppered with something. I don't crack, I roll it, and everybody solemnly Turns On. From there, they stare lugubriously and hangdoggish at one another, afraid to say they're turned on, afraid to say they ain't.

I was reminded of J.P., when he poured tons of nutmeg down me.

"You feel anything?" he asks.

"I got a headache," I says.

"That's it! That's the kick!"

Let's talk about yew, — Jim

Westchester, New York
AUGUST 25, 1963

Dear Angie:

You sounded happier in your last letter than you have for quite a while. The free-floating petulance was absent. That man must be good for you. Forget about his dinoysian kid, who seems to occupy your thoughts. If the little shit is flirting with frac-turing the statutes, the old man should let him go to jail. If he's got any brains it will do him good, if he hasn't he may at least pick up some pointers on lawbreaking and be more efficient at it.

Or, if he's so dazzling, why doesn't he become a professional coxter? (For women, I mean, faggots would burn him out.) Though maybe this is a crowded field in California.

I hope you made a lot of bread on August 4, your night at the hungry i (my god, is it that long ago I got your letter?).

Doug came East as I asked him to. Apparently he wangled a get-out-of-town donation from his ma and bought a station wagon. First I knew, he woke me one morning calling from White Plains. God, the heart-stopping joy of hearing his voice. And that mingling of shyness and fright and overflowing gladness to see him again. He was so huge, so beautiful, so brusquely awkward—and to look at his face and see mirrored there exactly the upheaval that was racking me. If life is not about this, it is not about anything.

I occupy a couple rooms at the top of the house and Doug stayed there with me. He slept in one room, me in another and all the resident neurotics here died to know if we were conjugally occupying my celibate couch. I never had so many requests for books and magazines.

I was determined (I can be so twisted) I would not broach the desire that was looming so large in my head I'm sure it stuck out of my ears. So we spent a couple of Paul et Virginie nights.

The third night we got stiffened on Dexies. I had all-night duty that night. There is an elaborate luxury suite here, vacant because the rich neurotic who lives in it is at the Vineyard for the summer. It has a screened porch that looks over miles of country to the sound. Here, in gayety and gravity, we discovered one another again.

Alas for re-runs. He is still the arrogant domineering seigneur, and I—I've changed. And when he went through all my mail, and manuscripts, as he used to do, I couldn't be the passive chattel I once was.

A quarrel. Sunday night he drove into New York to see

some cats, got turned on some hard shit, blew all his bread. He came back with a story of being mugged in Harlem. This blatant, sleazy shuck enraged me. He was obviously stoned out of his skull on H, eyes pinned and all, and his subsequent actions made me know he'd made a meet and copped. I was bitterly disappointed and said so. Another hassle, and I get belted.

I asked the exalted shrink who runs this joint to give Doug a job. He interviewed him and turned him down, possibly he feared the conjunction of two ex-cons. (He told me, "The young man has strong lines of willfulness in his face.") So Doug and I went to a posh Jewish sanitarium in the area, and he got on there, assistant to the grounds keeper. Physical labor outdoors, which is what he wants.

When he left, I could tell he was still simmering at my show of independence, though bland on the surface. For several days, I didn't see him, and of course could think of nothing else, he moves everything right out of my mind.

Last night he came by late, half bagged, towing a Cuban stud who works with him. The Cubano, one of those coal-eyed Latins, something else. I was on duty, whatever was afoot I never found out, but Doug was edgy, preoccupied, and the Cuban sat looking at me with a sort of horrified fascination. So I think I can guess what the projected ploy was.

Well, I asked for it. Is cyanide very expensive?

Love, — Jim

Westchester, New York
AUGUST 26, 1963

Dear Doug:

You've got me crawling again.

The theatrical exit you made was truly stunning, but I had some dialogue left over. Try to watch it?

Okay. Just two points and I'm done. If I was doing something underhanded, as you say, behind your rippling-muscled back (in writing your m----r), would I have told you about it?

My motive was purely pragmatic— you liked the job, I wanted in some way to help you keep it— and it baffles my prosaic mind how that should lead to an emotional hassle.

Further, you say that I want to see you remain dependent on your m----r. This is baked *merde*. If inversion is the principal force in my makeup, as you claim, would I want to see you anything less than independent of *all* women? You can't have it both ways, kiddo.

Your mother has instilled in you a regrettable provincial snobbery, and countless times I've been whipsawed by it. Fortunately, the wild blood of the highland chieftains flows in my veins, and I am above such squalid considerations as pedigree. And with inborn patrician courtesy, I have concealed my opinion that you are both upstart Americans.

My dealings with your mother have always been baldly opportunistic—it shames me to think of it. But they have had little to do with you—only that I hoped in a couple of instances to gain something for you by these detestable tactics.

Will you ever realize that my loyalty to you has never been touched by all these picayune maneuverings?

And at whatever risk, I will say that I hate to see you go back to a diaper-hung environment. It looks to me like this one isn't above the old tribal ploy that the other used. "I want to bear your chee-ild." Medea said it to Jason a while back, and recently I heard Anita Ekberg say it in a Tarzan picture. That's the stuff you got to watch, tootsie.

Come back, lil shoobie.   Jamie MacDuff Blake

Westchester, New York
SEPTEMBER 2, 1963

Dear Angie:

I'm full of bile, bleats, choked sobs, baffled rage—and just plain strung, this stud has got me homicidal.

Running from a hassle in Chicago, he came to me for help; I got him squared away with a job where he could spend a quiet winter in the country. But every time we're together it seems to wind up with him coming on hostile. He came by one recent midnight, blocked; I was on duty so I took him into a remote wing of the joint to keep the noise down.

He told me he'd talked to his mother in Lake Forest. She'd offered him a substantial bribe to come back home again. Seems she didn't figure he'd run to Blake, the detestable homosexual.

Kind of morbidly funny, really, that she pays him to clear off and let her deal with a chick he has knocked up, then she discovers he has run to the opposite pole. Close the door, they're coming down the chimney.

So I ask him what he's going to do, he says go back. Maybe at this point I shouldn't have mentioned Oedipus and Jocasta. Anyway he belted me and there ensued a tidy post-midnight row in what is supposed to be a haven for the mentally distoibed.

Naturally the Doctor got the word. Next day he swept me with a chilly glance in passing. For this aloof Olympian, this is like throwing me off the roof.

There's another thing about this imbroglio that salts me— I have been so careful to present an image of no-image. In a cannibal colony of neurotics like this one, they'll marinate you every time, just for being definite. And with the women, tricoteuse every one, the fact that Doug is huge and good-looking doesn't help— and when he falls up the fire escape into my room and stays and stays, it's fairly clear we ain't cutting up old bowling scores or reading aloud from Thoreau.

This is flabby behavior, and makes me edgy. If the joint taught me anything, it taught me never to leave myself in the open. But it was the same when Doug and I were together in the joint— while he's shooting up all the schmeck in sight and fucking off with the pachucos, I was flapping my wings and playing the chapel organ, trying to cool our scene with the brass and the hacks. And then getting needled for being square.

I've got a story I want to finish, I need the bread, but I can't work, I can't think of anything but him. Ridiculous, when I'd hung up the gloves on all that shit and was quite happy to forego it. Alone, my wants are simple, I can spend happy hours just digging the wax out of my ears.

My dear, I could tell you a tale of love's labor.

I know the chick he inseminated, a very shrewd and determined female who thinks that having a baybee is the way to anchor him. The poor cunt, what she ought to do is sell the kid to the gypsies, marry a yak-jockey and start a poppy ranch.

I forgot to tell you about the Cubano scene. Doug leeringly asked me what I thought of the young Cuban— how would I like to make it, milord wanted to know. Here I was supposed to say I don't want nobody but you, Daddy. But when somebody asks me a question with a built-in answer, I'll give a wrong answer if they kill me for it.

So I said, book it baby, and he did. And we did. Hoo-hah! The Bull pretended he wrote it that way—but I know he's a saver, and some day it will all come dripping out, little drops of acid. Meanwhile he burns up his insides.

By all means send pictures, I love pictures. And you may look at this one of Doug and send it back to me. Taken in Florida, he caught the fish. And dig, he's pinned out of his skull.

I wish I was single again.   Later, — Jim

Westchester, New York
SEPTEMBER 7, 1963

Dear Angie:

Why you should think about going to Hawaii I don't know. This is one place I've never had the least desire for, seems so spoiled and so bloody square. I knew a cat in Florida from the Honolulu Advertiser, nothing like the island, he used to say, and he was such a fearful blank I decided I'd never go there. Japan, now. If you go there send for me. A nation of schizos, fascinating.

Doug has gone back to his slavish clutch of adoring females, leaving as usual a shambles behind him. The physical aches sustained from the beating I got on the last night he was here are gone, but there remain a number of pains a little harder to lose.

I've puzzled ever since over the mad desperation that seemed to be gripping him during this last interlude. The sex with him was pure sorcery as always, but there was a new element in it of savagery and despair, and more than once I got a sharp disturbing whiff of awful finality in his actions.

There has always been in Doug a terrible compulsion to exhaust and drain everything he encounters. With lush, with H, anything, there is a feverish scramble to use up everything and abandon it.

And it is so with him in his human relationships. Find them, know them, seize, explore, fuck them, gut and discard them. It maddens him that there is a part of myself that belongs only to me. He's always had me hung up, sideways, but it is impossible for me to give him the kind of surrender he demands.

When we were together this latest time, he went through all my mail, manuscripts, everything. Searching, searching. Trying like a marauding tiger to get inside me, questions and questions, till at times I felt as if my mind were being ransacked and plundered. Not until he finds what he's seeking in me, examines it and possesses it, will he feel entirely able to abandon me.

It's upsetting, and frightening too, but mainly I feel it's sad, because even if I wanted to, I can't give him what he wants. It simply isn't within my control. So for that reason I know he'll be back for another attempt. None of the broads he's conquered and jettisoned have ever realized this about him and so they've lost him— but then I had two years of night and day to observe him and I know him completely.

He spoke nostalgically and at length of our life together in prison as cellmates. There I was able to give him a quiet haven and protection from abrasive experiences. And that only by unremitting effort, endless prison politicking and expediencies and compromises, at godknows what spiritual expense. He dominated me entirely, it was the only way to make the relationship work— but it fell to me to find the strength and cunning to keep the tide of violence and ugliness in the joint away from our life together. I still marvel at how the hell I ever did it, I don't actually know, but it was accomplished.

I think he expected me to provide again this same kind of surcease and serenity. Impossible, of course, I got a life to live, of sorts. But my failure to furnish this soothing cocoon baffled and embittered him. He is like Henderson the Rain King— "I want, I want, I want."

Neither here nor in the joint could I accept one thing with equanimity or even resignation, and that is his heroin addiction. He made a trip to Harlem one day to cop, and when I found he was making the scene again, I could only flip. Told him that rather than watch him commit suicide on the installment plan, I'd prefer to give him the barbiturates to do himself up properly. His answer was that he would like to kill himself, but that he was too young to die. And further that if I loved him as I said, the junk wouldn't make any difference.

The last evening was such a combination of farce and Gotter-dammerung I got to tell you about it. In the afternoon I had a call from New York, another Raiford grad, named Bob. This is a cat Doug always abominated in the joint and I always found fascinating. A very evil guy, but with formidable mental capacity. Incisive, retentive mind, a restless schemer—what riveted me was the bottomless amorality of the man, and his esoteric perversions. Doug bitterly resented the association and persisting in it brought me quite a few lumps. He always insisted Bob and I were making it sackwise. Couldn't understand, or didn't want to, that with Bob being geared, the chemistry wasn't there.

Bob told me he had just come off a check run with a score of over 2 grand. So I got maybe great expectations, and I told him come on up.

There's a lot of bitch in me, I'm aware, and when Doug came by that evening, I told him Bob was coming up, and also that he'd just wound up with 2 G's. Taunting, I suppose.

Actually, I expected Doug to say, later for all that, and leave me free to try for some of that bread. Uhuh. Doug said he'd meet Bob's train, have a forgive and forget reunion, take him out on a deserted road nearby, work him over and take what he had.

I'll give you half of what I get, he said. Don't do me no favors, I told him. Do yourself a favor and back off, this stud is too smart for you.

Wrong thing. So I walk the floor singing Where Are The Wandering Boys Tonight. I finally learned the full meaning of "misgivings."

My apartment is on the top floor of Lakeside, reached privately by a fire escape when necessary. First I hear feet on the iron steps, too many feet. Then Bob comes in, followed by Doug. All smiling.

I realized I've had hidden malice for Bob and had been hoping Doug would take him. To see them asshole buddies rather soured my outlook.

So we start drinking, friendly like. Doug tells of taking Bob out on the golf course, making him strip, and finding 40 bux. And a watch. Seems that when Bob learned it was a heist he didn't even lose a beat. Told Doug, you're too hip for these chicken-shit scores, work New York with me and I'll make you some real bread.

And we'll shack up, is the implicit hook.

Doug says to me, dazed, "He captured my imagination." Hands me the watch. "This is for you." It's a Macy watch, worth maybe $125. I give it back. "This is schlock, I don't want it." But he makes me keep it, to tag me conspirator in the action. I am pissed at the flabbiness of the whole bit. And of course jealous.

Meanwhile Bob is bleeding reproach from the eyes, all over me. "You set me up, mother-grabber."

I said, "I didn't set up a goddam thing. I told this amateur asshole to forget it."

Doug said, "I might have known it. A couple of faggots bumpin' pussies." A lot more of that style.

Bob is remembering being made to disrobe and coming on heavy at Doug. And Doug is livid with me for witnessing his failure.

I'm weary of the whole bad scene. "Why don't you two go somewhere and fuck?" I say.

Bob gives me a veiled wounded look and splits. Doug belts me around the room at length, calling me a ratfink, says I put him on a hummer.

While he's doing this, Bob is busy down in the driveway putting sand and foreign objects into Doug's gas tank.

Upshot: I get a bitter note from Doug, from somewhere in Pennsylvania. On the way back to mother. "Don't call or write," he says. He'll be back.

Bob phoned me later. "What was that all about?"

Truthfully I said, "I don't know."

He said, "Jesus, you ought to button your lip. I had 2 Grand on me, he might have found it."

I said, "I know what you mean. When are you coming up, tootsie?" You lose it on the swings, you gotta make it up on the roundabouts.   Zut alors, — Jim

Westchester, New York
SEPTEMBER 8, 1963

Dear Doug:

I'm still sizzling over that kick in the gut Friday night, before you took off with your fascinating little friend. You haven't been around for me to tell you. (By now, I wot, you must be turning a pretty penny, your looks, his brains, if you're not in the Tombs. Golly, think of going to Sing Sing with Kaplan as your rap partner. It could open up whole new vistas.

If you didn't go around in a narcissine dream, you'd have seen immediately from the watch and the way he was dressed that he was looking for an early bust. Wonderful time to get in on the ground floor, especially if you're going to the basement.

Instead of dumping the sonovabitch after he had de-balled you, you bring him around to bleed reproachfully all over me, while you indulge in manly invective, trying to salvage what you can.

And then, motheruhgod, you fawn all over him. And this is a line seared in my brain— "He captured my imagination." This ticktock, dingdong, jargon-hung, gimmick-headed little fat rotten egg "captured your imagination."

I'm sitting there thinking, this is the asinine sophomore, this meretricious mendacious mother-grabber who tells me how I should write. Where oh where did you go?

Kaplan, with an alleged $1500, in a rising monsoon, is trying to borrow remote acquaintances of mine to get out of the storm. Where are the marks of yesteryear?

Another memorable quote: "You put me on a hummer." This to me, before you kicked me in the gut. You put yourself on a hummer, kid, I told you exactly how it was. The whole thing was farcical; If you hadn't been such a solemn ass you'd have seen it. Instead, a contemptible piece of savagery towards me to restore your *amour-propre*.

You lost me my private monster. For years I've cherished and coddled Kaplan, and learned from him, about perfidy, iniquity, treachery—a human totally committed to bush warfare on his own species. And there was more to learn, always more, he was an inexhaustible trove. For years I parried, sparred with him, and picked his brain. While you denounced him with bombast, *molto furioso*. And then in your first real encounter with him, he hands you your head. This malign little clock-work gnome "captures your imagination."

Who was I talking to all those years, who was it I loved?

For years in Florida, Kaplan, envious of the attachment we felt for one another, envious and avid and cold as only a reptile can be, tried to subvert our relationship, in vain.

And in one stinking night of folly, you hand him what he wants. You always made too bloody much of my identity, who I really was. I'm here to tell you, Charlie, I'm the kiddo nobody kicks in the gut twice.

Ave, old son, *vale*. Lots of luck with your new little man. I envy you the years ahead, fresh daily enthrallments for your imagination. As a last gesture, be advised that Robert is hosting 150 generations of spirochetes. So hang loose, old friend. — Jim

Westchester, New York
MARCH 2, 1964

Dear Doug:

You said not to write, I know, but I really cannot be expected to go along with such soapy gothic pronouncements. (Incidentally, you forgot to include "never darken my door.")

Because there are a few answers I haven't been able to arrive at, which I aim deviously to elicit, all being well, in due course.

I've been wondering about you from time to time, actually every time I look over at the sanitarium. In some baffling and annoying way, your shadow hangs over that landscape for me, and it is one of my favorite vistas. When I read Donleavy's *A Singular Man* it brought the whole thing into focus— I wanted you to read the book and so I decided to write. Got your address from your mother.

Maybe I should put you in a cheerful frame of mind by giving you a piece of news you can gloat over, with that astounding vindictiveness that has always jolted me when I see it. Kaplan departed up the river to Ossining February 10 on a 2½ to 5 ride. Something about larceny, a lesser charge than they could have used. A real sad letter from him from the Tombs—you know, that Ave type, "I go to that bourne from which no traveller returns . . ." Well, partially sad. The rest of it was filled with the whirring of gears and the humming of wheels, Kap getting his new bit organized. I'll go along with it, do what he asks if I can. He's your bete noir, not mine.

You'll notice the Donleavy book is rather bloated. It was in a disastrous fire I had St Valentine's Day. I had a club date with Larry that night at the country club. When I was about to get dressed for it, I opened my closet door and found the closet a seething mass of flame. Biggest shock of my life. We fought the fire with extinguishers till official help arrived, and we held it pretty well in check. One of the guests and I were close to barbecue in that ghastly inferno, this dude really phenomenal, I never saw such abandon. Nor did I even think of danger somehow, felt only a terrible urgency to get the obscene thing put out. My mustache singed, my eyebrows, some smoke inhaled, but okay. Thousands of those volunteer assholes tramping around and they let the blaze spread, so a good deal of the room itself was burned, that lovely room. Lost all my clothes and left standing in shower slides and blue terry bathrobe. Worse, I lost the current manuscript I was on. Some others burned, too, and everything watersoaked.

The gallons of water cascading down from the top floor did a lot of damage in the south wing. All insured. But part of a beautiful old pegged planking floor buckled by the flood, not replaceable. Still, a number of those awful prints in the dining room are gone, providential.

The doctor stood around in the living room while the riot surged, looking like he was at a dull cocktail party and wondering how soon he could gracefully leave. Later though, he gave me a brief glacial interview, suggested in his clipped taciturn way that I give up smoking or methedrine. What started the fire I actually do not know, but it would, I feel, have been churlish of me not to shoulder the responsibility. The doctor wished it in order to simplify insurance claims. I think what really disturbed me most was that such a reticent reserved man should have been exposed to a roman holiday.

In sum a traumatic experience, they tell me I was in shock for a while. I know I felt the deepest most palpable depression I've ever known. I had a wild urge to run away, I don't know where, but I had no clothes.

Later I got bread from the doctor, and that fag Manhattan playwright sent me 100, unasked. Such a nice thing to do, I felt like I finally had to make some kind of commitment on the play he wants to do with the Raiford material. Now I've changed my mind again, don't quite know why. Either he's not the one to do it, or the material isn't suitable for a play, as he sees it.

Hereabouts at present all is bated and precarious. The Doctor is in the hospital, they're running a series of tests, and from the hush-hush fragmentary reports I'm able to get, I think they're trying for a biopsy, looking for cancer. But his heart is bad, difficult to operate. Everything is vague now, but if he goes, the joint goes, and I've put out a feeler or two to find out where is the next ice floe. I could go to Manhattan, too frantic, or stay here for a while.

All right. Tell me what you have been doing and cease this hateful boo-hooing. *I* am the wronged one. Shortly after you left (leaving me in a vulnerable dangerous and careless mood) Raoul came along, a rich cruel Arab who owns a camel ranch. Days of degradation on the burning desert sands, nights of Moslem madness under a desert moon. But sand got into the vaseline and the camels hated me. I barely escaped with my life, and all because of yoo-oo.

I had a strong feeling during and after your Westchester safari that something remained unsaid—either unasked or unstated, I couldn't say. What *was* bugging you?   Write, please—Jim

PART X

you *can* go home again

Jacksonville, Florida
JUNE 22, 1964

Dear Mike:

Probably from the wire you will have realized that I'm still on the bricks. Saturday night was a new low in the history of crime, though I must insist that it was not a conclusive test of strength.

Much has been made of New Yorkers' disengagement in the matter of law enforcement. In Jacksonville, as my tottering reason will attest, everybody is on The Force. How could I have forgotten that Southerners are insane?

I had a camera joint thoroughly cased and was satisfied that I could enter it through the wall from an empy store next it, to avoid hidden alarms. Figuring I could work at it into Sunday and emerge Sunday evening if necessary.

A sound plan by any measure. At 1 AM I sallied forth. Bar-closing time, people on the street, not too many, to keep me comparatively inconspicuous. One hangup, the people all stoned. I had to turn off Bay Street, through a short alley, to reach the rear of the joint.

Everything was quiet, only the distant sound of revelers on the street. I drew forth my favorite crowbar of the finest case-hardened steel. Trying it tentatively against the door, I was suddenly aware of stertorous breathing behind me. In the light from a naked bulb three floors up on the fire escape I saw a drunk, redfaced, rocking back and forth, staring intently at me and at the crowbar I held.

"What smatter, buddy, lose your key? Need nee help?"

I snarled. Bogey in "Key Largo." "Better get the fuck outa here, friend, y'might get hurt." I looked up at a darkened window. "Keep this cat covered, Lefty."

His head fell back, his mouth opened, he staggered back a step. "Yeah. Keep'm covered, Lefty." Gazing earnestly up. Then a bleary uncertain peer at me. "Lefty?"

"Yeah, Lefty. Kills yuh just the same as righty." In a soothing tone I called up, softly. "Take it easy up there, chum, the guy's bagged."

His face was congested with the effort to form a thought. "Are you guys—? You guys are breakin' in!" Suddenly stealthy, he called upwards. "Hey, Lefty, I'll give ya jiggers. I'll be look-out, okay, boy?" (He liked Lefty better than me.) His voice banged and rocketed off the walls of the surrounding buildings.

Briskly heading for the street, I called back, "Keep him covered, Wingy!" From the alley, movin' on, I could hear, "Hey, Lefty? Hey, Wingy? Hey, you guys?"

I returned to my modest cache-cache at the Inn Of The Five Pleasures and fumed and fretted for hours. Till I hit upon a new concept. I would return at daybreak, and work inside the store in full daylight. Armed with steel tape measure, chalk and my rain hat (to wear casually on the back of my head).

I returned to the scene of the (pending) crime. To my stupefaction, a guy was backing a red convertible into the space behind the building. He opened the trunk and took out a bucket and sponge. Intending, in the rosy Florida dawn, to wash his red motorcar. When he saw me, he gave me a cordial good morning. I said good morning and returned to the Inn.

Thine, — Blake

Jacksonville, Florida
JUNE 24, 1964

Dear Gertrude:

Thank you for the gold, little sister to the poor, you give a lovely light. I have been spreading terror in the ranks of all the little Dixie darlings down here. Their little feet must be just aching, I see them pounding the beat night after night. It's a mystery, I don't know where all the females in this town are kept.

Actually, I have little of this sort of commerce, it's so somehow hangdog and pointless. The article in the current *Life* said a lot and said nothing, though the parts about Los Angeles fuzz and the leather clothing boys were informative. All that leather must be very hot. I imagine they stink some, but it's kind of funky at that. Vast improvement on the sad little swishes.

And of course they have to line up the usual stable of bullshit psychiatrists to say the usual wild things, or else things that are long since vieux jeu. (I could a tale them weave of homos and quackotherapy. Hee hee.)

I'm still living at this Hotel (sic) on the riverbank. Most of the residents work at the adjacent shipyards and are wild drunken hard-breathing boys. This afternoon I kept hearing somebody walking up and down in the corridor outside my room. (The hotel is old southern style, windows looking out and jalousies on the corridors.) Somebody in boots. So when there came a tapping and a rapping, I wanted to know something before I unbolted. Sometimes they lunge. All I could hear was mumbling, it sounded pretty drunk, therefore harmless, so I opened the door. He's in jockey shorts and engineer boots, and healthy. Looked like the star high school athlete who turns out to be a marijuana fiend, a small boy quality about him. Though it was amply clear he was no small boy.

Very softly. "Can I come in, I wanna come in, I don't want nothing to drink I just wanna come in can I come in?"

My heart sang, any bleedin' day of the week you can come in. But one of the soi-disant house dicks rushed up and wanted to lead him away. "Let him alone," I said, "the boy isn't drunk, he's sick." In my ringing sincerity my voice was rising. "Sick, yes, sick to his soul with loneliness, as we are *all* soul-sick with loneliness!" A respectful admiring group had gathered, and there were many nods of agreement.

"And what is the cure for loneliness?" I asked, and a couple of yellow toadies said timidly, "Love?" and I seized on it.

"Love, yes, *love* is the cure for loneliness!" I declared, firmly drawing the invalid in and slowly closing the door. With just my head showing in the aperture, I gave them a saucy wink and a toss of my curls. "But I have just so much therapy to give, dear boys." And with much good-natured banter and hearty laughter, the group dispersed.

Most nights before bed I like to walk by the river, and sit and watch the shipyard activity, the garlands of working lights strung over the ships, the fountains of sparks, the flares, all reflected in the shining black water. And high overhead the humming of tires on the big bridge.

So I'm walking and the moon is mooning over the water, and there's a big interstate rig parked there, all dark. I look, but pass on and sit a little way from it. Pretty soon noises, and a stud gets down from the truck cab. Comes over and says, don't the moon look purty.

A hill person, rawboned, Indian hair hanging coarse and lank on his brow. Christopher Plummer as the Young Abe L. I've known them, a nice delicate feeling for things, and this stud was like that about the river, nothing awkward, nothing fancy. After a bit, it is disclosed that there is a bed behind the driver's seat.

Blake, I said, as sure as the wild blood of the highland chieftains is pounding in your veins, you got to make it into that sack with Young Abe. —I got to say that erotic frolic in one of those things opens up a whole new field.

I hope you won't think I'm loose. I also go to the public library quite a bit and take out good books.   Zut alors,—Blake

Jacksonville, Florida
JUNE 30, 1964

"Isn't that Nelson Algren, the movie star?"

"Yes. He's divine. He used to be a writer, you know."

"I know. The Horatio Alger bit, how about that?"

Dear Nelson:

Since my disengagement from the good and useful life in lushest Westchester County, and consequent traumatic dislocation of spirit, I have a wandering warlock been, seeking the keeper of the truth.

In green and peaceful Bala Cynwyd, with the twilight deepening, a flaxen-haired child of the rich pauses at the day's last croquet:

"Nanny, oh, Nanny, did you hear it? There was a sound in the sky!" The faithful old nurse draws the child closer and gazes fearfully into the lowering sky· "It is nothing, my little wren-child. Only the warlock, flying South. Let us go in."

In a waterfront dive in Norfolk, a taffy-haired child of the poor pauses over the night's first beer: "Did you hear a funny sound, Mummy? A rushing, flapping sound, like the wind?"

"Shut up and drink your beer. And call me Bernice."

In a bayfront park in Miami, a slender figure with reddish-gold hair sits on a bench gazing at the sun-glint on the water. His big myopic blue eyes mirror the tropic sky, and mirror nothing. From the pocket of his rumpled seersucker protrudes a worn copy of Gerard Manley Hopkins. A dark-haired child of Semitic aspect approaches, his boy's dark eyes full of a dream. His chubby knees are much scarred with the vigor of his play. One wears a Band-Aid, white on the glowing brown of child-skin. The boy's treble is true and unafraid.

"What's your name?"

"My name? Jim the Warlock. What's yours, son?"

"Sammy. But I'm changing it to Pierre as soon as I have my mother declared unfit."

"Is that kind?"

"Kind-schmind." His small brown nose sniffs. "Is that Gerard Hopkins I see? Good God."

"There is a failure of communication. The gulf between generations, the crying abyss—"

"Stop with the crying abyss and dig. As you know, your friendly FBI, J. Edgar Hoohoo, Director, has supplied a pamphlet for the protection of our most precious asset, the American child. This useful booklet is titled 'The Child-Molester, What To Do Till The Gendarme Comes.' If you will pardon me—"

In his chubby brown fist he holds the small booklet and reads, the childish treble clear and unabashed: "These symptoms will serve to indicate a child-molester—" (Reads silently.) "Hmm, yeah. Yeah. Yeahyeahyeah."

The big alert brown eyes are guilelessly candid, locked on the wide blue ones which hold a hint of pain. "Categorizing is always suspect of course, I'm hip, but friend, in your case I'd say paedophile, am I right?" (Consults book.) "Wet lips, shifty eyes, has a tendency to finger himself vacantly, yeahyeahyeah." (To Jim the Warlock.) "On the button, baby, child-molester."

He is suddenly brisk, impersonal, a changeling: "Just for the record, would you care to expose yourself indecently? Or decently, ce n'est egal. Alors, these squalid terms. —Well, Charlie?"

"I'll show you mine if you show me yours."

"Done and done. Oh where are the erogenous zones of yesteryear, eh, old thing? Precisely. —Now then, the busty female you see hoving to behind you is ma mere. A civic-minded dipsomaniacal duenna of Greater Miami. She will take it from here. —You're not a bad sort, Hopkins aside. Don't give her more than a fin, she'll only knock me down on it anyway. Ciao, Charlie. Happy groping."

"—Allow me to introduce myself, and also the technique of citizen's arrest. Your fly, I note, is awry. Your friendly FBI has provide—oh, you've had that. Well, old molester, I am the despoiled Samuel's mother, aroused and outraged civic-minded mother. Founder and President of the League of Marauding Matrons, Chairlady of the Committee for Comeuppance. But for this ripple, you can call me Rose the Bag Lady. Do I do my eagle-scream, G above high C, and we'll all go downtown?"

"I am Jim the Warlock. Did you say five?"

"Five it is, Hon. Warlock? God the beautiful Anglo-Saxon names these southern slobs— Thank you, tootsie, God bless. Is that Gerard Hopkins, for the creepingjesus?"

Really did meet a child agent provocateur. A few nights ago I was sitting on the concrete wall that borders the river, when a Honda motorcycle roared up and a young boy about 16 got off. A radiantly handsome boy, glowing with health, blond, and it seemed to me uncommonly extroverted for a child that age, adolescents are not often articulate with an older person. This one confided in dizzy succession that he was from Atlanta, that he had come all the way on the Honda, and that he also had an automobile that he had left at home. Interspersed with this were questions about me, where I was from, what was I doing, where did I stay. I made the observation that he must be a rich kid, to have both motorcyle and automobile, thinking to myself he was also a liar, if he had come 400 miles from Atlanta on a motorbike he would have been the color of cowhide, which he was not. The adolescent then made a gracious if veiled offer to share my lonely sack, and then all the bells that had been going off made a pattern. Agent provocateur of course, such a beautiful one I was almost tempted beyond prudence. However, I let him down lightly, just told him to get on his motorsickle and go back to his fuzz friends.

Not so with a quaint little cracker from Fort Pierce, who approached me on the riverbank quite guilelessly offering his body for a night's lodging. What really touched me was that he said he wanted to look around town but didn't want to attract the attention of the fuzz by carrying his bag, and asked if I would watch it for him. So I did, watched his bag for him till he got back, took him home, fed him, and let him stay all night. He told a story of too many children in the family, not enough attention for him, the imaginative one (he didn't say that), so he had set out to seek his fortune.

It would be nice to be able to say that we slept side-by-each,

Paul and Virginia the night through, but the imaginative urchin wanted more adventure than that, and so the morning saw him more or less sullied. He looked for a job the next day and came back in the afternoon, and already I could see him wondering what the overlarge family he'd left behind were doing. "If ah got a ride on a truck, ah could be home by dahk." I advised him to get a ride on a truck. And be home before dark.

Best,—Blake

Jacksonville, Florida
JULY 17, 1964

Dear Gertrude:

Tonight I learned that Ginger Rogers is older than I am, and it has given me renewed hope and vigor for the future.

I've been here for about a month now, living in a shaggy waterfront hotel. Most of the denizens work in the adjoining shipyards, headlong heedless boys who work like fiends all week and then try to kill themselves with alcohol on the weekend. But they are so *clean*. I've never seen anything to equal the sub-cutaneous glow they have.

Some time during the somber weekend festivity, one of them will remember me, the odd man out in this happy little group (I am always alone, and not really satisfactorily explained) and come and bang on my door with some unintelligible demand, challenge, denunciation. Then I have to be stern, clipped, peremptory, and demolish the antagonist before his blurred antipathy can get off the ground. Sometimes the knock is sneaky and clandestine, and then of course no sweat. I'm sort of resident madonna for the hardworking lads.

At one time I told them I was a Canadian abortionist hiding from Interpol. When one of them remembers he says if I'm a doctor I ought to listen to his heart, at least. I tell him I'm not licensed to practice in Florida and could be arrested.

Actually, I told them the bald truth when I first checked in, but for some reason it doesn't satisfy them. Maybe because I helped one of them one arid Sunday, an especially magnetic one who had an especially bad hangover. I gave him a glass of V-8, about fifty grams of B-12, ten grams of amphetamine and a big dollop of honey. Principally, I suppose it was the amphetamine and honey, though the B-12 probably did something to get his gonads stirring. As a result they think I'm a witch doctor, and come to me with their hangovers. For my own dubious reasons I carry on with the practice, but B-12 costs like the devil, even though I often purloin it. And as for the amphetamine, very hard to get, and in a few days I'll have to make a raid on a pharmacy I have lovingly reconnoitred.

I've joined the boys only once in their drunken bouts, not drinking and taking far less speed than I did in Westchester. Live very quietly, swim a lot, lie supine in the sun a good deal, write a good deal (and that seems to be going better) and otherwise just wander about looking, sometimes but not often pick somebody up and bring him to book.

About Lakeside, the doctor died, and black terrible secrets came pouring out of all the crevices; he was a conscienceless crook, really, a complete monumental fraud. Even though I had suspected it all along, and kept shoving it away from me, the discovery was rather traumatic and for a while nervous collapse loomed. (Oh well, I was taking too many pills, too, but the pressures and tensions were something else.) Miserable fucking shitbirds, those respectable people, and they had nibbled away at my spirit till I was almost gone.

Aside from a few anxieties, I'm more contented now than I ever was in Westchester. I just don't swing with respectable people, they're all murderers. The contentment is ephemeral, as what is not?   alors, — Blake

PS—I don't hear anything from Northrop. Fuck him too.

Jacksonville, Florida
JULY 19, 1964

Dear Mike:

The French navy is in town, off what is apparently a missile ship of some kind, and I, poor thing, am in trajectory myself. Quels Bijoux, they are living dolls. All so *young* and (what a nice change from the Murcan sailors, hoodlums all) they are so fresh and so wise. With their little red pompoms on their hats, tout a fait charmant. (I'm honing up on my French, you should excuse the expression, because they'll be here for a month.)

I ran into a couple of them on the street, they were hassling with some old man, and nobody could get over the language barrier. I didn't do so terrific either, language-wise. I asked them, with my Parisian French, if they wanted women. ("Ou est le bureau de tabac?") One of them, with hair and eyes as black as the raven's wing, asked me why did I want to know that? ("Pardon, monsieur, ou est le mensroom?") His eyes so bright and dancing with malice, I thought I would swoon clean away on the spot.

Well ultimately (and if I never hear the expression "faute de mieux" again, it will be fine with me) we played a French game called two-against-one. The *attitude* is so utterly delightful, they didn't want money, it would not be polite, they said, and the merry one said that Papa de Gaulle would not like it.

When they saw my hotel room, which is maybe a little raffish, they both exclaimed "Montmarte" and the young blond one asked me if I were beatnique. I said "Non, monsieur, een my countree I am wot you call arteest."

Oh to be in April now that France is here.

Les affaires sont les affaires, Blake

Jacksonville, Florida
SEPTEMBER 10, 1964

Dear Gertrude:

It is a little after midnight, and outside in Jax, Hurricane Dora is battering the town. Now and then the electric light goes a lurid orange, but I count myself lucky to have it at all, about 90 per cent of the city is dark. (I have candles in readiness.) It has been raining in horizontal sheets all day, the wind steadily rising, till it is now alternating between a banshee howl and a roar like a fast freight on a trestle. The shabby hotel I live in is what Floridians call a "boomer," that is, built around 1925. The rooms have windows facing outward and jalousies facing a central corridor. Very breezy and cool arrangement normally, but in this howling gale the wind seethes and whistles through it, one expects it to play a tune like a harmonica.

Instead, the building is behaving like an old palsied dog, it keeps up a constant throbbing shudder under the impact of the wind. Now and then it gives a little leap up into the air. I feel like a mouse in a box which is intermittently nudged and walloped by some monstrous unimaginable hand. Perhaps if I am very quiet, it will go away.

It's a drag to have to ride it out indoors, but the dirty ol fuzz have said they will arrest anyone caught on the street without a good reason. Even so, the radio says looting is going on, and from the business district I can hear the pealing of burglar alarms. These are snatch and grab artists, interlopers and summer soldiers, no feeling for form and finesse, not proper burglars at all. Upstarts and arrivistes. I laugh them to scorn.

This thing is really cooking now. The eye of it has crossed the coast with winds of 115 mph. I hear a torrent of shattering glass somewhere, and in the parking lot across the street, a motorcar has just turned languidly over on its side, like a restless sleeping beast.

A little while ago at high tide, I looked at the river, which is only about 150 feet from the hotel, and it's up over the bulkhead, way above normal. Over at the Atlantic Coast Building a block away, the Navy has moored two gigantic dredges weighing a little more than the Rocky Mountains. It will be interesting to see in the morning what the high water has done to them. I hope they're in the lobby, it's a dreadful building.

I'm being invaded. The rising river has forced the big river-roaches to move and they are scuttling around the room. Monsters. They look like armor-plated mice with antlers. Maybe I will find a beached mermaid in the morning. If I am alive.

—Okay, now it is 10 AM the next day. I couldn't resist the uproar, some time towards daylight I had to go out in it. All the bemuscled residents of the hotel were huddling in the lobby looking like sailors' wives waiting on the dock. They took a dim view of my expedition. It was honestly exhilarating, on this big plaza-parking lot along the river. The rain coming in horizontal sheets, the wind a palpable shoving force, but I could stay erect in it, by moving carefully. The river looked tormented, lashing, crashing, bashing, slopping in huge gulps over the bulkhead, not at all the river I know. I didn't stay out long, because big metal signs were wafting through the air like veils, and I didn't want to be beheaded.

The wind blew until daylight, but all is calm now, except that the hotel appears to be marooned. The old joint weathered the blow in good shape, they don't make firetraps like they used to, some of the other, newer hotels in town did not do so well.

The river seems to be pretty high as yet, hard to say how much, but there seems to be an awful lot of tugboat traffic past my window, and I thought I saw a catfish peering in at me.

The radio says the roof blew off the old County Jail. Rumor has it there was a mass Ascension, which I discount categorically.

In all, a nice satisfying little blow, I'm having a very good hurricane season. (Understand Ethel, the next one, is somewhere out there waiting.) Floridians love these things, everybody gets stoned and in general behaves in a loose manner.

Was that a submarine I saw just now? Passing the window? Perhaps I should get some sleep.   ciao, Blake

Jacksonville, Florida
NOVEMBER 10, 1964

Dear Mrs. Northrop:

I was shocked indeed to hear of Doug's trouble in California. I didn't even know he was out there, we haven't been corresponding lately. It's doubly bad that he had to get busted for drugs out there, the state is very rough on that sort of thing.

Perhaps one saving aspect of a bad situation is that the California penal system places heavy emphasis on psychiatry. Guys I know who have served time there have said they have two shrinks for every convict. It may be that this time psychotherapy will work for Doug.

I realize now that when he visited me in Westchester, he was looking for help, and I was too involved in my own problems to see it. For that I will always reproach myself.

I remember once when Doug and I were cellmates in Raiford, he said that you actually preferred him to be locked up, since then you could be certain where he was. Undoubtedly the accusation was unfair and extreme. But I do think that a cooling-off time is indicated for him. I know that you will continue to help him as you always have, and my sympathy and admiration, for what they are worth, go out to you.

Sincerely, Jim Blake

Jacksonville, Florida
DECEMBER 18, 1964

Dear Mike:

Sometimes I get this hellish feeling, sometimes I feel like a
motherless child. The town square here (that's a Where, not
a Who) is called Hemming Park, and right now it is all strum-
peted up with the expensive glitter of Christmas. Loudspeakers
bray incessantly oh come all ye faithful and jingle bells jingle
bells jingle all the way.

And I prowl like a dislocated mouse on the surface of it,
on the peripheral dazzle of it. Stealing to survive, making a
score here and there, but nothing important, nothing really
big.

A while ago I came to the (obvious) conclusion that burglary
was little more than a way of breaking your back. All that
property to remove—and then the fence beats your chops for
the bread. So I got myself a fake gun and went forth with
a high heart to try armed robbery.

Hideously embarrassing. I have to go into these places (all
of them chain stores, corporations, if you will, where I won't
feel so involved with the people, and where I won't really
be wresting any bread from individuals).

In a way it has worked, though I've hated going through
that Jimmy Cagney dialogue, that up-against-the-wall-mother
routine.

I think what really wiped me was the night I went into
the local department store, into the gourmet food department
—they seemed to do a lot of cash transactions there.

I strolled around, choosing lobster bisque and madrilene and
godknows what, and then at the cash register I showed the
piece to the fat lady in charge and told her in menacing tones
to put all the bread in the bag.

Well. She sagged, a deflating dirigible, slowly toward the
floor and lay there like a beached whale, out cold, of no

fucking use to anybody, especially me. I couldn't understand
the mechanism of the cash register, and so the money remained
out of my reach. There was nothing to do but walk out
into the warm Florida evening, into jingle bells jingle all the
way.

I think it was then I realized I wanted to go back to the
tribe, to my people, in the joint. And said to myself, home
is where, when you go there, they can't turn you away.

Homesick, how about that? And homesick is where, when
you go home, they make you sick.

No, Virginia, there is no Santa Claus. So dummy up and
drink your beer.   Love, Jim

TERM METED
IN ATTEMPTED
DRUG THEFT

Jacksonville, Fla., March 11, 1965—
James William Blake, 44, was sentenced yesterday to five
years in the state prison in connection with a burglary to
obtain barbiturate drugs.

Blake, who pleaded guilty, was sentenced by Criminal
Court Judge William T. Harvey.

Asst. State Atty. William M. Tomlinson said Blake was
arrested outside a medical office building at 225 W. Ashley St. last Dec. 18 after an attempted burglary there.

Blake pleaded guilty to attempted breaking and entering with intent to commit a misdemeanor and received
a 2½-year term on that count. He also pleaded guilty
to unlawfully possessing a barbiturate drug without a
prescription and received an additional 2½ years.

When the first selections of James Blake's letters from prison were published in the mid-fifties (in Jean-Paul Sartre's *Les Temps Modernes* and in the literary quarterly *The Paris Review*), the addressee of many of the letters was referred to simply as "X" . . . "Dear X." This device was used to shield the identity of the recipient, who, according to prison regulations, was required to be an immediate member of the prisoner's family. Blake was in prison on a second hitch when the letters were published. In fact, "X" was Nelson Algren, the distinguished author of *The Man with the Golden Arm*, etc., who in 1948 met Blake by chance in a Chicago nightclub named The Pink Poodle. Blake was playing the piano in the band. "He came in to look at the girls, I guess," Blake recalls, and the two became acquainted. After Blake was locked up in Raiford, convicted on breaking, entering, and larceny charges in Jacksonville, Florida, he wrote Algren a somewhat tentative letter, telling him what had happened, and when it was replied to, the correspondence began. Algren's letters to him were "funny," as Blake remembers, and, more important, continually urged him to keep on writing. Though comparatively well-read, Blake had had little experience with the written word until the restrictions of prison life left him with no other way to express himself. The stimulation of corresponding with a well-known author was important: it sharpened his efforts, not only in his letters to Algren but to others of his correspondents, largely his musician friends.

Publication of the letters came about mainly through the enthusiasm of Simone de Beauvoir, who saw a packet of them while visiting Algren in Chicago. She sent the letters to Jean-Paul Sartre, who had them translated and published in *Les Temps Modernes*. Shortly thereafter, the original letters appeared in *The Paris Review*, published in tandem with another prison chronicle—Jean Genet's.

Since the appearance of his first letters, Blake has kept to his letter-writing habit—through his three terms in jail, and on the outside. When possible, he made copies of his letters. These and the originals were collected from two sources in 1969—a closet in Algren's Chicago home and a shoe box of Blake's personal effects stored in a Bowery mission house while he completed a jail term. The selections for this volume were first culled and arranged by Janet Coleman and the undersigned. The author, with the guidance of editor Walter Bradbury, arranged and edited the final version.

George Plimpton